Gender and the Professions

This book examines gender and professions in the 21st century. Historically the professions encompassed law, medicine and the church, all of which excluded women from participation. Industry and the 20th century introduced new professions such as engineering and latterly information technology and, whilst the increase in credentialism and accreditations open up further avenues for professions to develop, many of the 'newer' professions exhibit similar gendered characteristics, still based on a perceived masculine identity of the professional workers. In contrast, professions such as teaching and nursing, characterised as women's professions which reflected women's socially acceptable role of caring, developed as regulated and lower status occupations from the late 19th century.

Since the 1970s and the women's movements, anti-discrimination and equal opportunity legislation and policies have aimed to break down the gendered bastion of the professions and grant women wider entry. With growing numbers of women employed in a range of professions and the political importance of gender equality gaining prominence globally, *Gender and the Professions* considers how women and men are faring in a diverse range of professional occupations.

Aimed at researchers, academics and policy makers in the fields of Professions, Gender Studies, Organizational Studies and related disciplines. *Gender and the Professions* provides new insights of women's experiences in the professions in both developed and less developed countries and in professions less often explored.

Kaye Broadbent is Associate in the Faculty of Arts and Social Sciences, University of Technology, Sydney, Australia.

Glenda Strachan is Professor Emerita in the Department of Employment Relations and Human Resources at Griffith University, Australia.

Geraldine Healy is Professor of Employment Relations and former Director of the Centre for Research in Equality and Diversity at Queen Mary University of London, UK.

Routledge Studies in Gender and Organizations
Series Editor: Elisabeth K. Kelan

Although still a fairly young field, the study of gender and organizations is increasingly popular and relevant. There are few areas of academic research that are as vibrant and dynamic as the study of gender and organizations. While much earlier research has focused on documenting the imbalances of women and men in organizations, more recently, research on gender and organizations has departed from counting men and women. Instead research in this area sees gender as a process: something that is done rather than something that people are. This perspective is important and meaningful as it takes researchers away from essentialist notions of gender and opens the possibility of analysing the process of how individuals become women and men. This is called 'gendering', 'practising gender', 'doing gender' or 'performing gender' and draws on rich philosophical traditions.

Whilst Routledge Studies in Gender and Organizations has a broad remit, it will be thematically and theoretically committed to exploring gender and organizations from a constructivist perspective. Rather than focusing on specific areas of organizations, the series is to be kept deliberately broad to showcase the most innovative research in this field. It is anticipated that the books in this series will make a theoretical contribution to the field of gender and organization based on rigorous empirical explorations.

1 Gender and the Professions
International and Contemporary Perspectives
Edited by Kaye Broadbent, Glenda Strachan and Geraldine Healy

Gender and the Professions
International and Contemporary
Perspectives

Edited by Kaye Broadbent, Glenda
Strachan and Geraldine Healy

Routledge
Taylor & Francis Group

LONDON AND NEW YORK

First published 2018 by Routledge

2 Park Square, Milton Park, Abingdon, Oxfordshire OX14 4RN

52 Vanderbilt Avenue, New York, NY 10017

Routledge is an imprint of the Taylor & Francis Group, an informa business

First issued in paperback 2019

Library of Congress Cataloging-in-Publication Data
A catalog record for this book has been requested

ISBN: 978-1-138-68057-9 (hbk)
ISBN: 978-0-367-87779-8 (pbk)

Typeset in Sabon
by Apex CoVantage, LLC

Contents

Tables and Figures

Tables

Figures

Contributors

Arosha Adikaram, *Faculty of Management and Finance, University of Colombo, Sri Lanka*, is Senior Lecturer in HRM. Additionally, she serves as a resource person and a visiting lecturer for a number of other government and private institutions and corporates. She is also an associate member of the Institute of Personnel Management, Sri Lanka and a member of the Center for Women's Research (CENWOR), Sri Lanka. Her research interests are in the areas of sexual harassment at the workplace, gender issues in organisations and employee relations.

Janis Bailey, *Department of Employment Relations and Human Resources, Griffith University, Australia*, is Adjunct Associate Professor with research interests including union strategy and campaigning, vulnerable workers including youth and women, and teaching and learning in business. She is currently working on projects on developing professional identity in ER and HR graduates, and gender equity in universities.

Kaye Broadbent, *Faculty of Arts and Social Sciences, University of Technology, Sydney, Australia*, is an associate whose research interests focus on gender and employment insecurity, women and union activism in Asia and labour dissent in wartime Japan. Most recently as a Chief Investigator on an ARC Linkage Grant (2009–2012) "Gender and Employment Equity: Strategies for Advancement in Australian Universities" she analysed fixed-term research academics. Publications include *Women and Labour Organizing in Asia: Diversity, Autonomy and Activism* (Routledge, 2008) and *Women's Employment in Japan: The Experiences of Part-time Workers* (Routledge Curzon, 2003) and a study of privatised home care work in Japan, appearing in *Work, Employment and Society* (2013).

Moira Calveley, *Hertfordshire Business School, University of Hertfordshire, UK*, is Principal Lecturer in HRM and is a member of the Work and Employment Research Unit. Her research interests are in the areas of equality and diversity and employment relations from a UK and international perspective. Her most recent projects have included an

investigation into the work experiences of people from socially disadvantaged and Black and minority ethnic backgrounds in the engineering
profession. She has recently published a paper with Keith Randle and
Cynthia Forson which looks at the social composition of the UK film and
television workforce using a Bourdieusian perspective.

Valerie Caven, *Nottingham Business School, Nottingham Trent University,
UK,* is Senior Lecturer in HRM, after an earlier career in the construction
industry. This has led to her research interests of women's careers in the
male-dominated construction industry professions. She has carried out
comparative studies of both men and women in the construction industry
in France, Spain and Lithuania. She has published widely in international
journals and is currently co-editing a book on *Hidden Inequalities in the
Workplace* to be published by Palgrave in 2018.

Linda Colley, *CQU Business School, Central Queensland University, Australia,* is Senior Lecturer in HRM and Industrial Relations. She brings
extensive practical experience from her career in HRM and industrial
relations in the Queensland public service and her research builds on this
career. She has published on topics such as merit, tenure, job security,
redundancy, gender and age at work, public management reform, privatisation and the effects of austerity measures on public employment. She
is active in two international networks, as co-convenor of a Permanent
Special Interest Group on 'Public Servants at Work' within the International Research Society for Public Management (IRSPM).

Anne Cox, *Faculty of Business, University of Wollongong, Australia,* is Senior
Lecturer researching and publishing in three main areas: the transfer of
multinational companies' IR/HRM policies and practices across borders,
the transformation of HR/IR systems in developing countries and gender
equity. Her book *The Transformation of HRM and Industrial Relations
in Vietnam* was published by Oxford Chandos Publishing in 2009. Her
current research addresses the implications of multinational companies'
management practices on the social and economic fabric of Australia.

Susan Durbin, *Faculty of Business and Law, University of the West of England,
UK,* researches gendered employment, specifically women in male-
dominated jobs and industries. She has published her work in a number of
journals and is the author of *Women Who Succeed: Strangers in Paradise?*
(2015), published by Palgrave Macmillan. She is an Associate Editor of the
journal *Gender, Work and Organization* and works closely with organisations in the public, private and not-for-profit organisations. She is a founding member of *alta,* a bespoke mentoring scheme for women/by women in
aviation and aerospace.

Cynthia Forson, *Organisational Behaviour and HRM and Deputy Provost
at Lancaster University, Ghana,* researches the work, leadership and

management experiences of women in the labour market and organisations and has published several articles in this area. She focuses particularly on gender, ethnicity, class and migrant status and the intersectional influence of these structures in the lives and careers of women. Her research interests now extend to the work and labour market encounters of African women in Africa and the diaspora with a particular interest in the development of management theories that reflect the lived work experiences of women in different African contexts.

Christeen George, *Department of Psychology, University of Hertfordshire, UK*, is a chartered occupational psychologist and her main interests focus around people's behaviour in the workplace and employment relationships. She is particularly interested in psychological contracts, organisational and professional commitment and positive psychology. In 2009 her book *The Psychological Contract: Managing and Developing Professional Groups*, concerned with the psychological contracts of professional workers, was published by Open University Press.

Anne-marie Greene, *School of Business, University of Leicester, UK*, researches employment relations and equality and diversity issues in areas of work that stand outside of the standard employment relationship. A particular interest is the interface between work, life, family and community, particularly in areas of work where a sense of calling, mission or activism are required. Recent research has looked at the work experiences of clergywomen, the careers of diversity consultants and the management of volunteers within the National Trust and other voluntary sector organisations. She is co-author of *The Dynamics of Managing Diversity: A Critical Approach* (fourth edition, Routledge, 2016).

Geraldine Healy, *Centre for Research in Equality and Diversity, School of Business and Management, Queen Mary University of London, UK*, has a particular interest in the interrelationship of a number of themes including the intersectional nature of discrimination and disadvantage, inequality regimes, individualism and collectivism, career, the gap between equality and diversity policies and practices and multiple rationalities. Her research recognises the importance of a multilayered analysis and the role of history. Her books include *Gender and Union Leadership*, Routledge 2013 (with Gill Kirton); *Ethnicity and Gender at Work*, Palgrave 2008 (with Harriet Bradley) and *Diversity, Ethnicity, Migration and Work: International Perspectives*, Palgrave Macmillan 2011 (with Franklin Oikelome). She is co-editor of *Equalities, Inequalites and Diversity* (Healy, G., G. Kirton and M. Noon 2011: Palgrave 2010) and *The Future of Worker Representation* (Palgrave 2004). She has also published widely in leading international journals.

Pavithra Kailasapathy, *Faculty of Management and Finance, University of Colombo, Sri Lanka*, is Senior Lecturer in HRM. She is an associate member of Institute of Personnel Management Sri Lanka and was a member of the IPM Council in 2002–2003. She was a member of the Board of Directors of Women's Education and Research Centre, Colombo. Her research interests are in the areas of work-family conflict and gender issues in organisations.

Uraiporn Kattiyapornpong, *Marketing, School of Management, Operations and Marketing, Faculty of Business, University of Wollongong, Australia,* is a Lecturer and also serves as academic program advisor for the postgraduate level (Marketing) and is acting Honours Coordinator. She teaches a variety of marketing subjects at undergraduate and postgraduate levels. She is on the editorial board of the *Journal of Business Research* and *Journal of Travel and Tourism Marketing.* Her research interests are International Marketing, Business to Business Marketing, Services Marketing, Tourism Marketing, and Consumer Behaviour. She has recently published a case study in an International Marketing textbook by Pearson Australia (2017).

Ana Lopes, *Newcastle University Business School, Newcastle University, UK,* gained her PhD in Sociology from UEL with a thesis on the sex industry and action research. Her research interests focus on gender and employment and include casualisation and precarious work, women's activism and voice in trade unions and women working in male-dominated industries. She is a founding member of *alta,* a bespoke mentoring scheme for women/by women in aviation and aerospace.

Robyn May, *Chancellery (Research), University of Melbourne, Australia,* submitted her PhD in 2013 when she examined the causes and implications of insecure academic employment in Australia's public universities. The research was part of a wider ARC Linkage project at Griffith University looking at gender and employment equity in the university sector. Before undertaking her PhD she worked for the National Tertiary Education Union, and she has also worked as a researcher and casual academic and in a range of research positions overseas.

Elena Navarro-Astor, *School of Building Engineering and the School of Architecture, Universitat Politècnica de València, Spain,* is Senior Lecturer in Applied Economics and HRM. Her research interest is broadly focused around job satisfaction and HRM in the construction industry, with a special interest in gender issues. She has published comparative studies in international journals of women architects in France, the UK and Spain, and also on career barriers confronted by women in the construction industry. Currently she is researching Lithuanian women architects.

Judith K. Pringle, *Department of Management, Auckland University of Technology, New Zealand,* is Professor of Organisation Studies. She researches workplace diversity, women's workplace experiences, bi-cultural methodologies, intersections of social identities (gender/ethnicity/sexuality/age) and reframing career theory. She was co-editor of the *Sage*

Handbook for Workplace Diversity (2006) and has published numerous book chapters and in scholarly journals. She established the Gender and Diversity Research Group at AUT University, and is also Adjunct Professor at Griffith University.

Susan Ressia, *Department of Employment Relations and Human Resources, Griffith University, Australia*, is Lecturer in HRM and Employment Relations. Her recent doctoral research focused on the job search experiences of independent non-English-speaking-background skilled migrants in Australia. Her research interests also include the areas of work-life balance, managing diversity, equality and social justice issues.

Stefanie Ruel, *Mission Manager, Canadian Space Agency*, is a doctoral candidate at Athabasca University, Canada. Most recently she was the Canadian Increment Payload Manager for Canadian Commander Chris Hadfield's mission aboard the International Space Station. Her research focus has included a critical examination of intersectionality and diversity in the science, technology, engineering and mathematics (STEM) context. She is currently working on her dissertation, an intersectionality study focused on the exclusion of STEM-professional women from the Canadian space industry's management positions.

Irene Ryan, *Business, Economics and Law Faculty, Auckland University of Technology, New Zealand*, is Senior Lecturer in Management. Inspired by feminist research in management, leadership and organisational studies, her current research interests revolve around gendered practices of leadership, diversity and careers. She has a particular interest in the sport context and the ways this can reveal what is often invisible in other contexts.

Steven Shelley, *Hertfordshire Business School, University of Hertfordshire, UK*, is Principal Lecturer in HRM and Senior School Research Tutor. He lectures and researches in vocational education and training and in the changing context of public services. His 2005 book *Working in Universities: The Realities from Porter to Professor* (Glasgow: Humming Earth) informed the early stages of the research project from which his chapter in this volume is derived.

Glenda Strachan, *Department of Employment Relations and Human Resources, Griffith University, Australia*, is Professor Emerita who continues to conduct research on contemporary and historical workplace change, especially issues relating to women's working experience. The impact of organisational and national employment policies, especially EEO and diversity management, is a focus of her work. She is co-author of *Managing Diversity in Australia: Theory and Practice*, 2010. Her recent work has focused on gender equity in university employment.

Acknowledgements

This book emerged from our research on women workers. Few studies of women workers have examined a range of professions and fewer still have widened this lens to look at gender issues. Our research on women workers in a range of industries was highlighting the precarious nature of professional work, a feature that these educated workers had not experienced in previous decades, or at least not to the same extent as we were finding. Thus the idea for this book was formed.

All work of this nature is a collaboration, and many people and organisations have helped us along the way. We would like to thank the commissioning editor David Varley and his team, and the editors at Routledge who have greatly assisted in the process of this book. All these people have been critical to the final outcome.

We are very grateful to all the authors who shared their research with us for the book. All academic staff are very busy with the demands of their work and we are appreciative that the authors dedicated so much time to this book. The contributors were wonderful throughout the process, particularly in responding to requests promptly and cheerfully. Throughout the chapters, the ideas and discussion are based on the information supplied by a range of professional workers, many of whom took the time to share their stories. We would like to thank them for their time and generosity.

It has been a great experience being a team of co-editors, and working together has taught us so much about working collaboratively, ensuring this volume is much richer as a result. As always, our families have played a crucial part in supporting us in this endeavour, and we thank them for their encouragement.

1 Introduction

Inequality Regimes and the Gendered Professional Context

Geraldine Healy, Kaye Broadbent and Glenda Strachan

> Occupational segregation by sex is detrimental to women. It has an important negative effect on how men view women and how women view themselves. This in turn negatively affects women's status and income and, consequently, many social variables such as mortality and morbidity, poverty and income inequality. The persistence of gender stereotypes also has negative effects on education and training and thus causes gender based inequalities to be perpetuated into future generations . . . occupational segregation is extensive in every region, at all economic development levels, under all political systems and in diverse religious, social and cultural environments.
>
> (Anker 1997, 315)

Our focus is gender and professions where status and credentials promise to protect professional workers and perhaps avoid the gendered experiences of their less qualified sisters. Indeed 'professions' also promise some protection from occupational and economic vicissitudes and that by implication professional workers will treated fairly regardless of sex. Extensive literature tells us that fair treatment may be more a promise than a reality, but arguably there is still an expectation that professional status will protect women from the worst effects of gendered organisations and of occupational segregation. We consider the extent to which women enter a gender-neutral space where they can subscribe to professional values, even those that may be explicitly patriarchal and disadvantage women. This book therefore explores how women and men are faring in a diverse range of professional occupations in a number of national settings, as well as the global movement of professional women. We question what employment in a profession means for women and examine whether they have changed the face of their professions or whether they are forced to conform to male definitions of the profession. We investigate the everyday experiences of women and men working in different professions in different countries and importantly consider issues of insecurity, masculine cultures and intersectionality.

Background

This book is about gender and professions in the 21st century. The concept of 'profession' is potentially a slippery concept but one which is widely used by different parties—whether the state, a professional association, the individual—to defend, persuade, legitimate, control, exclude and segregate. The relative importance of these concepts to different occupational groups varies with the nature of the profession itself, the national context and the historical moment in the history of the profession. These concepts are also underpinned by high levels of credentials and closure strategies so that access to professions may be, although not always, carefully controlled, thus maintaining an autonomy and access to tacit knowledge. What is striking about early studies on the professions is the invisibility of gender, implying instead that their emphasis infers that professions are gender-neutral.

We eschew gender neutrality as a way to understand professions, but recognise that early approaches have offered insights into professions, despite the invisibility of gender, in understanding the meaning and characteristics of the term 'profession'. Early studies focused on listing traits present in a profession (Millerson 1964, 5) or discussing which occupations are to be considered professions. Larson observed that a profession was the "means of earning an income on the basis of transacted services" (1977, 9). Johnson (1972) emphasised the concept of control by an occupation, which he acknowledged differs due to the historical development of the occupation (1972, 45–47). Freidson argued that major theoretical writing on the professions have focused on defining professions as "occupations which share characteristics of considerably greater specificity than higher education alone, and which are distinctive as separate occupations" (1994, 17). He also specifically identified control to be significant and defined a profession as "an occupation that controls its own work, organised by a special set of institutions sustained in part by a particular ideology of expertise and service" (1994, 10). He further considers that professions distinguish themselves from other occupations by "the particular tasks they claim, and by the special character of the knowledge and skill required to perform them" (1994, 36).

Studies such as Johnson's move away from defining professions in terms of attributes to focus on emphasising the process of professionalisation as a mechanism to explain the differences in prestige attached to a range of professions such as between law, medicine and social work (1972, 21). Professionalism, he argues, is an institutional control framework based on occupational authority. To discuss professionalism Johnson draws upon a typology focusing particularly on the resolution of tension in the 'producer-consumer' relationship and the extent to which the producer was able to control the relationship and benefit from it. Freidson (1994) focused on the political, economic and ideological forces on professions. He builds on Johnson's work where he defines professionalism as 'the ideology and special set of institutions' (1994, 10). Freidson (1970) focuses on the power professions gained to control the work granted by the state. For Schmidt in understanding the professional, it is important to understand 'ideology' or "thought that justifies action" (2000, 15). He argues that the criteria which deems an individual qualified to become a professional is not just technical knowledge drawn from their occupation but their attitude, in particular their ability to work within a certain political and ideological framework.

The contributions in our book do not treat 'profession' as a generic concept, but rather as a changing historical, cultural *and gendered* concept. We accept Crompton's (1987, 420) view that precise definitions of profession proved difficult given the heterogeneous group of occupations involved. We argue for the importance of understanding the gendered experiences of professions in a range of cultural contexts. We address the issues of horizontal and vertical gender segregation and question how integrated women are into all levels of the professions. Our book particularly relates to aspects of Johnson (1972) and Larson's (1977, 1980) arguments, as from them we take as our starting point that the development of modern professions is historically located. For us professions emerged as a product of the divisions which have developed within capitalist society, they are as Johnson argues "a product of state formation" (1982). In this way, the developments we are seeing—for example, proletarianisation and insecurity—are because of changes in capitalist society. So while some professions in some countries may still control the monopoly of knowledge such as medicine or architecture, control of the labour market is not necessarily guaranteed and so increases the risk of oversupply such as academics or lawyers (see Larson 1980) and tension between producer and consumer (Johnson 1972).

Larson (1977) also analyses control but in the light of both the state and profession. She discusses the development of professions in terms of the "professional project" (1977, 51), which she considers is one "of market control [which] underlines the central role of the state . . . most particularly its function of sponsoring monopolistic education systems" (1977, 18). The state also exercised control over the professions through regulation of qualifications and licensing. But by establishing a standard body of knowledge the professions were able to bind educational qualifications to occupational function, and established a "monopolization on competence and [demonstrated] that this competence is superior to others" (Larson 1977, 51). We also see the development of the professions as a 'project' as their knowledge and survival strategies are evolving to counter the changing contexts within which they operate. For example, the public service of the present does not resemble that of 40 years ago—(see chapter on Australia) as the number of women and older women is increasing.

The work of Friedson, Larson and Johnson is insightful particularly with the importance they attribute to control, power and ideology. Nevertheless, they neglect the gendered nature of professions and so we look to the work of Anne Witz (1992). In examining gender and the professions, Witz

(1992) updates Larson's research on the 'professional project'. Like Larson she examines the strategies professions develop for occupational closure, which enables them to gain occupational monopoly over the provision of certain skills and competencies in a market for services. Witz unpacks the specifically gendered dimensions of closure practices in professionalising occupations including exclusionary, inclusionary, demarcationary and dual closure strategies (Witz 1992). For Witz it is important to gender the agents of closure strategies and distinguish between male and female professional projects, as gender makes a difference in form and outcome of professional projects which are grounded in a capitalist society. Thus, our book is about gender and gendering at multi-levels of contemporary organisations and how gender shapes and is shaped by the intra-professional structures, opportunities and relations for women and men. But it is also about gender in context and, as we shall see, the context and the relational intersect.

We have seen a huge change in women's opportunities since the 1970s and the women's movements including anti-discrimination and equal opportunity legislation and policies which aimed to break down the gendered bastion of the professions and grant women entry and progression. While women are employed in an increasing range of professions (Anleu 1992; Cech, Pecenco and Blair-Loy 2013; Sang, Dainty and Ison 2014), they often remain underrepresented and often segregated in narrow specialisations. Therefore an increased numbers of women in professional employment does not necessarily translate into an equal spread across all sections of a profession. So while in many countries there is evidence of significant change—for example, women now form the majority of graduates in law, accounting and medicine, their career paths after graduation remain gendered. This applies to medicine, where women are more likely to be employed in general practice and less likely to be surgeons, and law, where women are more likely to specialise in family law and less likely to be in corporate law and to access senior positions in law and accounting firms (Anleu 1992). Stratification and segregation by and within professions is maintained and reproduced (Healy and Oikelome 2011; Cech, Pecenco and Blair-Loy 2013). These patterns also embody different career trajectories by gender and indeed in some cases, higher dropout rates of women compared to men after several years in a profession (including engineering) (Strachan, Troup, Peetz, Whitehouse, Broadbent and Bailey 2012). Moreover, there are gender differences within and between professional groups according to place of qualifications (Oikelome and Healy 2007; Healy and Oikelome 2011; Oikelome and Healy 2012) and migration (Oikelome and Healy 2012). Thus despite rapid and seemingly progressive change, we find a resilience of both horizontal segregation, where women are more likely to work with women and men with men, and vertical segregation, where men are more likely to remain at the top of their organisations, segregations that are maintained by gendered and inequality regimes.

Historically the professions in the Anglo-Saxon world encompassed law, medicine and the church; mobility was restricted and patronage dominated

(Larson 1977, 5) and professions excluded women from participation. Industry and the 20th century led to new professions such as engineering and latterly information technology (see Larson 1977; MacDonald 1995). Moreover the increase in credentialism and accreditation opened up further avenues for professions to develop (see Larson 1980). Many of the 'newer' professions exhibit similar gendered characteristics, still based on a perceived masculine identity of the professional worker and the association of the professional with high-level credentials based on university and professional body qualifications.

In contrast, professions such as teaching and nursing, characterised as women's professions which reflected women's socially acceptable role of caring, developed as state-regulated occupations from the late 19th century. They struggled to achieve the status of being called a profession and to be granted entry into university education. Indeed these professions were often ascribed the gendered and somewhat pejorative description of 'semi-profession', a description determined primarily by the main sex of the professional work, a term which Hearn argued reflected the patriarchy of the "full profession" (Hearn 1982). Pay structures and status in traditionally female dominated professions were much lower than those of law and medicine, attended by the fact that the major employer of some female-dominated professions, for example, teachers and nurses, is the state. In the case of these gendered professional groups, there is little doubt that their credentials provide some protection from the uncertainties of the labour market. Nevertheless, in this neoliberal era, the intensification of controls and the marketisation of professions, such as teaching and nursing have sustained a high degree of collectivism amongst women and men. Moreover, professional workers may defend their terms and conditions through the discourse of their professionalism and thereby challenge attacks on their autonomy (Healy and Kirton 2002).

Moreover, we see a convergence of gendered experiences mediated by the gendered structures that are evident in the professions that disadvantage women, more intensely experienced by those who follow other than conventional choices, such as those professions dominated by men.

Professions and professional work itself are not static and recent decades have seen huge changes in professional work. The concept of a profession embodied the idea of autonomy of operation has been challenged by the external forces of competition, capitalist and technological developments. The computerisation of aspects of work and the surveillance and monitoring of professional workers has reduced individual autonomy in many areas.

Thus the employment of professional groups is increasingly characterised by a struggle for autonomy. This applies in both the private sector with the growth of the international legal and accountancy firms, and in the public sector with the increasing privatisation of professional work and the centralised prescription of much professional work (Muzio, Brock and Suddaby 2013). At the same time, we see professionals, traditionally employed in the public sector, demonstrating a strong allegiance to unions, whose role has been important in uncovering the dangers of privatisation and insecure work. Thus, the marketisation of professional work has become an important feature of the professional project.

Our Approach

The neglect of gender in many accounts on professions is notable. Davies (1996) provided an influential account of placing gender in the sociology of professions. By drawing on recent work on the gendering of organisation and bureaucracy, she suggests a key issue for consideration is not so much the exclusions of women from work defined as professional, but rather their routine inclusion in ill-defined support roles (Davies 1996, 661). For Davies, to claim that institutions and practices are gendered is to argue that they call upon notions of masculinity and femininity for their construction and that gender, as a set of cultural understanding around masculinity and femininity, is constitutive of social relations (Davies 1996, 671). A theme that comes through in this book is the relevance of gendered relations in understanding men and women's positions in organisations and professions.

Acker has had a profound impact on our understanding of gender relations in organisations (Acker 1990; 2006a; 2006b) and thereby professions. In her influential work on inequality regimes, Acker (Acker 2006a; Acker 2006b) points to the different constituent components[1] that conspire to mutually constitute an inequality regime. Inequality regimes are defined as "loosely interrelated practices, processes, actions, and meanings that result in and maintain class, gender and racial inequalities within particular organizations" (Acker 1990). Thus Acker is challenging the binary that so often characterises work on gender. While our book is about gender we move beyond the binary of female/male or woman/man. We recognise that our identities are intersectional with other identities, such as identities linked to our sex, age, ethnicity, nationality, migrancy, sexuality, disability, religion. However, while important, these categorical intersections, tell only part of the intersectional story (Crenshaw 1991; McCall 2005; Simien 2007). Acker's (2006a) concept of inequality regimes addresses two feminist issues: first, how to conceptualise intersectionality, the mutual reproduction of class, gender and racial relations of inequality,[2] and second, how to identify barriers to creating equality in work organisations. She develops one answer to both issues, suggesting the idea of "inequality regimes" as an analytic approach to understanding the creation of inequalities in work organisations. Acker's work on inequality regimes and intersectionality has been foundational in the work of a number of researchers seeking to explore the complexity of gender alongside other identities (for example, Atewologun, Sealy and Vinnicombe 2016; Healy, Bradley and Forson 2011; Seierstad and Healy 2012; Tatli and Özbilgin 2012; Wright 2013; Wright 2014; Tatli, Ozturk and Woo 2017; Wright 2016). Her influence has been equally strong in the different chapters in this book, either directly or indirectly.

While the book is about women, it is also about men and the gendered organisational practices that affect women and men differentially. To broaden the empirical research field on professions, we have chosen for consideration professions and countries which do not regularly feature in the literature.

We examine professions in a range of national and cultural contexts to understand the interaction between professions and the state—and to shed light on similarities which may exist within the 'professional project'.

The book provides new insights of women's experiences in the professions in both developed and less developed countries and in professions less often explored. We showcase under-researched professional groups in less developed countries (see chapters on women in information technology (IT) in Sri Lanka, nurses in Thailand and academics in Ghana), and we recognise the heterogeneity of women, for example, older women workers in Australia, migrant women and women working in male-dominated professions such as aviation and the clergy in the UK and Canada's space agency. Moreover, we consider the importance of inequality regimes at the organisational level including their masculine practices such as in the legal profession in New Zealand. Moreover, the increasing insecurity among professional workers including migrant professional workers is a strong theme indicating the tension between producer and consumer (Johnson 1972) has turned to favour the consumer. We have chosen to examine a range of professions in a number of countries to understand how the experience of the gendered professional workers is common or different. Cross-cultural comparison is important and provides a deeper understanding of the relation between the state and professional occupations and allows us to consider the social and cultural context which formed the background to the profession and the impact this has had on the formation on both the gender culture and inequality regime which developed. Our focus is on those who work in a profession rather than the profession and its institutions.

A key theme is the social construction of gender and the shape it develops in a range of countries and occupations. Despite the undoubted increased entry of women to previously viewed 'male occupations', the book exposes the resilience of inequality regimes in their different forms operating in a number of occupations and country contexts despite in some cases high levels of regulation.

The broad questions the chapters address include:

1. What is the historical and contemporary context of the professional worker?
2. How does the professional worker experience gender in their organisation life?
3. What is the social and cultural context of the professional worker?

There are three dominant interrelated themes emerging from our chapters. These are the importance of intersectional approaches, the gendered flexible professional worker and resilience of gendered societal organisational and masculine practices. We introduce each chapter in turn under these dominant themes.

Intersectional Approaches and the Professional Worker

The importance of intersectional approaches and the professional worker is particularly strong in the next first two chapters, which discuss the gendered pay gap in Australia and then the intersection of age, gender and culture in Ghana.

Gender Pay Gap and Inequality Regimes

Curiously, pay is missing from much research on professions, where it is assumed that professional status will lead to high economic rewards. It is also missing or underplayed in some studies of gender and professions, where it is accepted that women will be earning less than males as a result of vertical and horizontal segregation, but such assumptions are not accompanied by detailed analysis. While scholarly papers tend to talk about vertical and horizontal segregation, discrimination and disadvantage and theories on the reasons for gender inequality, stories in the media citing the latest in gendered employment inequalities adopt a more visceral approach and call it out in tabloid terms. "Let's play add a penis"[3] was the graphic used by the Australian group Destroy the Joint for a piece comparing starting salaries by gender. This was a powerful message and because of its absurdity one that underscored basic inequalities. It doesn't seem to matter which country you look at, women earn less than men. For dentists in Australia women started on AUD$77,000 but by 'adding a penis' the amount increased to AUD$91,000. In the UK, 'adding a penis' means that for £100 women earn £87. This simplistic and catchy binary is a fraction of the story and of course no longer represents the world in which live[4] nor does it capture the complexity of women's inequality. While critiquing the binary we do not undermine the importance of challenging the gender pay gap, bearing in mind that some countries (e.g. UK) have had equal pay legislation since 1965. Under the more recent 2010 UK Equality Act, organisations with over 250 staff are required to publish their gender pay gap by April 2018. Schroders fund managers were the first FTSE 100 company to go public. The group revealed that fixed pay for its female staff was 33 per cent lower on average than for their male staff, while there was a bonus gap of 66 per cent.[5]

Linda Colley in Chapter 2 brings further complexities into understanding the nature of the gender pay gap and segregation. Colley begins by exploring the gender pay gap with respect to female-dominated public agencies and age. She builds on existing literature on gender inequality analysing data in the highly regulated Australian state public service to understand whether inequality is exacerbated by age. She concludes that despite decades of equal opportunity policies, a gender pay gap (GPG) exists which, while lower than that found in the broader labour market, conceals a significant gender pay gap in the senior levels of the organisation, with female-dominated agencies registering the largest gaps. Colley's chapter reveals that while women are gaining access to a wider range of jobs in the public sector, the effects of gender and age begin in the early stages of careers.

Colley's chapter is important by drawing attention to the apparently 'good employer' still not demonstrating equality in pay. Tentative hypotheses tested were that women would have prospered in female-dominated agencies and that inequalities would only be evident amongst the oldest cohort of the workforce. These pointed to the importance of gender segregation and pay as well as the cohort effect. Colley's chapter supports other research findings that women working in female-dominated workplaces is an important element of women's lower wages in comparison with men and that women receive more wage growth in male-dominated areas (Dex, Ward and Joshi 2008). This is not to suggest that women cannot prosper in female-dominated areas, just not to the same extent as do men. Colley's research also highlighted the relevance of Acker's (2006a, 2006b) inequality regimes, which were shown to be evident in that the women in her study struggled to gain access to steep career hierarchies due to discriminatory allocative processes and the within-group bias where male managers promote male employees.

A strong defence of gender inequality is that time will resolve the inequities between the sexes. If this were the case, then it is reasonable that Colley's research would show that the greatest inequalities would show in the older cohorts, that is, cohorts that did not fully benefit from embedded equality structures and legislation. In fact this was not the case, and the professional women in Colley's study experienced inequality post 35 years. She argues that the younger age groups receive some protection from the fixed-entry salaries for most professions. Thus a level playing field is maintained until the processes and practices associated with inequality regimes underpinned by masculinist organisational cultures starts to take effect. Colley closes by questioning whether equal employment policies are having an impact beyond the point of recruitment. This is not dissimilar the findings of a UK study investigating the experiences of Caribbean, Pakistani and Bangladeshi women working in the public sector (Healy, Bradley and Forson 2011).

Intersectional Approaches—Age, Gender and Culture in Ghana

In Chapter 6, Cynthia Forson, Moira Calveley, Steven Shelley and Christeen George combine age and gender in examining the experiences of academics in Ghana. History and culture are shown to intertwine in that their colonial antecedents shaped the masculinist organisation and philosophy of African universities. Forson et al. find that women are moving into the Ghanaian academy in greater numbers but their progress has been slow. Unlike Western culture, Ghanaian culture reveres maturity and this chapter highlights the disadvantages experienced by younger women and men in trying to establish a career in universities. For young women and men appointed to managerial positions, they face resistance from mature colleagues, which is exacerbated for women as they try to navigate their role within a patriarchal culture.

Forson et al. adopt an intersectional approach focusing particularly on gender, age and seniority. While they found frustration amongst the young academics, both male and female, it was evident that young women's professional status was not recognised on three fronts: firstly, as women they were viewed as having less power, both as tutors (by students) and managers (by colleagues); secondly, their youth delegitimises their authority in the classroom and in the academic community. Finally, they are expected to take on the undervalued responsibilities of home-related caring, which compounds the struggle to achieve the respect and recognition in the academic community. While young women academics have some similar experiences in Western countries, the strong patriarchal African culture provides even greater challenges to the young Ghanaian female academic whose aspirations and achievements are never fully valued. Drawing on Evetts (2000) framework of cultural, structure and action and on how behaviour is influenced and even controlled by cultural belief systems, Forson et al. demonstrate that Ghanaian society is characterised by a deep reverence towards age maturity; to pay respect, honour and give privilege to elders is a time-honoured convention. These attitudes are so embedded within workplaces that not to act in this way would almost be deemed as deviant behaviour. This intersection of cultural beliefs and attitudes impacts the approach taken to age and gender in the workplace, even in the 'enlightened' sphere of academia.

The Intersections of Migration, Gender, Ethnicity and Family

The increasing global reach of firms (engineering, legal and accounting) together with the global movement of labour means that professionals may choose to work overseas for a period of time or migrate permanently. Many national migration programs are based on attracting skilled migrants and specifically focus on skilled professional workers. Women are now overtaking men as primary applicants in skilled migration streams (Docquier, Lowell and Marfouk 2009; IOM 2010), as their human capital attributes including skill, language and qualifications meet the requirements to fill identified skill gaps within Western labour markets. Many women are migrating with substantial work experience in high-level professional positions, including professions traditionally dominated by men. Professional migration is an important characteristic of the skilled labour market. Medical migration from the Global South to the Global North is widespread in the US, Australia and the UK. One of the fears of the outcome of the UK Brexit election is how will the UK make up for the loss of skilled labour, unless it makes some provision for migration.

Despite the widespread increase in professional migration, we understand little about the experiences and outcomes of job seeking for skilled migrant women (Kofman 2013; Phan, Banerjee, Deacon and Taraky 2015). One study seeking to fill this gap is Oikelome and Healy (2012), who compare UK-based doctors who qualified outside the UK with UK-based doctors who qualified in the UK with respect to perceptions of inequality, morale and career aspiration. Their paper argued that the human capital protection of qualifications, profession and status was not sufficient to equal the experiences of migrant doctors with those of doctors who qualified in the UK. Moreover, drawing on intersectional insights shows that women migrant doctors are the most disadvantaged despite the apparent protection of high human capital (Oikelome and Healy 2012).

However, high human capital enables successful migration. In her study of Sierra Leonean women scientists, Beoku-Betts (2008) found that while they experienced discriminatory practices based on their race, gender and nationality, their socio-economic status and marketability as skilled labour put them in a relatively better position to compete for particular jobs and to access rights and entitlements such as permanent immigration status. Thus acceptance of the positives and underplaying the negatives was an important characteristic of gendered migration. However, this was not always the case as the next chapter reveals.

Chapter 7 by Susan Ressia, Glenda Strachan and Janis Bailey focuses on the gender impact of skilled migration to Australia, which is a major pathway attracting immigrants based on their human capital while fulfilling skills shortages. Their interviews revealed that a number of professionally skilled women experienced adverse outcomes after migrating due to the intersection of gender, race and family compounded by the lack of quality services assisting their integration into the labour market.

Ressia et al. also draw on intersectionality as an analytical approach to understanding the experiences of skilled migration through the intersection of race, gender and family. They use a subset of migrant women who are neither sponsored nor from Anglophone countries, that is, migrants who are likely to face the greatest challenges. Ressia et al. show that this is indeed the case by showing that this group of highly skilled professional women experience severe downward mobility, far greater than their male counterparts. This is all the more surprising given that it might be expected that the well-known stringency of the Australian immigration system would put structures in place to ensure that their new professional migrants make an effective contribution to the country. Again we are reminded of the diversity of professional women. It is not their profession and its particular characteristics that determine the conditions of work; rather it is their gender, race and always for women their family responsibilities. The migrants in this chapter sought to improve the quality of their lives and went to Australia with great expectations and experienced severe disappointment when these were dashed. Ressia et al.'s chapter differs from most of the chapters in this book, as they seek to show how women, despite their human capital acquisition, struggle to *find* work rather than how they struggle to be treated fairly within work. Ressia et al.'s analysis reveals the value of an intersectional sensibility in understanding how inequality is produced, maintained and reproduced.

Gendered Flexible and Precarious Professional Work

What is emerging in the capitalist organisation of labour is the increasing move to a flexible labour force even in the professions. While there is 'good' flexibility which offers what we might call 'worker-driven' flexible work, much flexible work is what we would call 'bad' flexibility', which heightens insecurity and works mainly in the interests of the employers. In contemporary society flexible work may also be associated with internships which, if unpaid will secure routes of access to work for those who are able to afford to work for long periods for nothing. In this section we focus on an example of highly qualified flexible workers, academics in Australia, the precarity of architectural practice in Spain and the important case of work which seems to have no boundaries, clergywomen.

Insecure work is now a feature of professional employment in some industries; indeed Kalleberg (2009) argues that precarious work has spread to all sectors of the economy and has become much more pervasive and generalised and now includes professional and managerial jobs which are also precarious these days. For him, precarity is "employment that is uncertain, unpredictable, and risky from the point of view of the worker" (2009, 2) so that they are living in a state of permanent fear that their jobs will disappear or partially disappear and thereby threaten their economic security. Precarity can involve employment on fixed-term, temporary contracts or casualised work, rather than permanent employment. Engineers and architects in professional firms, for example, may be employed on a contract basis and dependent on the firm's winning contracts. This issue is important to investigate as women are traditionally linked to forms of insecure employment in lower levels of organisations (Healy and Bergfeld 2015). New professions such as those in IT are also linked to contract employment, which for some with scarce skills are well paid, but still insecure work (Grey and Healy 2004).

Research indicates that between 20 and 30 per cent of managerial and professional jobs are temporary (Doogan 2009). This is particularly the case within state employment as governments opt to outsource and privatise former state agencies. As a result, there is a greater percentage of highly qualified staff employed on fixed-term contracts and hourly paid work compared to permanent employment (see in this volume Broadbent, Strachan and May; Navarro-Astor and Caven). In private sector organisations such as engineering, consultancy and IT firms there is a plethora of project work, which means constantly forming teams with inherent insecurity (Grey and Healy 2004). The latter point is a current one as professions absorb ideas of flexibility including the nature of the employment contract. But least expected might be the casualisation of university academics leading to a two-tier system.

The Flexible Academic

The research of Kaye Broadbent, Glenda Strachan and Robyn May (Chapter 3) in research-intensive universities in Australia focuses on a highly regulated industry with market-leading equal opportunity policies. Their chapter examines employment insecurity and gender for highly qualified academics employed on fixed-term and casual contracts who perform core functions in contemporary universities. Their conclusions indicate that despite the advances made by women in academia, they have had to accommodate to insecurity, at the expense of career advancement or development.

Broadbent et al. point to the binary nature of much academic employment where the privileged, on open-ended contracts, are able to build their research careers because there is a temporary labour force, what we might recognise as a reluctant reserve army of labour eager to gather the experience that might just give them the opportunity to access the much coveted open-ended contract. Along the way, they are forced to confront difficult choices, all the more so if they have taken leave to care for children or elders. Casual academic work may lead to a career plateau and the intensity of the academic labour process means that academics on casual contracts will increasingly find it difficult to get more permanent appointments. This is not to say that some casual work may not provide the experience necessary to jump to a full-time academic appointment. It does for some who are able to capitalise quickly on that experience. But life gets in the way and even more so for women who may find the period of casual work far longer than they expected due to caring responsibilities and that casual work becomes an effective career 'dead end'. Moreover, women working on casual contracts may well find that they are more likely to be excluded from influential networks, normally dominated by males (Seierstad and Healy 2012). It is noteworthy that casualisation is not just an issue for Australian academics; for example, it is noteworthy that the University and College Union in the UK has launched an anti-casualisation campaign to protect and improve the conditions of casualised academic staff (University and College Union 2017).

It is also worth reflecting on this chapter, that despite high-level qualifications, the trap of casualised work may still ensnare those with the highest credentials, credentials which, from our earlier discussion, were supposed to promise security of employment and fair (even superior) pay. The first two chapters question both of these premises.

The Impact of the Market on the Precarity of Architectural Careers

Elena Navarro-Astor and Valerie Caven (Chapter 5) introduce the conditions of employment for women architects affected by Spain's economic crisis—specifically they focus on gender and precariousness in both the private and public sectors. Private sector architects were affected by the initial economic downturn as construction demand dropped sharply, while public sector architects were affected when public sector jobs were cut as the recession deepened. Their interviews revealed women fared badly in labour market indicators, salaries and working conditions but continued to remain committed to their professional development.

The economic context and increasing neoliberalism has been crucial to the context of earlier Chapters 2, 3, 4 and now Chapter 5. The fundamental relationship between the profession of architecture and the economy underpins Chapter 5 and the volatile supply and demand for architectural services and the relationship of the economic downturn and gender equality in Spain is well explored. Segregation continues as a theme with female architects following different career paths to men and experiencing discrimination and exclusion. It is recognised that architects may work in both the private and public sector, the latter offering more security but less aesthetic satisfaction and lower pay. Nevertheless, it was shown that many women may settle for a more secure environment that is better regulated with respect to equality.

Unbounded Gendered Flexibility Linked to a Professional Calling

Anne-marie Greene's (Chapter 8) examination of the clergywomen in the UK Methodist church provides a remarkable picture of a life dominated by their professional and spiritual calling. Greene shows how the unbounded nature of clergy work is even more the case for clergywomen than for their male counterparts. They experience an extraordinary level of gendered behaviour whether from their male counterparts, their congregation or even the general public. Reading this chapter one cannot but be amazed by the total gendered nature of their experience, which seems to tap into almost every moment of their lives and thinking.

Clergywomen are immediately disadvantaged by not having 'a wife'. Greene points to the expectation on clergy wives to bake cakes for parishioners and undertake the administrative work for the congregation. When the congregation get a female minister who takes over a parish (or more likely today a number of parishes), she is bundled up into one: 'wife plus minister' and expected to undertake the ministers role *and* the role of the minister's wife. Moreover, clergywomen's motherhood roles are also highly visible through schools, church events and shopping, which potentially leaves them open to the critical eyes of the congregation, who may have superhuman expectations of clergywomen to comply with the "expected ways of behaving, modes of action, attitudes, beliefs and form of body" (Greene in this volume). Unlike most professional groups, they are never off duty.

What was also notable from Greene's research was the level of acceptance of the discriminatory treatment the clergywomen faced. For them, the advantages of their work largely outweigh the disadvantages, in that their ministry work is deemed to be satisfying and represents a life recovery for them. Perhaps there is a level of gratitude that despite centuries of exclusion, they are now able to practise their calling, where sacrifice is an inherent virtue. Thus the importance of ideology in the professional project (raised by Freidson earlier) but in this case through religious belief in the professional context of the clergywoman is profound and powerful. Although Greene also notes the context of continuing declining attendance, which means that clergy are having to work over multiple parishes and congregations alongside decline in finances as attendance declines and churches close and wonders what impact this work intensification may have on clergywomen.

Gendered Societal, Organisational and Masculine Practices

At this point it is worth reiterating that these sections are interrelated and that many of the gendered experiences already identified will have relevance in this section and vice versa. Here we focus on the impact of society on the opportunities offered (or not) and the day-to-day experiences of masculine practices through the experience of women partners in New Zealand law firms. These are women who have 'made it' by climbing to the top of their careers and therefore their experiences are particularly insightful. The section moves to discuss the experience of IT workers in Sri Lanka, engineers in the UK and space engineers in Canada and finishes with a female-dominated occupation, nursing in Thailand.

Masculine Business Practices and the Gendered Cultures

Masculine business practices have permeated our chapters in different ways. We now turn initially to the relevance of masculine practices in the legal profession. In their chapter on women in law in New Zealand, Irene Ryan and Judith Pringle investigate the perceptions and experience of female and male managing partners, in other words those who have successfully navigated career hurdles to achieve the elevated position of managing partner. Ryan and Pringle argue that it is not the underrepresentation of women at the high-paying partner levels of law firms that is the issue any longer, but the masculine practices that underpin the business structures of law firms which frustrate women's career goals. Combined with the neoliberal economic policies adopted in New Zealand from the early 1980s, the 'business case' and 'merit' work in tandem with beliefs about appropriate age and stage for promotion to partner to create gender equality in the large law firms examined.

Ryan and Pringle's study shows how the acculturation of professional workers leads to the acceptance of the masculinist values and culture which have traditionally characterised professional workers. Moreover, their study seems to show that there does not seem to be a divide between men and women in the acceptance of these values, which Acker (1990, 151) would associate with "the abstract bodiless worker, who occupies the abstract, gender-neutral job has no sexuality, no emotions, and does not procreate" (Acker 1990, 151). It is noteworthy that Ryan and Pringle indicate the class differences between those who achieved the level of partner and those below that level who, while demonstrating frustration with the masculine culture, did not indicate the capacity for agency to make changes (Pringle et al. 2017). If change is to take place, it would seem it has to be led from the top, but there lies the conundrum which closes the chapter: the privileging of law as a 'special' profession requiring extraordinary demands from extraordinary people is neither serving the profession nor the sustainability of its people.

The impact of society on organisation practices and resulting masculine practices is particularly entrenched in male-dominated professions but begins in cultural practices in societies which impact crucially on the home and education context.

Societal and Organisational Practices in Information Technology in Sri Lanka

Arosha Adikram and Pavithra Kailasapathy (Chapter 9) explore the experiences of women working in IT in Sri Lanka, which needs to bring in more women to respond to the increasing demand for IT workers. They note that IT is an extremely important and growing industry in Sri Lanka with the employment of professions increasing from 15,586 in 2003 to 82,824 in 2014 with the vision to create 200,000 jobs and 1,000 start-ups by 2022 (Adikram and Kailasapathy in this volume). In this context of growth, IT potentially offers significant opportunities for women, who make up 51.6 per cent of the total Sri Lankan workforce. Adikram and Kailasapathy employ social cognitive career theory (SCCT) in order to explore how women form interest, select and perform in the field of IT within an Asian setting in the context of cultural and social barriers. They show that women are constrained in forming an interest and selecting IT in the masculinist image of IT and then again in their performance in the field of IT. Cultural forces such as gender role stereotyping beliefs lead to less self-efficacy. Work-life balance and the social support they received at work (client, manager, peers) and the family (husband, parents, in-laws) influenced their contentment and retention in the field. For IT-based organisations, it seems clear that if they are to grow and develop according to the vision, they will need to recruit more women and to do so they will need to ensure that they adopt sophisticated work-life balance policies and practices and that schools and universities need to work on challenging the gender stereotypes associated with IT.

Societal and Organisational Practices in UK Engineering

Susan Durbin and Ana Lopes's chapter 11 continues the theme of the underrepresentation of women in STEM through an examination of engineering in the UK. Their findings suggest that engineering is a highly segregated industry with segregation beginning in the school years and the choice of subjects. The Royal Academy of Engineering indicates that 92 per cent of engineers are male and equally worrying, 94 per cent are white (Royal Academy of Engineering 2016). According to Engineering UK,[6] engineering companies are projected to need 182,000 people with engineering skills each year to 2022. They suggest that the UK needs to double the number of graduates and apprentices entering engineering to fill this potential skills gap. There are echoes here of the Sri Lankan IT industries. The demand for more engineers means that the lack of women and Black and Minority Ethic (BME) professionals is a major problem for UK engineering both from a business perspective but also in denying talented people opportunities.

In their study of this highly segregated profession, Durbin and Lopes found there was a general awareness of the token status of women in the profession and that this had serious implications for attracting young women and retaining those already employed. As a result attitudes towards men's roles in childcare and domestic chores meant that organisations failed to encourage and value part-time and flexible working. They discuss the underrepresentation of women in engineering and how women engineers are perceived and treated including having to confront some of the negative stereotypes and gendered treatments that persist through blatant sexual harassment. Durbin and Lopes also highlighted the personal challenges that are particularly prevalent in male-dominated sectors (although not exclusively) through the need to 'prove yourself' as a woman, men's resistance to being managed by a woman and the general sexism experiences. Moreover, women were judged by their perceived reproductive capacity and the fear that they would leave or request part-time work. Durbin and Lopez cautiously suggest that if engineering were able to move to a more gender-balanced environment, this may lead to a more supportive environment where women were assessed as engineers, not by their gender. While they recognise that some of the problems lie with organisational practices, they also take the long view. They point to the challenges women face from their educational practices, their teachers' and career advisers' gendered career approaches, which all play out at the critical formative years. Thus the appeal for change is necessary and urgent.

Gendered Discourses and 'Doing Space'

Following on from the male-dominated IT industry of Sri Lanka, and the UK engineering industry, Stefanie Ruel considers the male-dominated science, technology, engineering and mathematics (STEM)-trained women managers in the Canadian space industry. She examines the impact of gendered discourses on the identities of these women and what it was like for them 'doing space'. She uses the critical sense-making framework (CSM) to consider how gender discourses shape the interaction between STEM-professional women and men in order to reveal the lived, ordered experiences of these highly qualified women and their intersecting identities. Interestingly, Ruel presents her own act of reflexivity to demonstrate what she calls the first 'I' in intersectionality and a possible range of ephemeral anchor points and also shares the emotional toll that the interviews have on her as the interviewer. This chapter is insightful as it provides a sense of the minutiae of everyday gendered interactions of women's experience of working in space and while recognising there is more to be done in revealing the power-effects on self and social identity.

Gendered Cultures and Nursing

The gendered experience of nursing in Thailand brings in an example of a female-dominated sector and is the focus of Uraiporn Kattiyapornpong and Anne Cox's chapter. They note that the nursing profession in Thailand is transforming but still is operating within a largely traditional society and point out that women's role in Thai society continues to be influenced by Buddhist beliefs and cultural norms that emphasise the superiority of men. Thai girls are brought up to contribute to the care of their family and to serve their brothers. Their findings focused on two themes: tradition defines career choices, and gender defines relationships and power at work and discrimination against male nurses. Nursing is seen as a suitable career for women as it aligns with the gendered values of caring. Interviewees stated that they were aware of discrimination in employment conditions but that patients preferred female nurses. The perception of women nurses was that male nurses struggled not only in relationship to patients but with women doctors. Kattiyapornpong and Cox's paper brings into sharp relief the impact of the society in which the profession is practised and in this has resonance with Greene's paper on clergywomen. The Thai patriarchal societal values play out in the social and career dynamics of nursing in Thailand. As might be expected, male doctors prefer female nurses as the doctor-nurse relationship has long been associated with paternalism. Moreover, the female nurses also promoted patient support of female nurses to ensure closure on a certain specialism in nursing and thereby exercise their gendered power. However, the impact of cultural norms on the socialisation of boys and subsequently men was also drawn out in the chapter. Male nurses were less compliant with both male and female doctors. So while female nurses respect the credentialism of women doctors, gender norms trump credentialism for male nurses, leading to more difficult relationships with female doctors, but also with male doctors.

In Conclusion

Our book about gender in professions and professional workers has begun and ended with credentialism. But we have covered much ground in between and contributed to a more contemporary understanding of gendered professional work in practice, where credentialism is only part of the story. We have tried to capture of the gendered context of professional work, diagrammatically incorporating the three themes emerging from the research in our chapters on professional workers. The wedges in Figure 1.1 below show the dominant interactional themes of professional context: inequality regimes, culture and intersectionality. The figure spells out elements of the dominant themes: for example, (a) professional context includes credentialism, (b) inequality regimes include masculine practices, (c) culture includes national culture and intersectionality (which is also an essential part of inequality regimes), which includes the (d) categorical intersections, such as gender, ethnicity and class.

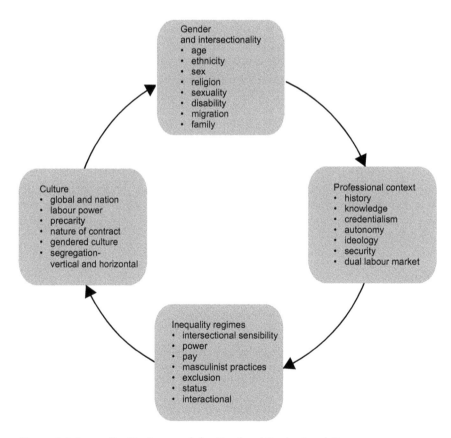

Figure 1.1 Inequality Regimes and the Gendered Professional Context

While professional identity in some cases does provide some protection from the worst effects of employment change, professional workers are not immune and women professional workers remain most vulnerable. Family and children continue to be used as obstacles and excuses to exclude women, but our chapters show that the gendered hegemony, while encompassing family and children, is much wider and deeper. The chapters in our book have exposed some of the gendered and ethnicised concerns that permeate organisations and institutions for professional workers in the contemporary global capitalist context. The focus on control and autonomy appeared less key to the chapters than in earlier work on professions (Freidson 1970; Johnson 1972). However, this is not to suggest that control, autonomy and power did not remain important; however it is the context of exclusion and masculine practices, even for those who had reached the top of their profession, that particularly comes to the fore. Credentials remain important and offer status and opportunities for many in our study but still they are not sufficient to overcome the gendered barriers in gendered professions. The creeping insecurity in the professions means that survival may often be more important than autonomy and control with professional workers. Thus we see professions creating flexible reserve armies (often gendered) experiencing the very worst effects of insecurity. However, our book reveals that there is a vast array of experiences that professional workers undergo and in different ways and in different cultural and national contexts. Sadly, despite women's progress in the professions, the resilience of gendered inequality regimes remains strong in all the countries studied. This book certainly offers a new take and emphasis on the link between gender and professions, a topic of considerable contemporary significance.

We believe that the chapters in this book offer a new picture of the changing face of professions and professional work and provide fresh evidence and thoughtful reflection on the complexity of what we understand by gender and the conditions of professional work in our contemporary global environment.

Notes

1. Including the bases of inequality, the shape and degree of inequality, organising processes that create and recreate inequalities, the invisibility of inequalities, the legitimacy of inequalities and the controls that prevent protest against inequalities. Acker 2006a.
2. Elsewhere Acker brings in sexuality. However, we would include multiple intersections including sex, race, class, race/ethnicity, religion, sexuality, nationality and go beyond to include place of qualifications and other emerging intersections of disadvantage.
3. Destroy the Joint graphic using January 2013 Australian Bureau of Statistics Gender Indicators.
4. A world where gender is a more fluid concept and such binaries do not take account of those who for example have transitioned or see themselves as non-binary.

5. Thelwell, E. 2017. "Gender Pay Gap: What Every Woman Should Know." Accessed April 28, 2017. www.bbc.co.uk/news/uk-39513573.
6. Engineering UK Report 2016. www.engineeringuk.com/Research/Engineering-UK-Report-2016/

References

Acker, J. 1990. "Hierarchies, Jobs, Bodies: A Theory of Gendered Organizations." *Gender and Society* 4(2): 139–158.
Acker, J. 2006a. "Inequality Regimes: Gender, Class, and Race in Organizations." *Gender and Society* 20(4): 441–464.
Acker, J. 2006b. *Class Questions: Feminist Answers*. Lanham, MD: Rowman & Littlefield Publishers Inc.
Anker, R. 1997. "Theories of Occupational Segregation by Sex: An Overview." *International Labour Review* 136: 315.
Anleu, S. 1992. "Women in Law: Theory, Research and Practice." *Journal of Sociology* 28(3).
Atewologun, D., Sealy, R. and Vinnicombe, S. 2016. "Revealing Intersectional Dynamics in Organizations: Introducing 'Intersectional Identity Work'." *Gender, Work and Organization* 23(3): 223–247.
Beoku-Betts, J. 2008. "African Women Scientists and the Politics of Location: The Case of Four Sierra Leonean Women Scientists." *African and Asian Studies* 7(4): 343–366.
Crenshaw, K. 1991. "Mapping the Margins: Intersectionality, Identity Politics and Violence Against Women of Color." *Stanford Law Review* 43(6): 1241–1299.
Crompton, R. 1987. "Gender, Status and Professionalism." *Sociology* 21(3): 413–428.
Davies, C. 1996. "The Sociology of Professions and the Profession of Gender." *Sociology*, November 1996.
Dex, S., Ward, K. and Joshi, H. 2008. "Gender Differences in Occupational Wage Mobility in the 1958 Cohort." *Work, Employment and Society* 22(2): 263–280.
Docquier, F., Lowell, B. and Marfouk, A. 2009. "A Gendered Assessment of Highly Skilled Emigration." *Population and Development Review* 35(2): 297–321.
Doogan, K. 2009. *New Capitalism? The Transformation of Work*. Cambridge: Polity Press.
Evetts, J. 2000. "Analysing Change in Women's Careers: Culture, Structure and Action Dimensions." *Gender, Work and Organization* 7(1): 57–67.
Freidson, E. 1970. *Medical Dominance*. Chicago: Aldine-Atherton.
Freidson, E. 1994. *Professionalism Reborn: Theory, Prophecy, Policy*. Chicago: University of Chicago Press.
Grey, S. and Healy, G. 2004. "Women and IT Contracting Work: A Testing Process." *New Technology, Work and Employment* 19(1): 30–42.
Healy, G. and Bergfeld, M. 2015. *The Organising Challenges Presented by Increased Casualisation of Women's Work*. London: Trade Union Congress.
Healy, G., Bradley, H. and Forson, C. 2011. "Intersectional Sensibilities in Analysing Inequality Regimes in Public Sector Organizations." *Gender, Work and Organization* 18(5): 467–487.
Healy, G. and Kirton, G. 2002. "Professional and Highly Qualified Women in Two Contrasting Unions." In *Gender, Diversity and Trade Unions—International Perspectives*, edited by F. Colgan and S. Ledwith. London and New York: Routledge.

Healy, G. and Oikelome, F. 2011. *Diversity, Ethnicity, Migration and Work*. London: Palgrave Macmillan.

Hearn, J. 1982. "Notes on Patriarchy, Professionalization and the Semi-Professions." *Sociology* 16(2): 184–202.

International Organisation for Migration. 2010. *World Migration Report 2010: The Future of Migration: Building Capacities for Change*. UN Migration Agency. Accessed January 10, 2017. https://www.iom.int/world-migration-report-2010.

Johnson, T. 1972. *Professions and Power*. London: Palgrave Macmillan.

Johnson, T. 1982. "The State and the Professions: Peculiarities of the British." In *Social Class and the Division of Labour*, edited by A. Giddens and G. Mackenzie. Cambridge: Cambridge University Press.

Kalleberg, A. L. 2009. "Precarious Work, Insecure Workers: Employment Relations in Transition." *American Sociological Review* 74(1): 1–22.

Kofman, E. 2013. "Towards a Gendered Evaluation of Highly Skilled Immigration Policies in Europe." *International Migration* 52(3): 116–128.

Larson, M. 1977. *The Rise of Professionalism: A Sociological Analysis*. Berkeley: University of California Press.

Larson, M. 1980. "Proletarianization and Educated Labour." *Theory and Society* 9(1): 131–175.

MacDonald, K. 1995. *The Sociology of the Professions*. London: Sage.

McCall, L. 2005. "The Complexity of Intersectionality." *Signs: Journal of Women in Culture and Society* 30(3): 1771–1800.

Millerson, G. 1964. *The Qualifying Professions*. London: Routledge & Kegan Paul.

Muzio, D., Brock, D. M. and Suddaby, R. 2013. "Professions and Institutional Change: Towards an Institutionalist Sociology of the Professions." *Journal of Management Studies* 50(5): 699–721.

Oikelome, F. and Healy, G. 2007. "Second-Class Doctors? The Impact of a Professional Career Structure on the Employment Conditions of Overseas- and UK-Qualified Doctors." *Human Resource Management Journal* 17(2): 134–154.

Oikelome, F. and Healy, G. 2012. "Gender, Migration and Place of Qualification of Doctors in the UK: Perceptions of Inequality, Morale and Career Aspiration." *Journal of Ethnic and Migration Studies* 39(4): 557–577.

Phan, M. B., Banerjee, R., Deacon, L. and Taraky, L. 2015. "Family Dynamics and the Integration of Professional Immigrants in Canada." *Journal of Ethnic and Migration Studies* 41(13): 2061–2080.

Pringle, J. K., Harris, C., Ravenswood, K., Giddings, L., Ryan, I. and Jaeger, S. 2017. "Women's Career Progression in Law Firms: Views from the Top, Views from Below." *Gender, Work and Organization* 24(4): 435–449. DOI: 10.1111/gwao.12180.

Royal Academy of Engineering. 2016. *Diversity Programme Report 2011–2016*. London: Royal Academy of Engineering.

Sang, K., Dainty, A. and Ison, S. 2014. "Gender in the UK Architectural Profession: (Re)producing and Challenging Hegemonic Masculinity." *Work, Employment and Society* 28(2): 247–264.

Schmidt, J. 2000. *Disciplined Minds*. Lanham, MD: Rowman and Littlefield.

Seierstad, C. and Healy, G. 2012. "Women's Equality in the Scandinavian Academy: A Distant Dream?" *Work, Employment & Society* 26(2): 296–313.

Simien, E. M. 2007. "Doing Intersectionality Research: From Conceptual Issues to Practical Examples." *Politics & Gender* 3(2): 264–271.

Strachan, G., Troup, C., Peetz, D., Whitehouse, G., Broadbent, K. and Bailey, J. 2012. *Work and Careers in Australian Universities: Report on Employee Survey*. Brisbane: Centre for Work, Organisation and Well-Being, Griffith University. www.griffith.edu.au/business-government/centre-work-organisation-wellbeing/research.regulation-institutions/projects/work-careers-australian-universities.

Tatli, A. and Özbilgin, M. F. 2012. "An Emic Approach to Intersectional Study of Diversity at Work: A Bourdieuan Framing." *International Journal of Management Reviews* 14(2): 180–200.

Tatli, A., Ozturk, M. B. and Woo, H. S. 2017. "Individualization and Marketization of Responsibility for Gender Equality: The Case of Female Managers in China." *Human Resource Management* 56(3): 407–430.

University and College Union. 2017. Accessed 17 April, 2017. www.ucu.org.uk/stampout.

Witz, A. 1992. *Professions and Patriarchy*. London and New York: Routledge.

Wright, T. 2013. "Uncovering Sexuality and Gender: An Intersectional Examination of Women's Experience in UK Construction." *Construction Management and Economics* 31(8): 832–844.

Wright, T. 2014. "Gender, Sexuality and Male-Dominated Work: The Intersection of Long-Hours Working and Domestic Life." *Work, Employment & Society* 28(6): 985–1002.

Wright, T. 2016. "Women's Experience of Workplace Interactions in Male-Dominated Work: The Intersections of Gender, Sexuality and Occupational Group." *Gender, Work and Organization* 23(3): 348–362.

2 Does Gender Equity at Work Have an Age Dimension? A Study of the Queensland Public Service

Linda Colley

Introduction

Public services are large employers of women, especially semi-professional and professional women. They have favourable conditions—such as highly regulated employment frameworks, merit-based recruitment and advancement and comprehensive adoption of equal employment policies during the 1980s and 1990s—which could be expected to support gender equality in the workplace. This research considers pay equity within one state public sector and asks why, despite these favourable conditions, the gender pay gap persists.

Traditional analysis of the gender pay gap tends to examine the progress of women compared to men. While an important starting point, this between-gender comparison can conceal important trends and inequalities, such as the intersection of gender and age and the potential addition of ageism to sexism. The concept of intersecting inequalities is not new. In the 1990s, (Crenshaw 1991) pioneered ideas of political intersectionality with her work on gender and race. She urged policy makers and activists to consider the intersection of different inequalities, and warned that privileging the treatment of some inequalities, rather than recognising that they are often mutually constitutive, can lead to marginalisation. Hooyman, Browne, Ray and Richardson (2002) noted the continued neglect of the field, and encouraged a feminist gerontology perspective in research and policy making. However, intersectional inequalities seem to fall between the cracks of our laws, institutions and even analysis.

This research builds on previous literature related to gender equality by adding an age dimension to the analysis and asking whether gender inequalities are exacerbated by age. It will study one jurisdiction to examine gender, age and advancement across the Queensland Public Service (QPS) as a whole, and in selected agencies with a predominantly female workforce. It goes beyond considering occupations, which often compares women to other women, to consider the potential career paths within major agencies. The research identifies intersectional differences according to age, and finds that younger women are faring comparatively better than older women.

Success in increasing the participation of women entering the public service has not been paralleled by advancement up the career ladder, and there is an apparent age barrier to gender equality at work in the QPS. There is continued vertical segregation as women do not rise proportionately to the top levels, even in female-dominated agencies.

Gender Inequality Regimes at Work

Governments have taken action to increase the participation of women in the public sector workplace. The first wave of reform in the 1960s and 1970s included the introduction of equal pay policies and removal of some formal barriers to the participation of women, especially married women, at work (Colley 2013). The next wave of reform in the 1980s and 1990s included legislation against discrimination and in favour of equal employment opportunity. Welfare state activities towards defamilialisation, through policies such as childcare, parental leave and flexible working hours, enable women to take part in paid employment by reducing the clash between domestic and work obligations (Gornick and Jacobs 1998; Mandel and Shalev 2009). Despite these government commitments and actions, women have not achieved equality in the workplace.

The gender pay gap is the most studied indicator of gender inequality at work and in Australia women continue to earn less than men. The convergence in pay that began in the 1970s, when the gap narrowed rapidly from 41 per cent to 19.4 per cent in the decade to 1979, narrowed slowly since then to 15 per cent in 2004, widened to more than 17 per cent by 2015 and is narrowing again to 16.2 per cent in 2016 (WGEA 2012, 2016a). The gender-wage gap depends on the extent of class inequality in the wage structure, the distance between the top and bottom of the wage structure, and women's placement in that structure (Whitehouse 1992; Gornick and Jacobs 1998; Rubery, Grimshaw and Figueiredo 2005). Australia's labour market institutions, including compulsory arbitration and a comprehensive award system for much of the 20th century, reduced the extent of class inequality in the Australian labour market. Since the 1960s, evolving equal pay principles led to the removal of some tangible forms of discrimination (Lewis and Shorten 1987; Evans and Kelley 2008) and the traditional male breadwinner family model has given way to a growing number of married women in the workplace (Chesters, Baxter and Western 2009). More recent trends to decentralise industrial relations in favour of enterprise and individual-level agreements may undermine these gains (Peetz 1998; Peetz and Bailey 2012).

Economic theorists attribute gender inequality and the gender pay gap to human capital explanations including women's lower investment in their own education and training, or employers placing lower value on education and training in women (Anker 1997). Hakim (1991) adds that women's own choices and preferences lead to their different labour market outcomes. These theories focus on individual choices and skills of women. Human capital explanations become less valid as women gain equal qualifications and increasingly remain attached to the labour market when they have children (Blau and Kahn 2007). Recent inquiries in Australia and elsewhere find that less than one-quarter of the gender-wage gap is due to human capital differences between men and women. The remainder is better explained by frameworks for wage setting, organisation allocation processes and the way capitalist societies treat the institution of the family (Anker 1997; Rubery et al. 2005; Todd and Preston 2012). Peetz (2015, 345) notes that "existing theories on human capital, labour market segmentation and discrimination fail to fully explain gender gaps [such as] the large gender gap in elite occupations where women apparently possess high labour market power".

The gender pay gap is more likely a result of inequality regimes (Acker 2009) where women do not have access to the career structures or the opportunities to progress to higher salaries. Societal inequalities from the domestic sphere are reproduced in the organisational domain and result in continuing inequalities at work (Acker 2006). Organisations may have increased their recruitment of women, but organisational contexts continue to shape women's careers and sustain inequalities through differential power relations and still-gendered employment practices (Acker 2006; Huffman 2013). Organisations shape career outcomes by creating opportunities with different rewards, and then making decisions to match workers to these positions (Huffman 2013). Under organisational inequality regimes, women struggle to gain access to steep career hierarchies due to gendered processes (Acker 2006), such as continuing perceptions of lower labour market attachment affecting promotions and the within-group bias where male managers promote male employees. The presence of female leaders is associated with less pronounced inequality, as they provide positive mentoring to women and bring fewer negative perceptions, such as lesser pregnancy-related job biases (Huffman 2013).

This research considers the intersection of gender and age. Age is another means of stratification in society but is often invisible in studies of gender inequality at work. Women's experience of the labour market is highly cohort-dependent, influenced by the labour market policies of the time, starting conditions and path-dependent processes of career formation. Older women have a very different experience from younger women, being more likely to have encountered barriers to education and training, to remaining in the workforce once married and to promotion (Pocock 2003; Hoffmeister, Blossfeld and Mills 2006). Thus older women may be in an economically worse position than others due to the cumulative effects of lower access to education, employment opportunities, parental leave and support for work-life balance (Spratlin and Holden 2000; Duncan and Loretto 2004).

Gender at Work in Public Services

This research examines the issues of gender inequality regimes and age within public services. Public services are large employers of women, and the post-war expansion of welfare state regimes created employment opportunities for women in health, education and welfare (Gornick and Jacobs 1998; Spratlin and Holden 2000). In Australia, women comprise two-thirds of most state and federal public services and outnumber men in many agencies. The QPS, which is studied in this chapter, is a large employer of more than 250,000 staff, of which 70 per cent are women, and of which around 170,000 are employed in two female-dominated agencies of Health and Education.

Governments have traditionally been regarded as good employers. High levels of regulation and unionisation provide uniform wages and good conditions and keep the lower end of the wage structure higher than other sectors while compressing the overall range and hence the gender pay gap (Mandel and Shalev 2009; Fairbrother, O'Brien, Junor, O'Donnell and Williams 2012). Peetz (2015) proposes that this reduced distance from regulation should improve gender equality outcomes. Governments have often used public service workforces to model gender equality policies across the labour market. This has led to a smaller gender wage gap in the public sector than in the private sector (see summary in Peetz (2015)). The Workplace Gender Equality Agency (WGEA) data shown in Table 2.1 reports the lowest gender pay gap is in public administration (7.1 per cent) with other industry sectors ranging from 9.1 to 30.2 per cent (WGEA 2016a). But the gender pay gap persists even in this favourable policy environment. Public service EEO programs removed formal and procedural barriers to

Table 2.1 Gender Pay Gap by Industry, May 2015–May 2016

Financial and Insurance Services	30.2
Rental, Hiring and Real Estate Services	24.6
Health Care and Social Assistance	23.7
Professional, Scientific and Technical Services	23.5
Information Media and Telecommunications	19.5
Construction	19.3
Arts and Recreation Services	19.3
Mining	18.7
Wholesale Trade	17.9
Transport, Postal and Warehousing	16.3
Manufacturing	15.5
Education and Training	12.2
Electricity, Gas, Water and Waste Services	12.0
Accommodation and Food Services	10.1
Retail Trade	9.9
Other Services	9.5
Administrative and Support Services	9.2
Public Administration and Safety	7.1

Source: WGEA 2016a

women gaining jobs, but have had less success in removing discriminatory allocative processes and attitudes in promotion—the glass ceiling seems to persist (Acker 2006; Castilla 2008; Mandel and Shalev 2009). Public services provide more professional and semi-professional job opportunities but, perversely, the overall effect has been to bundle women into feminised occupations and jobs that attract lower earnings due to the social devaluation of women's work (Castilla 2008; Mandel and Shalev 2009).

Drawing on the discussion to this point the analysis begins with two tentative hypotheses or expectations. First, despite extensive occupational segregation in the major professions, the female-dominated nature of the public sector will have resulted in women prospering in higher-level jobs within those female-dominated agencies. Second, given the longstanding gender equality policies and comprehensive maternity leave provisions since the 1990s, gender inequalities should only be evident amongst the oldest cohort of the workforce.

The study is based on the Queensland Public Service (QPS) because Queensland is one of the largest, most populous and most prosperous Australian states. It has a large population living in the south-east corner, but active mining and agricultural sectors in rural and remote parts of the state. Further, a combination of prosperity and political factors (being led by Labor governments for 21 of the past 26 years) resulted in eschewing of the radical reforms undertaken in some other states and instead a general acceptance of the public workforce as the preferred provider of public services (QPSC 2000).

The research uses a primary dataset on the QPS workforce, the Minimum Obligatory Human Resource Information dataset, both for the most recent year (QPS MOHRI 2015) and for trends from 2000 to 2015 (QPS MOHRI 2000–2015). This centrally managed quarterly data collection of the whole QPS workforce (approximately 250,000 employees) is linked to the payroll system and hence has a high degree of accuracy and completeness. The dataset contains variables related to individual characteristics (such as age, gender, length of service), employment type (such as permanent or casual, part-time or full-time), organisational characteristics (such as position held, agency of employment, salary level) and employee behaviour (including work arrangements and sick leave). This research draws on variables related to salary, classification and age. While the data is of a high quality in terms of accuracy and completeness, there are limits to the extent to which descriptive data can be applied to complex social and political processes addressed in the literature.

The gender pay gap is calculated as the difference between the average of all male and all female earnings expressed as a percentage of male earnings. In Australia, the gender pay gap is usually calculated on full-time weekly earnings before tax and excludes factors like overtime and pay that is salary sacrificed. Because the gender pay gap does not take into account part-time workers' earnings, it gives us a value that is comparing like with like.

WGEA identifies that gender pay gaps can include differences between men and women doing the same work, men and women doing comparable work or organisation-wide gaps between the average remuneration of women and men across an organisation (WGEA 2016b). This research focuses on organisation and agency-wide gaps.

For the purpose of analysis, the research uses a framework around the proportion of women employed in an agency: female-dominated agencies being those with more than 60 per cent women; mixed agencies being those with 40 per cent to 60 per cent women; and male-dominated agencies being those with less than 40 per cent women.

Queensland Public Service Gender Pay Gap

Given the highly skilled and professional or semi-professional status of many public sector jobs, the research begins with an analysis of the sector as a whole. Like most public services, the QPS has a high degree of vertical segregation, as highlighted in Table 2.2. Women comprise around 70 per cent of the workforce, and are proportionately represented or over-represented at the lowest six levels, but underrepresented at management levels (7–8) and even more so at executive levels (9–10).

This gendered distribution across classification levels is reflected in average salaries across the sector, as displayed in Table 2.3. In 2015, the average annual salary for women was $73,649 compared to $80,869 for men, representing an overall gender pay gap of around 9 per cent. This gap is lower around the median salary levels (around 5 per cent, with women earning $70,798 compared to men $74,619) and distorted by the wider gaps for the higher-earning 10 per cent of the workforce (women $100,686 compared to men $112,240). This is a narrower gap than the average Australian gender

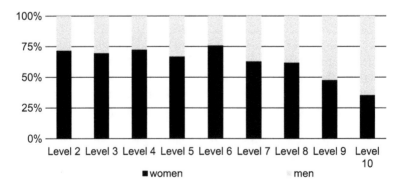

Table 2.2 QPS, Proportion of Women at Each Skill Level, 2015
Source: QPS MOHRI 2015

Table 2.3 QPS, Descriptive Statistics on Salary, 2015

Sex	No	Mean	p25	p50	p75	p90
F	177,517	73,649	55,756	70,798	88,142	100,686
M	78,875	80,869	56,896	74,619	91,585	112,240
Total	256,392	75,870	56,371	72,887	88,432	102,707
Gap		8.9%	2.0%	5.1%	3.8%	10.3%

Source: QPS MOHRI 2015

pay gap of 16.2 per cent, but poor for a sector that has a largely female workforce and has had equality policies in place for decades.

In the diverse QPS workforce, it is expected that there would be some correlation between the gap and the proportion of women in each agency, with male-dominated agencies more likely to have larger gaps than female-dominated agencies. However, the data reveals no such trend. Some of the lower gender pay gaps are in male-dominated agencies (such as Fire/Emergency services, 1.5 per cent) and the higher wage gaps in female-dominated agencies (such as Health, 15 per cent). The highest gaps occur in each of the male-dominated, female-dominated and mixed departments.

Analysis of the gender pay gap by age identifies distinctly gendered trends. Figure 2.1 provides a snapshot of the gap by age in 2015, charting wage trends for men and women as well as the gender pay gap. It identifies that younger women have higher average earnings than their male counterparts. But this is only up until the age 30–34 bracket, and there is a widening gender pay gap beyond this younger age group fuelled by two trends. First, the average salary for men continues to increase up to age 55 years, most likely as a result of career progression up until the earliest retirement age (with public servants being able to access their superannuation at 55 years up to 2015). Second, the average salary for women not only falls behind men but declines after age 35–39 years, potentially due to a combination of career interruptions plus management decisions around their career progression.

At face value, it might seem like this is evidence of improving gender equality, with the gap conquered for younger, often recently graduated, women, albeit not available to their older counterparts. However when placed into historical context (see Figure 2.2) it is clear this is not a recent phenomenon. In the lower age groups up to 30 years, younger women in the QPS have been earning more than younger men for a long period, and since the data available in the MOHRI dataset from 2001 to 2015. There is no gender pay gap in these age brackets. The absence of a gender pay gap is likely to be due to a combination of factors such as: the regulated nature of awards and agreements, providing standardised wages; the likelihood of many younger women employees being entry-level graduates in major professions such as nursing and teaching; and the large proportion of the QPS workforce employed in these agencies (around 180,000 of 250,000

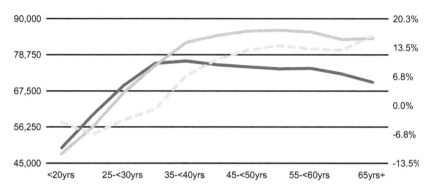

Figure 2.1 QPS Gender Pay Gap and Mean Salary by Age, 2015
Source: QPS MOHRI 2015

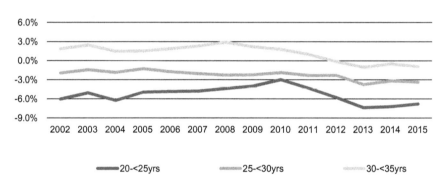

Figure 2.2 QPS Gender Pay Gap by Age, 2001–2015
Source: QPS MOHRI 2000–2015

employees). The change in the gap since the onset of the global financial crisis (GFC) is not related to improvements in the position of women and is related to a decline in the position of men during downsizing programs.

Similarly, there has been little change over time from 2001 to 2015 in the gender pay gap for women aged over 35 years. Analysis identifies that the historical trend for the gender pay gap for those employees aged 35 years and over is between 5 per cent and 10 per cent for those aged 35 to 40 years, and has declined a little since the onset of the GFC. For employees aged over 40 years, the gap is much higher, although with a similar trend of declining a little through the GFC and subsequent years of recruitment freezes and redundancy.

Against this overview of the whole QPS, the research now turns to the two largest female-dominated agencies—Health and Education. It examines the progress of professional women not within their professions, which usually results in comparing women to other women, but within the wider departments that 'house' their occupations.

Health

The Health department has the largest workforce in the QPS and is the most female-dominated with more than 75 per cent of its workforce being women (69,154 of 93,307 employees). The department workforce includes medical professionals such as doctors and nurses, allied health professionals, hospital administration and operational staff and general administrative staff. Many of the senior administration roles are filled from professional roles.

Table 2.4 provides descriptive statistics for the department for 2015. Based on average (mean) salaries for the department, there is a large gender pay gap of around 15 per cent, with men earning an average of $91,805 compared to women earning an average of $78,013. This far exceeds the gender pay gap of around 9 per cent for the whole QPS and is closer to the gender pay gap for the Australian labour market in general. In the lowest-earning quartile, women earn more than men and there is no gender pay gap. The gap remains quite small at 4.4 per cent for the lower-earning half of the workforce ($75,901 for women and $79,401 for men). The gap widens at higher levels, being 16.5 per cent ($17,588) for the top quartile of earners in the department and 34.4 per cent ($56,157) for the top decile. This is consistent with Peetz's (2015) observations regarding the large gap for women in elite occupations with high market power.

This trend is even more evident when the data is analysed across age groups. Figure 2.3 provides data for the Health department by age and sex, including the average salary (*F mean* for women and *M mean* for men) and the top decile (*F p90* for women and *M p90* for men). Analysis of the average (mean) indicates that there is no gender pay gap for younger employees, who are most likely in entry-level positions. The gender pay gap begins around 30–34 years and is fuelled by similar trends that occurred across the QPS. First, the average salary for men continues to increase up to 40–44 years (lower than the QPS trajectory of increasing up to 54 years)

Table 2.4 QPS Health Department, Mean Salary by Sex, 2015

Sex	N	Mean	p25	p50	p75	p90
F	69,154	78,013	60,078	75,901	89,225	106,932
M	24,153	91,805	58,314	79,411	106,813	163,089
Total	93,307	81,583	59,682	75,901	89,225	111,076
Gap		15.0 per cent	−3.0 per cent	4.4 per cent	16.5 per cent	34.4 per cent

Source: QPS MOHRI 2015

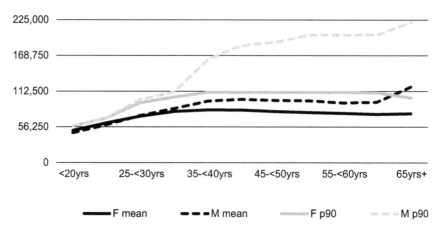

Figure 2.3 QPS Health Department, Salary by Age by Sex, by Mean and p90, 2015
Source: QPS MOHRI 2015

as a result of career progression. Second, the average salary for women falls behind men and declines after age 30–34 years, which is younger than the trend to decline from 35–39 years across the QPS but potentially due to similar reasons of career interruptions plus management decisions around their career progression.

Analysis of the top decile of earners in the department shows the stark gender difference in career trajectory—masked by the average figures—with the gender pay gap beginning around 30–35 years and widening quickly to 32 per cent and then in excess of 40 per cent from age 40 years. For the top decile of men, there is a substantial change in career trajectory from age 35 years. For the top decile of women, their career progression plateaus between the ages of 35 and 60 years and then declines, which differs from the continual decline for average women's income discussed earlier. Given there are more than 7,500 women in each of these age groups, the data is not skewed by small numbers and this is the average of more than 700 women in senior roles. It appears that there are different opportunities open to men than women, and this begins at a very young age. My tentative hypothesis that the gap would have been virtually eliminated for everyone except older women is not upheld, and gender differences in opportunity begin at younger age groups potentially due to inequality regimes.

Education

Education is another large QPS agency and is the most female-dominated with around 80 per cent of its workforce being women (71,864 of 90,289 employees). Table 2.5 provides descriptive statistics for Education. The average gender pay gap is smaller than in Health (8.9 per cent compared to 15 per cent), but the trend across the workforce differs, being wider for the lower-earning half of the workforce, narrower for the top quartile and widest for the top decile (albeit much smaller than Health at 1.3 per cent compared to 34.4 per cent).

Analysis of the gender pay gap by age reveals both similarities and differences from Health (see Figure 2.4). Women earn more than men in the youngest cohorts until their peak average salary between 30 and 34 years, with a drop in average salary between 35 and 54 years potentially due to childbearing and raising, and increases from 55 to 65 years. This differs from the trend in Health, where average pay for women declined continuously after 35 years. Men earn marginally less in their younger years, but their average salary continues to increase up until 50 years and remains high up until 60 years before falling for retirement-aged groups. Given the size of the workforce, there are in excess of 10,000 women in many of these age cohorts and around 2,000 men.

Table 2.5 QPS Education Department, Mean Salary by Sex, 2015

Sex	N	Mean	p25	p50	p75	p90
F	71,864	70,548.0	50,956.3	69,710.6	88,142.7	90,242.8
M	18,425	77,436.5	56,370.6	81,346.4	90,242.8	106,587.8
Total	90,289	71,953.7	51,433.5	73,037.0	88,142.7	93,243.1
Gap		8.9 per cent	9.6 per cent	14.3 per cent	2.3 per cent	15.3 per cent

Source: QPS MOHRI 2015

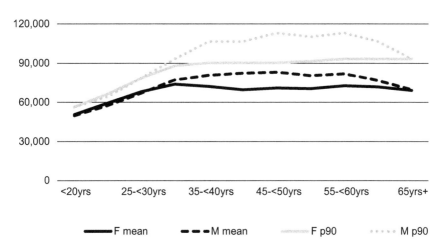

Figure 2.4 QPS Education Department, Salary by Age by Sex by Average Salary, 2015
Source: QPS MOHRI 2015

The trend for the top decile of earners is as distinctive as in Health, although the differences are smaller. As with average incomes, there is little gender difference for the highest earners up to 35 years. After that point, salaries for the top decile of women is slightly higher than the average for women across the department but relatively static until it begins to rise after age 50 years. The income/career trend for the top decile of men departs substantially from that of women, with gaps of between $16,000 and $25,000 across age groups up to 65 years. Despite women holding 80 per cent of the jobs in the department, they do not have proportionate access to higher-level jobs. For example, they hold around half the roles of education manager and 40 per cent of general manager roles—in both cases the pay gap is high at around 20 per cent.

Discussion and Conclusion

This article has examined pay equity within a public sector environment, with an in-depth study of two female-dominated agencies. The study identified that public services are expected to be conducive to gender equality based on factors such as highly regulated classification and wage structures and decades of equal opportunity policies. The analysis began with two tentative hypotheses that women would have prospered in female-dominated agencies and inequalities would only be evident amongst the oldest cohort of the workforce.

The study indicated that the gender pay gap persists despite decades of equal employment opportunity. The gap for the QPS as a whole was lower than that of the broader labour market, but the aggregated data concealed a wide gender gap amongst the top earners. The gap was not lower in female-dominated agencies, and in some instances these were amongst the highest gaps in the sector. The gender pay gap in Health was almost the same as the broader labour market, but followed the same trend of reducing slightly since the onset of the GFC. This is consistent with organisational inequality regimes, with women gaining access to professional positions based on their qualifications, but facing different career trajectories that limit their access to executive positions within agencies. In Health and Education, the widest gap is for the highest earners, suggesting that women do not gain proportionate, or even equal, access to higher-level jobs such as education managers or general managers. This confirms Acker's concept of inequality regimes, under which women struggle to gain access to steep career hierarchies due to discriminatory allocative processes and the within-group bias where male managers promote male employees (Acker 2006; Castilla 2008; Mandel and Shalev 2009). It also confirms Peetz's observation of the large gender gap in elite occupations where women have high-level qualifications and some market power, which cannot be explained by human capital and labour market segmentation theories. The proportion of women in an agency did not correlate to the gender pay gap or the number of women holding executive positions.

The data also identified that averages concealed wide differences in trends across age groups. Considering the longstanding equity and anti-discrimination policies in this and other public services, the research expected that any gender pay gap would be restricted to women in the oldest age cohort. Younger women are faring well, but this is not a new phenomenon and has occurred since at least before data collection in 2001. The relative equality for this group is more likely explained by the fixed entry-level salaries for most professions such as nurses, teachers and other professional officers where no discretionary decision-making is allowed, rather than the positive impact of equal opportunity policies. Contrary to my tentative hypothesis, inequality is evident for all age groups beyond 35 years. As employees gain more professional experience and potentially move into higher-level professional roles or administrative and executive roles, it appears that discretionary decisions support male progress in ways that differentiate their career trajectories from that of women. This is also consistent with Acker's concept of inequality regimes.

This research confirms that women have made gains in access to public service jobs and there is no gender pay gap in many of these professions at the entry level, but analysis by gender and age confirms that inequality regimes 'kick in' at early stages in careers and challenges whether equal employment policies are having an impact beyond the point of recruitment.

References

Acker, J. 2006. "Inequality Regimes: Gender, Class, and Race in Organizations." *Gender & Society* 20(4): 441–464.

Acker, J. 2009. "From Glass Ceiling to Inequality Regimes." *Sociologie du Travail* 51(2): 199–217.

Anker, R. 1997. "Theories of Occupational Segregation by Sex: An Overview." *International Labour Review* 136(3): 315–340.

Blau, F. D. and Kahn, L. M. 2007. "The Gender Pay Gap: Have Women Gone as Far as They Can?" *Academy of Management Perspectives* 21(1): 7–23.

Castilla, E. J. 2008. "Gender, Race, and Meritocracy in Organizational Careers." *American Journal of Sociology* 113(6): 1479–1526.

Chesters, J., Baxter, J. and Western, M. 2009. "Paid and Unpaid Work in Australian Households: Trends in the Gender Division of Labour, 1986–2005." *Australian Journal of Labour Economics* 12(1): 89–107.

Colley, L. 2013. "Not Codgers in Cardigans! Female Workforce Participation and Ageing Public Services." *Gender, Work and Organization* 20(3): 327–348.

Crenshaw, K. 1991. "Mapping the Margins: Intersectionality, Identity Politics, and Violence Against Women of Color." *Stanford Law Review* 43(6): 1241–1299.

Duncan, C. and Loretto, W. 2004. "Never the Right Age? Gender and Age-Based Discrimination in Employment." *Gender, Work and Organization* 11(1): 95–115.

Evans, M. D. R. and Kelley, J. 2008. "Trends in Women's Labor Force Participation in Australia: 1984–2002." *Social Science Research* 37: 287–310.

Fairbrother, P., O'Brien, J., Junor, A., O'Donnell, M. and Williams, G. 2012. *Unions and Globalisation: Governments, Management and the State at Work.* New York: Routledge.

Gornick, J. C. and Jacobs, J. A. 1998. "Gender, the Welfare State, and Public Employment: A Comparative Study of Seven Industrialized Countries." *American Sociological Review* 63(5): 688–710.

Hakim, C. 1991. "Grateful Slaves and Self-Made Women: Fact and Fantasy in Women's Work Orientations." *European Sociological Review* 7(2): 101–121.

Hoffmeister, H., Blossfeld, H. P. and Mills, M. 2006. "Globalization, Uncertainty and Women's Mid-Career Life Courses: A Theoretical Framework." In *Globalization, Uncertainty and Women's Careers: An International Comparison*, edited by H. P. Blossfeld and H. Hoffmeister, 3–31. Cheltenham, UK: Edward Elgar Publishing.

Hooyman, N., Browne, C. V., Ray, R. and Richardson, V. 2002. "Feminist Gerontology and the Life Course." *Gerontology & Geriatrics Education* 22(4): 3–26.

Huffman, M. L. 2013. "Organizations, Managers, and Wage Inequality." *Sex Roles* 68(3–4): 216–222.

Lewis, D. E. and Shorten, B. 1987. "Female Participation in the Australian Labour Force." *Australian Bulletin of Labour* 13: 237–263.

Mandel, H. and Shalev, M. 2009. "How Welfare States Shape the Gender Pay Gap: A Theoretical and Comparative Analysis." *Social Forces* 87(4): 1873–1911.

Peetz, D. 1998. *Unions in a Contrary World: The Future of the Australian Trade Union Movement*. Cambridge: Cambridge University Press.

Peetz, D. 2015. "Regulation Distance, Labour Segmentation and Gender Gaps." *Cambridge Journal of Economics* 39(2): 345–362.

Peetz, D. and Bailey, J. 2012. "Dancing Alone: The Australian Union Movement over Three Decades." *Journal of Industrial Relations* 54(4): 525–541.

Pocock, B. 2003. *The Work/Life Collision: What Work Is Doing to Australians and What to Do About It*. Annandale NSW: Federation Press.

QPSC. 2000. *Employment Security Policy*, Queensland Public Service Commission, April 20, 2000. www.psc.qld.gov.au/library/document/policy/employment-security.pdf.

QPS MOHRI. 2000–2015. Minimum Obligatory Human Resource Information dataset, collected quarterly by the Queensland Public Service Commission.

QPS MOHRI. 2015. Minimum Obligatory Human Resource Information dataset, collected quarterly by the Queensland Public Service Commission.

Rubery, J., Grimshaw, D. and Figueiredo, H. 2005. "How to Close the Gender Pay Gap in Europe: Towards the Gender Mainstreaming of Pay Policy." *Industrial Relations Journal* 36(3): 184–213.

Spratlin, J. and Holden, K. C. 2000. "Women and Economic Security in Retirement: Implications for Social Security Reform." *Journal of Family and Economic Issues* 21(1): 37–63.

Todd, P. and Preston, A. 2012. "Gender Pay Equity in Australia: Where Are We Now and Where Are We Heading?" *Australian Bulletin of Labour* 38(3): 251–267.

WGEA. 2012. *Gender Pay Gap Fact Sheet*. Workplace Gender Equality Agency (WGEA). www.wgea.gov.au/Research_And_Resources.asp.

WGEA. 2016a. *Gender Pay Gap Fact Sheet*. Workplace Gender Equality Agency (WGEA). www.wgea.gov.au/sites/default/files/Gender_Pay_Gap_Factsheet_final.pdf.

WGEA. 2016b. *What Is the Gender Pay Gap?* Canberra: Workplace Gender Equality Agency. www.wgea.gov.au/addressing-pay-equity/what-gender-pay-gap.

Whitehouse, G. 1992. "Legislation and Labour Market Gender Inequality: An Analysis of OECD Countries." *Work, Employment and Society* 6(1): 65–86.

3 Academic Staff on Insecure Contracts and the Interplay of Gender in Australian Universities

Kaye Broadbent, Glenda Strachan and Robyn May

Introduction

Historically, academic work in universities was seen as one of the professions reserved for men. Universities were bastions of male dominance (Larson 1977, 100) where women had to fight to gain a place. In many countries women were not allowed to enroll as students until the last quarter of the 19th century and were first admitted to the Universities of Cambridge, London and Oxford in the 1860s and 1870s (Hearn 2001, 71), and in Australia in the 1880s at the Universities of Melbourne and Sydney (Mackinnon nd). The representation of women has changed and in the 21st century women form the majority of students in many countries, although they are often a minority in the sciences (UNESCO 2010, 77). As university staff, women academics were seen as "outsiders in the sacred grove" (Aisenberg and Harrington 1988) and few were employed as academic staff until the final decades of the 20th century. While women now form over one-third of the academic staff in many countries, men continue to dominate the senior positions (Blackmore and Sachs 2007; Bell and Yates 2015; Strachan et al. 2016).

The composition of academic work itself has changed. Historically, there was "a deep, widely shared and seemingly unwavering commitment of academics to scholarly values, expressed through both teaching and research" (Bexley, James and Arkoudis 2011, 13). This nexus of teaching and research has been decoupled, and today in many countries there are academic staff whose work is totally, or mostly, *either* teaching or research. This change is relatively recent, and has come about since the 1990s at a time when the male domination of academic work has been questioned.

Until the last few decades, employment of academic staff has been on a secure, permanent basis, that is, a continuing contract of employment usually referred to as tenure, which offered a "well-defined career and promotion possibilities and pathways" (Bexley 2013, 97). However, since the 1980s universities globally have shifted significantly from elite (Larson 1977, 100) to mass systems of education (for example, Parker and Jary 1995; Marginson and Considine 2000; Dias 2015) often accompanied by a decline in public funding (Robinson 2006) and the growth and application of digital technology (Sappey and Relf 2010). As Marginson (2000, 23) argues, universities have become corporatised with their focus now on "mergers, managerialism and marketization". These changes have had a major impact on staffing models in many countries, which has resulted in an increasing number of non-permanent appointments, passing the burden of insecurity to employees (Keep and Sisson 1992, 68; Bryson 2004a; Bousquet 2008; Enders and Musselin 2008; Hughes 2015). The decoupling of teaching and research has assisted and most insecure contracts specify either teaching or research work. These changes have affected both women and men, but, like other employment arrangements, they have a gendered impact.

This chapter examines the structuring of the academic workforce in Australian universities into two tiers of staff—permanent and insecure. It examines the impact of insecure employment on two groups of academics—fixed-term research staff and casual academic teaching staff—and uncovers the gender story. To understand the issue of insecure employment and the gender dimension we asked: What is the impact of employment insecurity for academics? Is there an effect on career development? Does gender make a difference in the impact of insecure employment? To address these questions, the paper draws on data from the Work and Careers in Australian Universities (WACAU) survey[1] of over 11,000 academic staff from 19 public universities (Strachan et al. 2012) and qualitative interviews conducted with academic staff employed on insecure contracts. This chapter argues that employers have developed a segmented workforce and for many academics there is no choice—insecure employment is the only option they have. In addition to insecurity, this form of employment does not offer additional pay for years of experience and an extremely limited career path. As the survey and interview data shows, while the major impacts affect all staff, there are some gender differences around aspects of this insecurity.

Insecure Employment and Gender

In Australia insecure work, the term we use in this chapter, has been defined as

> Poor quality work that provides workers with little economic security, and little control over their working lives. The characteristics of these jobs can include unpredictable and fluctuating pay, limited or no access to paid leave, lack of security and uncertainty over the length of the job and lack of any say at work.
>
> (ACTU 2012, 14)

The term "precarious employment" has gained widespread currency with Standing's (2011) book on the "precariat" the subject of discussion and debate and similarly encompasses "lack of protective regulation, short or uncertain duration, lack of 'standard' employment benefits and ambiguous or unprotected legal status" (Burgess and Campbell 1998, 8). Traditionally, insecure or precarious employment was linked to work with few formally recognised skills and often precarious populations such as newly arrived migrants (see Broadbent 2003; Sengupta, Edwards and Tsai 2009). Studies in the 1970s and 1980s described the inequality in the labour market based on the creation of primary and secondary labour markets, resulting in a permanent 'core' and insecure 'periphery' which were the outcome of employers' search for flexibility (Reich, Gordon and Edwards 1973; Atkinson 1984).This has changed and insecure labour "can no longer be described in any sense 'peripheral', but rather as *central* to production today" (Trott 2013, 4: original emphasis). Some studies have analysed insecure employment in highly skilled and highly educated workforces (Carnoy, Castells and Benner 1997; Hoque and Kirkpatrick 2003; McKeown 2005) and in this chapter we see the spread and impact of insecure work into a highly educated population, most of whom have gained, or are studying for, a PhD.

Literature examining the gender impact of insecure employment is extensive, with a developing body of work analysing the impact in professions (Whittock, Edwards, McLaren and Robinson 2002). This research frequently discusses part-time work, which is prominent in many countries and is a way that parents (usually mothers) meet paid work and family care demands (Epstein, Soren, Oglensky and Saute 1999), and many employees on less than full-time hours work on an insecure employment arrangement. Much of the debate focuses on whether women voluntarily 'choose' part-time work (Hakim 1995) or whether the reasons for women's lower rates of full-time employment are more complex (see Broadbent 2003; Crompton and Lyonette 2005). Once in part-time employment, studies indicate that this form of work seriously limits women's careers (Crompton and Lyonette 2011). Debate has emerged as to whether insecure employment is temporary and a bridge to permanent employment (Burchell and Rubery 1990; Scherer 2004), or whether it negatively affects future employment options (Junor 2004; Watson 2013). Gender equity for academic staff in universities has been widely discussed (for example, Aisenberg and Harrington 1988; Fletcher 1999; Morley 1999; Brooks and Mackinnon 2001; Currie, Thiele and Harris 2002; Knights and Richards 2003; Acker 2010; Wilson, Marks, Noone and Hamilton-Mackenzie 2010; O'Connor 2014) as has consideration of insecure employment (Kimber 2003; Altbach 2009). Few studies, however, address both gender and employment insecurity in universities.

Insecure Employment in Australian Universities

Insecure employment in the context of the neoliberal agenda (see Pollert 1988), where restructuring the university workforce is a response to rapid expansion and resource constraints, has had a significant impact on universities globally (see Deem, Hillyard and Reed 2007) and in Australia (Marginson 2000). Combined with the growth in student numbers, university managements supported by deregulated labour markets to manage the competing demands for resources have restructured academic work, often in the face of union resistance (NTEU 2013). By decoupling teaching and research activities and "outsourcing" them to insecurely employed academics (Cloonan 2004), university managements created a tiered workforce based on employment status with different access to equity and employment policies.

The shape of insecurity varies in each national context, determined by the form of employment contract. Two main forms of insecure employment exist in Australian universities: employees on fixed-term contracts (mainly research staff) and employees on casual, hourly paid contracts (mainly teaching staff).

For research academics contracts can vary from as short as one month up to five years, with no guarantee of contract renewal. Casual academic teaching staff are contractually employed on an hourly basis, although they are typically engaged for a semester (12 to 13 weeks). Pay rates are not linked to an increase in experience. Casuals are employed on a fixed hourly rate. Fixed-term research academics' pay is determined by the level of their appointment, which is dependent on the level of funding granted and are usually equivalent to the two lowest ranks of the academic pay scale (85 per cent of women and 80 per cent of men in the WCAU survey) (Broadbent, Troup and Strachan 2013, 285). The differences in these employment contracts affect an individual's access to regulatory protections. For example, casual staff are ineligible for a number of benefits such as annual and sick leave, and maternity protection is limited to a period of unpaid leave. Under some circumstances only they are eligible for the national requirement of 9 per cent employer contribution to superannuation (see Table 3.1). In lieu of these entitlements they receive an additional payment (loading) of 25 per cent of their hourly pay. Fixed-term employees, depending on their length of contract, may be eligible for benefits and an increased employer contribution to superannuation as outlined in Table 3.1.

Both types of insecure work in Australian universities have expanded since the 1990s. From 2002 to 2012, the proportion of academic appointments combining teaching and research declined from 61 per cent to 51 per cent while research academic numbers grew by 63 per cent (Broadbent and Strachan 2016, 252). The number of academics employed on a non-permanent basis (not including casuals) in 2015 was 38.6 per cent (Department of Education and Training 2016). The WCAU survey revealed that 45 per cent of academic staff (excluding casual staff) were employed on fixed-term contracts (Strachan et al. 2016, 24). Of those academics classified as research-intensive (that is staff who spent 80 per cent or more of their time on research), 84 per cent were employed on fixed-term contracts (Broadbent, Troup and Strachan 2013), generally between one and three years in length. The proportion of casual academic staff (on a full-time equivalent [FTE] basis) increased from 11 per cent in 1990 to 22 per cent in 2011,

Table 3.1 Contractual Differences Between Permanent, Fixed-term and Casual Academics in Australia in 2016

	Permanent	Fixed-term	Casual
Appointment	After probation on a continuing basis	For the length of the contract—varies depending on the needs of the project	On a semester basis (12–13 weeks) or on a needs basis, but technically employment is hourly hire
Salary	Percentage increases determined through collective bargaining	Percentage increases determined through collective bargaining	Percentage increases determined through collective bargaining. Fixed loading (currently 25 per cent) to cover ineligibility for other benefits (see below)
Superannuation	17 per cent employer contribution	9.5 or 17 per cent employer contribution depending on contract length	Eligible when earnings exceed a monthly threshold of $450 (before tax) but then employer contribution is at the statutory minimum, which is currently 9.5 per cent
Annual leave	4 weeks	4 weeks	No entitlement
Sick leave	15 days annually	15 days	No entitlement
Parental leave	Varies by university and is between 26 and 36 weeks and structured in a variety of ways. Some universities allow primary carer to access the entitlement and not just birth mother	Entitlement is dependent on timing of pregnancy/leave within the contract. If the birth takes place at the end of the contract then entitlement to leave is unclear	Eligible for an unpaid entitlement only

outstripping the growth in tenured academics. Survey data revealed over 21 per cent of (FTE) academics were employed on a casual contract (May, Peetz and Strachan 2013, 260). It is estimated that casual academic teaching staff, on a headcount basis, are the majority of academic staff in the sector (May, Peetz and Strachan 2013).

These trends have a gendered face. The proportion of academic staff (tenured and fixed-term) who are women increased from 30 per cent in 1990 to 45 per cent in 2010, and 54 per cent of casual academic staff were women in 2010 (May 2014, 42–45). The WCAU survey indicated women are slightly more likely than men to be in insecure employment in Australian universities. Women are represented in all disciplines, but in some disciplines (not all) they are the majority of research academic and casual teaching academic workforces (Strachan et al. 2016).

Methods

To understand the employment issues facing insecure academics we draw on the WCAU survey and interviews with academic staff on insecure contracts. The survey was conducted in 2011 across 19 Australian universities and examined employment issues and gender equity. The survey received over 8,000 responses from academic staff and almost 3,000 responses from casual academic teaching staff. The response rate for academic staff was 35 per cent and 13 per cent for the casual staff (Strachan et al. 2012).

Interviews were conducted in two research-intensive universities in order to gain rich data on issues affecting fixed-term research and casual academics. Research-intensive universities were selected as interview sites as the WCAU survey revealed that this type of university is the major employer of research academics (Broadbent, Troup and Strachan 2013, 283). Due to their large size they also employ the majority of casual teaching staff, although the proportion is higher in newer and smaller universities. Both Research University and Old University rank highly in international surveys of universities and attract millions of dollars in research funding. In Australia, most competitive research funding or 'soft money' is concentrated in research-intensive universities, which affects their staffing profiles as high proportions of research academics are employed through research grants.

Eighteen research academics (14 women, four men) were interviewed in 2012 at Research University and 12 casual teaching academics (eight women, four men) at Old University in 2011. Pseudonyms have been assigned to each of the participants in order to preserve their anonymity. Semi-structured interviews focused on why these academics remained in the university sector, how they adapted to insecure employment and how they accommodated it in their daily lives. These were people who, by dint of remaining in the sector, had made their insecure employment situations "work" for them, and we have no information on those unable to make it work.

How Does Insecure Employment Affect Casual Academic Teaching Staff?

The WCAU survey of casuals elicited 3,163 responses. Of this group 57 per cent were women, the median age was 36 years and 16 per cent were PhD qualified while 38 per cent were studying for a PhD (May, Peetz and Strachan 2013). Eight of the 12 interviewees at Old University had completed their PhD and seven of the eight were actively searching for continuing or fixed-term academic positions.

Insecurity is a significant issue for casual academic teaching staff. The WCAU survey revealed that less than 1 per cent had secured an appointment offering more than one year of casual employment. Nearly one-half had appointments that were contracted for three months or less, one-half had contracts of between three and six months and 10 per cent had a contract of between six and 12 months' duration. Yet, two-thirds had worked within a single institution in a casual teaching appointment for more than one year: 16 per cent had worked for six or more years, 29 per cent for three to five years, 18 per cent for one to two years. To overcome the negative economic impact of employment insecurity, 20 per cent of casuals surveyed worked in more than one university (Strachan et al. 2012).

The impact of academic casual employment on a total life could be devastating. Annie and Lee were both casuals in their late 50s and studying for a PhD. Both women told a similar story of the personal toll their study and casual work had taken on their lives. Annie revealed that

> It has destroyed me financially. I work seven days a week. I can't afford to fix my house. I can't afford to fix a car that is falling apart. I can't afford some health things I need to do, but I am supposed to be in a really well paid job. I could not do any more hours if I tried. I don't have the hours left. I don't have a private life. I can't afford a private life.

Lee's comment illustrated the long-term negative impact of casual employment: "my superannuation is probably about one-tenth of my partner's. I can see that I will need to work on some kind of part-time basis until I am quite old".

The WCAU survey showed that casual academics are a diverse group but 56 per cent, and slightly more women than men, aspired to a continuing academic position (May, Peetz and Strachan 2013). The casual academics interviewed saw their employment as a temporary status and as part of their strategy to gain more secure academic employment. A third had applied for a fixed-term appointment (generally seen as a pre-cursor to a permanent appointment) and about two-thirds desired a fixed-term appointment that was either full-time or part-time. But over half agreed that casual work was all they could obtain. Only one of the 12 interviewees 'chose' the casual life. Kim, a woman in her 30s with two children, reported 'choosing' the casual life. She wished to remain in casual employment because it suited her circumstances, which involved caring for young children and a partner in a demanding full-time position. The choice, however, had a career cost: "it's a career plateau . . . and the pay is significantly reduced", but she hoped to return to her corporate career in the future.

The WCAU survey revealed that access to induction, career supports and professional development was patchy (May, Peetz and Strachan 2013) and many interviewees commented that they did not receive structured mentoring and career support. The semester-to-semester mode of employment limited their career development, especially for the transition to secure employment. Casual employment rendered them "marginal, temporary employees with no past and no future beyond the immediate term" (Gappa and Leslie 1993, 63). The work they performed contributed to their career development and resembled the skills needed for the transition to secure academic employment, but there was much that negatively affected their careers. Their CVs contained evidence of teaching experience but employment as a casual academic, while necessary for economic survival, reduced their research time, and the constant search for work, cultivating networks, managing student expectations and worrying about finances was exacerbated when applying for permanent positions was added.

Does Gender Have an Impact for Academics Employed Insecurely?

The WCAU data suggested that after two years working as a casual post-PhD, respondents' perceptions of gaining more secure employment were significantly reduced. Casual teaching, rather than being seen as a career stepping stone, acted as a barrier to career progress. There was a gendered element to this impact. Women reported particular difficulty limiting how long they would continue in casual employment while male interviewees concluded earlier that teaching was not assisting their career ambitions and so were quicker to limit their casual teaching commitments. Jed, a man in his 30s with one small child, was completing his PhD and had decided to stop casual teaching work and instead deliberately seek out research work because teaching was a "downward spiral": "I've actually said no to tutoring now. I love teaching, but the amount of time proportionate to pay is ridiculous". It is clear that the lack of pay increase to account for the experience is influencing the decisions of casuals to leave.

Gender differences were apparent in the way that women and men framed their casual working experience. Women appeared to focus on their deficiencies while men were generally more optimistic about the future and seemed more confident. Many women reported that they strived to be seen as "good" in every aspect of their work and hoped that someone would notice. They were acutely aware of the importance of a strong research profile, but were quick to point out their deficiencies. Lee commented that her research was "not so good. When I teach I tend not to do much research, and some of my teaching is away from my area, so I need to go back to basics". In contrast, Mohan, a man in his 30s who had a heavy teaching load, played down his lack of publications: "If I had to put a finger on one weakness it is that my research and publication record is not extensive. . . . The strength of my application is my broad teaching experience".

Women's childbearing and childcare responsibilities were significant. Abigail, a woman in her 40s with twins, described the difficulties of having children and trying to focus on study, and how this resulted in her taking much longer to finish her PhD than she had hoped:

> I really enjoyed having something to focus on that wasn't about the children; it was very rewarding. What I found is that it was only in the past year that I got back the capacity to really write the thesis and do it justice.

How Does Insecure Employment Affect Research Academics on Fixed-Term Contracts?

In total, 8,737 participants from the WCAU academic staff survey completed all three questions on the nature of their contract—55 per cent (n=4,824) combine teaching and research and 83 per cent of this group are on continuing contracts. Research academics were the next largest group (n=3,020) but only 16 per cent hold continuing positions. The overwhelming majority of research academics, 84 per cent (n=2,578), were employed on a fixed-term contract. Of these, 48 per cent were women. Eighty per cent of research academics (n=2,098) were PhD qualified (Broadbent, Troup and Strachan 2013).

The interviews at Research University revealed that only two research academics 'chose' contract work. Moira and Martha had chosen fixed-term contracts to boost their publications record, with Moira hoping it would increase her competitiveness for future grants. Three women research academics worked part-time for household/family reasons, compared with only one of the four men, because that was all he was offered.

The sheer numbers of research academics on contract was obvious to all interviewees, especially to those working in a research institute where few, and only senior managers and administrative staff, were permanent. Therefore, the focus for many was accommodating employment insecurity and making life choices which allowed them to work on contracts, including the reality that contract renewals rarely included promotion or recognition of increased experience. Only Bob (Professor) and Jocelyn (Associate Professor) had been promoted while employed on fixed-term contracts. The temporary nature of fixed-term employment contracts frequently left research academics feeling forgotten and isolated to the point of feeling 'invisible'. Jess reported that "in the time I was here only one lectureship was ever offered in my discipline area and that was offered at exactly the time that I went on maternity leave with nobody having talked to me about it".

The WCAU data showed that the access to career opportunities, new jobs and research collaborations was slightly gendered. On all of these measures, slightly more women reported problems compared to men (8 per cent women compared to 6 per cent men) (Broadbent, Troup and Strachan 2013). Only Carly's head of institute had developed a career plan for research academics. Career advancement was not discussed. All of the fixed-term academics had been on more than one contract, and only Nancy had gained a permanent position (but at the same level of appointment).

Fixed-term academics, like permanent academics, reported long working hours, an indication of the greedy and open-ended nature of academic work (Strachan et al. 2012). For fixed-term academics the situation was exacerbated by the approaching contract deadline. Alicia, a woman in her early 30s with one small child, recounted that "I . . . tag team with my husband and we have to . . . juggle . . . I've had one weekend in the last two or three months where I've been home for the whole weekend".

Does Gender Have an Impact for Academics Employed Insecurely?

The impact of child and elder care on a career was greater for women than men. The WCAU survey revealed that 46 per cent of women academics, compared to 4 per cent of men, were mainly responsible for childcare. Seventeen per cent of women and 11 per cent of men said they had responsibilities for an adult needing regular care, although it is unclear who was mainly responsible for the care (Strachan et al. 2012, 50–51). Women interviewed followed this pattern. Carly, a woman in her mid-30s with one small child, said it was "just crazy to chase my career" when deciding to have children. Nancy said that a research position, compared to a teaching and research position, made it easier to manage her responsibilities: "You've got a lot more flexibility than when you have to be on campus and you have to produce a lecture every week for 13 weeks". For those who worked part-time there were disadvantages. Nita, who like Carly was in her mid-30s with one small child, discussed the disadvantage of part-time work:

> while the school [department] attempts to make allowances for me being part-time and having carer responsibilities, I sometimes feel like we're just viewed as slightly, as less productive full-time staff members.

Geographic mobility, often seen as essential for advancement in an academic career, was frequently tied to family issues. The WCAU survey revealed 51 per cent of women compared to 40 per cent of men reported that they could not move interstate for their job (Strachan et al. 2012, 46). Women and men can be affected, as Yohan, a man in his mid-30s with two school-aged children, mentioned that he did not want to uproot his family.

But the difficulty of geographic mobility was reported most by women interviewees. Alison, a woman in her 50s with no children, commented that "I'd move if my husband moved. [But] he needs to stay where he is [and] I wouldn't move him at all". Jess, also in her 50s with two school-aged children, dealt with the limited opportunities in research and geographic immobility by retraining as a secondary teacher. Lucy resolved the tension of elder care responsibilities and her desire to remain in the university by going down the career ladder: "I'm probably prepared to work my way down to research assistant jobs".

Discussion and Conclusions

The experience of insecure academic work reveals high levels of insecurity and poor conditions of employment, lack of resources and support, which are consistent with jobs in the secondary labour market. The interviews reveal that the majority of insecurely employed academics have had to accommodate to employment insecurity, with little prospect of career advancement, because there are other few options for them in universities. Both casual and fixed-term contract interviewees appeared to have reconciled themselves to the insecurity of contracts and the resulting impact on their work, private lives and futures, including their competitiveness (or lack of it) in seeking permanent employment, an issue found in the UK (Bryson 2004b).

Casual and fixed-term academics perform key functions critical to universities. They share the experience of employment insecurity but differ in how pay is determined, access to leave and applicability of equity policies. Both groups, however, do not receive increased pay based on increased abilities. While in some universities some fixed-term research staff may have an entitlement to apply for promotion, in reality very few are promoted. Only two interviewees had been promoted and thus had their experience recognised. The majority of interviewees had not received the annual salary increases permanent academics receive.

Casual and fixed-term academic staff, like other insecure employees, are building "career capital" (Mallon and Duberley 2000), but there is a limit to this. Indications are that several years of employment on a fixed-term or casual basis negatively affects opportunities for promotion, career development and ultimately financial rewards. The WCAU data revealed that 62 per cent of research academics had been on multiple contracts and at the same level. The casuals interviewed acknowledged there was little financial gain or career advancement from years of casual teaching, the reason why many male interviewees placed limits on the number of years they would teach on a casual basis.

The WCAU survey indicates that numerically the gender breakdown for research academics is relatively even while women employed as casuals outnumber men, an indication that the growth of women in higher education is flowing through to employment in the sector. The gender story, however, is complex and this research reveals that its impact differs depending on employment status and length of contract. Women's prospects were further limited as the WCAU survey revealed that they are not as mobile geographically and are more likely than men to assume primary family care responsibilities. Theoretically, women and men are equally affected by employment insecurity, but interviews revealed women remained in casual employment longer and tended to view their casual employment negatively. Women research academics, especially those with care responsibilities or limited geographic mobility, tended to accommodate to employment insecurity by deferring their career aspirations.

It is clear that the primary gender impact of insecure employment involves accommodating to insecurity and making adjustments, especially for women. Women suffer a "cumulative disadvantage" (Primack and O'Leary 1993) as gender shapes and magnifies the unsteady navigations of the career and life cycle. With universities under increasing attack from neoliberal reforms, women are especially vulnerable (Leišytė 2016). More research is needed to determine if casual or fixed-term employment in universities is a bridge to permanent employment or a trap into an insecurely employed ghetto. What is clear is that insecure employment negatively affects the development of the skills considered necessary for securing permanent academic employment.

Note

1. Three groups of university workers (academic staff, casual academic teaching staff and professional staff) were surveyed examining the specific nature of jobs, careers and related issues (see Strachan et al 2012; Strachan et al 2016). The research was funded by a Linkage Grant from the Australian Research Council. The views expressed herein are those of the authors and are not necessarily those of the Australian Research Council.

References

Acker, S. 2010. "Gendered Games in Academic Leadership." *International Studies in Sociology of Education* 20(2): 129–152.
Aisenberg, N. and Harrington, M. 1988. *Women of Academe: Outsiders in the Sacred Grove.* Amherst, MA: University of Massachusetts Press.
Altbach, P. 2009. "Peripheries and Centers: Research Universities in Developing Countries." *Asia Pacific Education Review* 10: 15–27.
Atkinson, J. 1984. "Manpower Strategies for Flexible Organisations." *Personnel Management* 16(8): 28–31.
Australian Council of Trade Unions (ACTU). 2012. *Lives on Hold: Unlocking the Potential of Australia's Workforce.* Report of the Independent Inquiry into Insecure Work in Australia. Melbourne: ACTU. www.actu.org.au/media/609158/lives-on-hold-final.pdf.

Bell, S. and Yates, L. 2015. *Women in the Science Workforce: Identifying and Sustaining the Diversity Advantage*. Melbourne: LH Martin Institute, University of Melbourne.

Bexley, E. 2013. "On the Fragmentation and Decline of Academic Work." In *Tertiary Education Policy in Australia*, edited by S. Marginson, 97–104. Melbourne: Centre for the Study of Higher Education. http://melbourne-cshe.unimelb.edu. au/__data/assets/pdf_file/0007/1489174/Tert_Edu_Policy_Aus.pdf.

Bexley, E., James, R. and Arkoudis, S. 2011. *The Australian Academic Profession in Transition*. Melbourne: Centre for the Study of Higher Education. http://melbourne-cshe.unimelb.edu.au/__data/assets/pdf_file/0011/1714718/The_Academic_Profession_in_Transition_Sept2011.pdf.

Blackmore, J. and Sachs, J. 2007. *Performing and Reforming Leaders: Gender, Educational Restructuring and Organisational Change*. Albany: State University of New York Press.

Bousquet, M. 2008. *How the University Works: Higher Education and the Low-Wage Nation*. New York: New York University Press.

Broadbent, K. 2003. *Women's Employment in Japan: The Experience of Part-Time Workers*. London: RoutledgeCurzon.

Broadbent, K. and Strachan, G. 2016. " 'It's difficult to forecast your longer term career milestone': Career Development and Insecure Employment for Research Academics in Australian Universities." *Labour and Industry* 26(4): 251–265.

Broadbent, K., Troup, C. and Strachan, G. 2013. "Research Staff in Australian Universities: Is There a Career Path?" *Labour and Industry* 23(3): 276–295.

Brooks, A. and Mackinnon, A. 2001. *Gender and the Restructured University*. Buckingham: Open University Press.

Bryson, C. 2004a. "What About the Workers? The Expansion of Higher Education and the Transformation of Academic Work." *Industrial Relations Journal* 35(3): 38–57.

Bryson, C. 2004b. "The Consequences for Women in the Academic Profession of the Widespread Use of Fixed Term Contracts." *Gender, Work and Organization* 11(2): 187–206.

Burchell, B. and Rubery, J. 1990. "An Empirical Investigation into the Segmentation of the Labour Supply." *Work, Employment and Society* 4(4): 551–575.

Burgess, J. and Campbell, I. 1998. "The Nature and Dimensions of Precarious Employment in Australia." *Labour and Industry* 8(3): 5–21.

Carnoy, M., Castells, M. and Benner, C. 1997. "Labour Markets and Employment Practices in the Age of Flexibility: A Case of Silicon Valley." *International Labour Review* 136(1): 27–48.

Cloonan, M. 2004. "Notions of Flexibility in UK Higher Education: Core and Periphery Re-Visited?" *Higher Education Quarterly* 58(2 and 3): 176–197.

Crompton, R. and Lyonette, C. 2005. "The New Gender Essentialism: Domestic and Family 'Choices' and Their Relation to Attitudes." *The British Journal of Sociology* 56(4): 601–620.

Crompton, R. and Lyonette, C. 2011. "Women's Career Success and Work-Life Adaptations in the Accountancy and Medical Professions in Britain." *Gender, Work and Organisation* 18(2): 231–254s.

Currie, J., Thiele, B. and Harris, P. 2002. *Gendered Universities in Globalized Economies*. Lanham, MD: Lexington Books.

Deem, R., Hillyard, S. and Reed, M. 2007. *Knowledge, Higher Education and the New Managerialism*. Oxford: Oxford University Press.

Department of Education and Training. 2016. "Selected Higher Education Statistics—2015 Staff Data." www.education.gov.au/selected-higher-education-statistics-2015-staff-data.

Dias, D. 2015. "Has Massification Led to More Equity? Clues to a Reflection on Portuguese Education Arena." *International Journal of Inclusive Education* 19(2): 103–120.

Enders, J. and Musselin, C. 2008. "Back to the Future? The Academic Professions in the 21st Century." In *Higher Education to 2030, Volume 1 Demography*. Geneva: OECD.

Epstein, C. F., Soren, C., Oglensky, B. and Saute, R. 1999. *The Part-Time Paradox: Time-Norms, Professional Life, Family and Gender*. London: Routledge.

Fletcher, J. 1999. *Disappearing Acts: Gender, Power and Relational Practice at Work*. Cambridge, MA: MIT Press.

Gappa, J. and Leslie, D. 1993. *The Invisible Faculty: Improving the Status of Part-Timers in Higher Education*. San Francisco: Jossey-Bass.

Hakim, C. 1995. "Five Feminist Myths About Women's Employment." *The British Journal of Sociology* 46(3): 429–455.

Hearn, J. 2001. "Academia, Management and Men: Making the Connections, Exploring the Implications." In *Gender and the Restructured University: Changing Management and Culture in Higher Education*, edited by A. Brooks and A. Mackinnon, 69–89. Buckingham, UK: Open University Press.

Hoque, K. and Kirkpatrick, I. 2003. "Non-Standard Employment in the Professional and Managerial Workforce: Training, Consultation and Gender Implications." *Work, Employment and Society* 17(4): 667–689.

Hughes, D. 2015. "Fumbled Response to Grade-Fixing Affects Students, Faculty Alike." *NJ Spotlight*, October 22. Accessed October 26, 2015. www.Njspotlight.com/stories/15/10/21/fumbled-response-to-Rutgers-grade-fixing-affects-students-faculty-alike.

Junor, A. 2004. "Casual University Work: Choice, Risk, Inequity and the Case for Regulation." *The Economic and Labour Relations Review* 14(2): 276–304.

Keep, E. and Sisson, K. 1992. "Owning the Problem: Personnel Issues in Higher Education Policy Making in the 1990s." *Oxford Review of Economic Policy* 8(2): 67–78.

Kimber, M. 2003. "The Tenured 'Core' and Tenuous 'Periphery': The Casualisation of Academic Work in Australian Universities." *Journal of Higher Education Policy and Management* 25(1): 41–50.

Knights, D. and Richards, W. 2003. "Sex Discrimination in UK Academia." *Gender, Work and Organization* 10(2): 213–238.

Larson, M. 1977. *The Rise of Professionalism: A Sociological Analysis*. Berkeley, CA: University of California Press.

Leišytė, L. 2016. "New Public Management and Research Productivity—a Precarious State of Affairs of Academic Work in the Netherlands." *Studies in Higher Education* 41(5): 828–846.

Mackinnon, A. n.d. "Early Graduates." In *The Encyclopedia of Women and Leadership in Twentieth-Century Australia*. www.womenaustralia.info/leaders/biogs/WLE0432b.htm.

Mallon, M. and Duberley, J. 2000. "Managers and Professionals in the Contingent Workforce." *Human Resource Management Journal* 10(1): 33–47.

Marginson, S. 2000. "Rethinking Academic Work in the Global Era." *Journal of Higher Education Policy and Management* 22(1): 23–35.

Marginson, S. and Considine, M. 2000. *The Enterprise University: Power, Governance and Reinvention in Australia.* Cambridge: Cambridge University Press.

May, R. 2014. "An Investigation of the Casualisation of Academic Work in Australia." PhD thesis, Griffith University.

May, R., Peetz, D. and Strachan, G. 2013. "The Casual Academic Workforce and Labour Market Segmentation in Australia." *Labour and Industry* 23(3): 258–275.

Mckeown, T. 2005. "Non-Standard Employment: When Even the Elite Are Precarious." *Journal of Industrial Relations* 47(3): 276–293.

Morley, L. 1999. *Organising Feminisms: The Micropolitics of the Academy.* Basingstoke: Palgrave Macmillan.

National Tertiary Education Union (NTEU). 2013. *NTEU Submission on the Fair Work Amendment (Tackling Job Insecurity) Bill 2012.* Accessed November 12, 2015. www.aphref.aph.gov.au-house-committee-ee-fairwork-subs-sub3.pdf.

O'Connor, P. 2014. *Management and Gender in Higher Education.* Manchester: Manchester University Press.

Parker, M. and Jary, D. 1995. "The McUniversity: Organization, Management and Academic Subjectivity." *Organization* 2: 319–338.

Pollert, A. 1988. "The 'Flexible Firm': Fixation or Fact?" *Work, Employment and Society* 2(3): 281–316.

Primack, R.B. and O'Leary, V. 1993. "Cumulative Disadvantages in the Careers of Women Ecologists." *BioScience* 43(3): 158–165.

Reich, M., Gordon, D. and Edwards, R. 1973. "A Theory of Labour Market Segmentation." *American Economic Review* 63(2): 359–365.

Robinson, D. 2006. *The Status of Higher Education Teaching Personnel in Australia, Canada, New Zealand, the United Kingdom and the United States.* Report produced for Education International.

Sappey, J. and Relf, S. 2010. "Digital Technology Education and Its Impact on Traditional Academic Roles." *Journal of University Teaching and Learning Practice* 7(1): 1–17.

Scherer, S. 2004. "Stepping Stones or Traps? The Consequences of Labour Market Entry Positions on Future Careers in West Germany, Great Britain and Italy." *Work, Employment and Society* 18(2): 369–394.

Sengupta, S., Edwards, P. and Tsai, C. 2009. "The Good, the Bad and the Ordinary: Work Identities in 'Good' and 'Bad' Jobs in the United Kingdom." *Work and Occupations* 36(1): 26–55.

Standing, G. 2011. *The Precariat: The New Dangerous Class.* London: Bloomsbury Academic.

Strachan, G., Peetz, D., Whitehouse, G., Troup, C., Bailey, J., Broadbent, K., May, R. and Nesic, M. 2016. *Women, Careers and Universities: Where to from Here?* Brisbane: Centre for Work, Organisation and Wellbeing, Griffith University. www.griffith.edu.au/__data/assets/pdf_file/0010/915589/UA-FINAL-Report-Digital-4-April-2016.pdf.

Strachan, G., Troup, C., Peetz, D., Whitehouse, G., Broadbent, K. and Bailey, J. 2012. *Work and Careers in Australian Universities: Report on Employee Survey.*

Brisbane: Centre for Work, Organisation and Wellbeing, Griffith University. www.griffith.edu.au/__data/assets/pdf_file/0004/469192/Work-and-Career-Report-on-Employee-Survey_Final-v2.pdf.

Trott, B. 2013. "From the Precariat to the Multitude." *Global Discourse: An Interdisciplinary Journal of Current Affairs and Applied Contemporary Thought* 3(3–4): 406–425.

UNESCO. 2010. *Global Education Digest 2010: Comparing Education Statistics Across the World*. Montreal: UNESCO Institute for Statistics. www.uis.unesco.org/Library/Documents/GED_2010_EN.pdf.

Watson, I. 2013. "Bridges or Traps? Casualisation and Labour Market Transitions in Australia." *Journal of Industrial Relations* 55(6): 6–37.

Whittock, M., Edwards, C., McLaren, S. and Robinson, O. 2002. "The Tender Trap': Gender, Part-Time Nursing and the Effects of 'Family-Friendly' Policies on Career Advancement." *Sociology of Health and Illness* 24(3): 305–326.

Wilson, J., Marks, G., Noone, L. and Hamilton-Mackenzie, J. 2010. "Retaining a Foothold on the Slippery Paths of Academia: University Women, Indirect Discrimination, and the Academic Marketplace." *Gender and Education* 22(5): 535–545.

4   The Gendered Law Profession

The Perceptions and Experiences of Female Partners and Male Managing Partners

Irene Ryan and Judith K. Pringle

Introduction

In principle, the legal profession should be an institution deeply committed to equality and social justice (Rhode 2011). Yet in practice, this appears to not be the case. Evidence is captured in a lead article in New Zealand's influential current affairs magazine, which opened with the statement: "Legal Discrimination: They dominate the profession and are some of its best and brightest, yet research confirms female lawyers are often subject to unfair biases" (Vaughan 2016, 30). A journalistic play on words, perhaps, but one that has a familiar tone: the persistence of gendered inequities in the legal profession is positioned as a 'women problem' (Vaughan 2016). Here we argue that the problem is not the underrepresentation of women in the lucrative partner echelons, but the dominant presence of influential men and valued forms of masculine business practices. It is these masculine practices that underpin the business structures of large law firms and provide the focus for this chapter.

The number of female law graduates has, since the 1990s, exceeded the number of male law graduates. At entry level, law is a New Zealand (NZ) success story, which is replicated in other comparable jurisdictions (Kumra 2015; Pringle, Giddings, Harris, Jaeger, Lin, Ravenswood and Ryan 2014; Rhode 2011; Sommerlad 2016). In 2015, 61 per cent of new admissions to the Bar were women (cf. 1980 = 26.3 per cent) (Adlam and Jacombs 2016) and 44.2 per cent held practising certificates. In spite of these proportions, only 27.1 per cent of partners and directors in law firms were female. In the largest law firms, where 19.6 per cent of all law firm lawyers work, almost half of all lawyers were women (49.3 per cent), but only 21.7 per cent of partners and directors were women (NZ Law Society 2015). As women graduates have been streaming into law for more than two decades they have not filled all levels of the hierarchy in the expected proportions.

The numerical disparity in the ratio of female to male partners is not unique to NZ. The same disparities are found in similar jurisdictions, for example, Australia (New South Wales, 18 per cent) (NSW Law Society 2012), England and Wales (22 per cent) (Walsh 2012) and the US (19 per cent) (Pinnington and Sandberg 2013). Nor is it unique to professional service firms, of which law firms constitute a substantial part. Explanations as to why this disparity remains is best illustrated in literature on the gendered patterns of careers in law (Lying 2010; Rhode 2011; Sommerlad 2016). Three decades of research, benchmarking and analysis, all directed primarily at women, precedes the current discussion. The working environments where lawyers practice are far from homogenous. The barriers to career promotion are particularly prevalent in the hierarchical structures of large law firms. Those barriers most frequently identified in the research include inflexible work hours, expectations of long hours, high workloads, organisational models of billing, care and family responsibilities, poor work/life balance, cultures of presenteeism and gendered constructions of meritocracy (Baron 2015; Kumra 2015; Pringle et al. 2014; Sommerlad 2016). All of these features are exacerbated by the timing of career progression structures coinciding with the biological imperative of childbearing. The life course priorities of women in their 30s provide a crucial decision dilemma (and to a lesser extent men) deciding on whether or not to 'go up' for partner. Despite rhetorical discussion of the need to redesign work structures and opportunities, the large law firms in the UK have shown little inclination to alter the traditional business model that shapes their practices (Kumra 2015).

Given the extensive literature on women within professional service firms and law, the focus we take in this chapter is to question the all too familiar response: that gender equity in the legal profession is a 'women problem' that has to be solved by women. Men are clearly present, especially in having children, but fade from sight replaced by discussions of the numbers of women and the paucity of women at senior levels of the firm and the profession. We concur with Sinclair (2014, 24) who asks, "Why is it still more comfortable to keep the 'problem' of gender located in women and to hold women responsible for fixing their own exclusion?"

In the following sections we sketch the wider national and cultural context of employment and its impact on the law profession. We then describe a comprehensive research study of gender issues arising in the large law firms in Auckland, NZ. This empirical research, commissioned in 2012, included surveys and interviews with women and men below partnership level, women partners and some of the managing partners.[1] The purpose of the wider study was to investigate the low proportions of women at senior levels and the reasons for this situation. In this chapter we discuss a part of this research that is less studied and discussed in the wider occupational literature. We examine the responses of those above partner level, women who have 'made it' and the perceptions of the managing partners, the leaders of these influential corporate law firms. We ask for their views on how the representations of women and men at senior levels may be more equitable.

National and Cultural Context

The backdrop against which we consider law as a gendered profession is neoliberalism, an ideology embraced by the leaders of the country since the mid-1980s (Callaghan 2009; Roper, Ganesh and Inkson 2010; Kelsey 2015).

The outcome is that "after three decades, New Zealand is one of the most neoliberal countries in the OECD" (Kelsey 2015, 121–122). A whole raft of supposedly 'common-sense' values: individual choice, individual initiative, individual responsibility and meritocracy are part of everyday societal discourse on fairness and equity. The law profession fits the neoliberal mould through its status as a 'special career' for highly competitive, achievement-orientated, exceptional individuals whose primary function is now to facilitate market economics (Collier 2014, 216). Thus the enduring inequities between groups of men and most women are rendered invisible by the individualising tendencies of neoliberalism. Equality of opportunity, not outcome (Jewson and Mason 1986), dominates the equity discourse (Jewson and Mason 1986; Sen 1992). New Zealand is now 17th among 36 OECD countries in the representation of women in management roles, having been fourth in 2003. The legal profession and the position of women within it provide a vivid exemplar of how women are an integral part of this "capitalist service industry" yet still suffer "archaic attitudes to gender" (Sommerlad 2016, 62).

In light of the patchy, slow pace of change, the National Council for Women of New Zealand has labelled gender equality, in policy terms, a wicked, systemic problem (National Council of Women of New Zealand 2015, 20). This is quite ironic given their founding president in 1896 was Kate Sheppard, who was at the forefront of women's suffrage, won in 1893 (National Council of Women of New Zealand 2016, 20). The same year Ethel Benjamin, known as NZ's female legal pioneer, began her law degree at the University of Otago. Her graduation gave effect to The Female Law Practitioners Act 1896 when she was admitted as a barrister and solicitor to the Supreme Court in 1897 (Brown 2013). From what is known of her legal practice experiences, historical accounts report that she was an astute commercial and property lawyer and businesswoman (November 2009). Nonetheless, Ethel struggled as the only woman in a conservative 'gentlemen's' profession. Now, in the 21st century, the early legal pioneers such as Ethel Benjamin would be pleased with the numerical transformation but perhaps dismayed and perplexed by the numerical disparity at the higher levels of large law firms. The much used analogy of the 'pipeline effect' and efforts to stem the leakage of women has failed to materialise.[2]

It was concerns over the 'leaking pipeline' that prompted the Auckland Women Lawyers' Association (AWLA) to contract members of the Gender and Diversity Research Group[3] to explore the reasons for the scarcity of women at senior levels in large law firms. While the paucity of female partners in law firms has generated much research interest, the research design of this study had the advantage of providing multiple perspectives on the crucial career transition, promotion to partner. The study explored the factors influencing careers of women 'below' the partnership line, and women partners situated 'above' it.

For the purpose of this chapter we draw on the interviews with five male managing partners who talk of their perceptions of women's experiences and 28 female partners, all of whom work in the eleven top large law firms in the competitive Auckland market. This group provided detailed insights into internal firm processes and with career longevity, they were able to reflect on changes in the profession including the external, strategic landscape of law. In the next section we outline the methodology and methods. Following this we intertwine the findings and discussion to further explain the disparities between female and male lawyers and the gendered patterns of career progression in law.

Methodology and Methods

The methodology chosen for the research was post positivist research, specifically interpretive qualitative (Smythe 2012). The study was structured in three phases: first, a short online survey of 136 volunteer respondents (105 women and 31 men) from eleven large Auckland law firms was carried out. Second, in-depth, semi-structured one-on-one interviews were carried out with 26 female and four male volunteers who held positions below partnership level and who fulfilled defined selection criteria. Third, similar style interviews were completed with 29 women partner volunteers and five male managing partners (for further information on participants refer to tables in Pringle et al. 2014, 41 and 61). All interviewees were from the same eleven large Auckland law firms. The semi-structured format to the interviews enabled greater consistency across multiple interviewers than, for example, the more open-ended conversational interviews. For the purpose of this chapter our focus is the interview data collected in the third phase with women partners and managing partners—29 female partners and five male managing partners (Pringle et al. 2014).

Content analysis of the interview transcripts was carried out. Thematic coding templates were developed for the two sample groups and analysed by two groups of three researchers. The completed coding templates were used as the basis for summarising the main themes from all the interviews (Braun and Clarke 2006). There was homogeneity across the total sample in terms of demographic characteristics. The average women partner (n=29) was aged 44 years, a European New Zealander, six years in their current position, 11 years working in the firm. She was most likely working full-time, 50–60 hours per week, earning $NZ397,222, married with at least one child, and a quarter were working part-time. Seventy-five per cent had overseas experience in law, most commonly in London or New York.

There were six volunteers (five men and one woman) from six of the 11 law firms in the study. Availability was a key reason for non-participation. For the purpose of this chapter we use the interview data from the five male managing partners. The five male managing partners were married; most had children and primarily their wife/partner looked after home concerns. All typically worked 55–65 hours per week earning 'managing partner or CEO salaries'. All managing partners had spent time overseas in law firms.

Findings and Discussion

In this section we use a selection of the key findings to discuss women's and men's accounts of 'views from the top' of large law firms. We sought to better understand the dominant presence of men at senior levels and the valued forms of masculine business practices that sustain the gendered nature of careers in law.

Characteristics of a Successful Lawyer and Partner

The primary characteristics required to be a 'good lawyer' and a successful partner identified by women partners focused on personal characteristics: intelligence, determination, dedication, mental toughness, resilience, drive, client orientation and clarity of thinking. The term 'rainmaker' was cited a number of times as key for succeeding as a partner. Other female partners articulated the importance of women having ambition to be partner, having strong support at home and maintaining unbroken careers.

> So everyone expects you to be a top-shelf scholar, very smart. How you look after your client—looking after your team and developing your team is a really big one now . . . There are lots of really good lawyers. What additional [aspect] is it that they're adding to the partnership? . . . When you see someone coming through you just know if they've got it or not. And it's very hard to articulate it, but you just know it.
>
> (#2)

A lack of assertiveness by women in general was considered by one female partner:

> And I think there is a gendered aspect to that, that worries me a little bit . . . we're not as good at shoving ourselves forward the way that guys are and I think that holds us back.
>
> (#27)

Not all references to gender were as explicit as this response, with one interviewee analysing in more detail the nature of merit:

> In this commercial high-level legal world, there is a very strong culture that merit is equated with super-confidence, bit loud, never wrong or never think you're wrong. A lot of traits that go with males, or that go with a certain kind of male. So it also excludes a whole lot of other males as well as many women. Because it's what's perceived as being a great lawyer . . . and the men don't realise it's happening. They do not realise it. They say, 'Don't know what we're doing. How can we retain more women?' They do not understand it, that it's a very subtle thing.

That what is seen as merit, is often a classic, stereotypical, loud, confident, articulate, probably working in court or great rainmaker male person. And some of the traits that women have, which actually make them into either better lawyers or better client relationship people, are not perceived as merit.

(#8)

Managing partners also talked about the challenging nature of a career in law, illustrated with this reflective and telling comment: "I do think that law is a really tough career; I mean it's worked for me. I wouldn't recommend it to my children". (#11MP)[4]

Another stated that for a female lawyer to have a baby "then all sorts of trouble happens" (#31MP).

The 'challenge' was perceived to intensify as one progressed. In order to succeed, women who have children have to decide what they need to give up for career progression to partner:

And to be a partner, you need to meet the criteria for partnership, and it requires so much of them, that a lot of women who are trying to have a balance in their lives will struggle with that. And therefore the choice they have to make is how much are they going to give up in order to adopt the full responsibilities of being a partner.

(#32MP)

The Partnership Model

The main business partnership models in law are: parity or equity partners (equal owners of the firm) differentiated from salaried partners who are paid at a lower rate, but the rewards are not dependent on the work flow. Parity partners are based on a principle of equality, sharing the risks and rewards. The two main partnership equity structures of law firms internationally (including Auckland) were described in colourful metaphors by one interviewee as "either 'eat what you kill', 'performance based' or 'lock-step' models—the English and the New York top tier firm model" (#34MP).

There was mixed opinion on the inevitability of the parity model for the profession, raising the question: is the partnership structure of large law firms changeable? When reflecting on the partnership structure, one female partner interviewee commented:

And I mean a partnership is a terrible way to run a business, a terrible structure to have all of the owners be all of the managers and all of the shareholders, you know, concentrating the power in that way is just retarded, like no commercial operation would succeed if it was run this way and it produces some really perverse outcomes.

(#27)

Such comment moots the question of whether the partnership structure of large law firms can be changed. One interviewee was a clear advocate for change:

> We've got more women law grads coming through each year by far . . . a number of those work part-time so it makes it harder for them [women] to progress to partnership, which is why the part-time partner model is helpful.
>
> (#14)

The challenges to the status quo and the limitations of the local market, caused reflections on the ways in which law is changing, but also how the profession is 'stuck in terms of the model' with client demands higher than they have ever been (#11MP).

Promotion Processes

The surface description of the promotion process by female partners and managing partners was largely devoid of gender; rather they emphasised the business case. As one female partner commented:

> Well, you need to do a business case . . . demonstrate your performance in terms of financial performance and technical performance, and get referees from clients and you have to be put up and supported by your group, your practice area, then you're voted on by the partnership.
>
> (#9)

The pre-partner phase, when the aspirant is demonstrating their worth, takes place over at least two years:

> It's really hard maintaining intensity and scrutiny that all your work gets over that period for an extended period of time. It's quite a challenge and it's not one that's a female challenge.
>
> (#30)

A common thread through reflections on the promotion process was the relentless pressure it created. Also the lack of movement of partners coupled with a tight economic market means partnership opportunities are most likely to come from the space created by existing partners retiring. The principle of merit was reiterated by managing partner interviewees as a baseline for any promotion:

> I've never heard these words in a partner meeting or a board meeting— Gosh, that's good, that's another woman. Never heard that. In other words, it's never—we're very meritocracy-driven. We don't care if

people are male, female, black, white, yellow, blind, deaf. If they're smart, driven people who are what we call viable—someone wants what they're selling—we don't mind. It's all around excellence.

(#31MP)

The merit-based action can create unexpected gender issues:

We just recruit on the basis of the best candidate, and the fact of the matter is the best candidates are usually women. And that happened in my last firm: it was the same; we did the same thing, and the best candidate was generally a woman. So over half the lawyers here are women, but it is not a form of positive discrimination. It is just the way it works out.

(#32MP)

A further unexpected gendered issue raised by the women interviewees was the lack of high-achieving male graduates presenting at recruitment.

The comments from interviewees highlight how the promotion processes are intertwined with the prevailing organisation culture, the focus of the next section. To illustrate, one woman partner's description of culture was couched in terms of the merit ethos:

I've always felt that it's a meritocracy. So the culture is all about people working hard and being—and we aspire to be basically the best, is our aspiration . . . if you're good you get recognised for it. You get rewarded.

(#10)

Organisational Culture

The interviewees from the 'top', whether male or female, clearly signalled the significance of organisational culture in sustaining the underlying masculine norms and justified it by citing by the business imperative prevalent in these law firms. Not surprisingly, the dominant cultural description recognised "the board as key and driven by the partners" (#12). Male managing partners spoke of the need to "bring people in who are consistent, that subscribe to the culture and are going to preserve it" (#34MP). It was clear that in the main, our interviewees were consciously trying to manage the organisational culture:

We have spent a lot of time thinking about our culture and working on our culture. Historically, we have been a firm that is very focused on individuals and less so on teams and collective effort and we've moved slightly.

(#5MP)

When women partners were asked to describe their firm's culture in a few words there was a great deal of similarity in how organisational culture was portrayed in spite of espoused differences between the firms. A number of women discussed the high-performance culture of firms, which included striving for excellence:

> It's a high-performing organisation. I think it's a demanding organisation. So it's a high-performance culture which has its pros and cons. But I like it. It suited me because you know the rules. It's really clear.
>
> (#7)

One interviewee reflected on how the culture has become tougher over time: "It has changed. It's much more ruthless and much more cut-throat than it used to be. And it's all about fee generation and revenue. And it's highly competitive" (#20).

While among the women partners there was little support for the notion of the 'old boy's network' there was recognition that a considerable amount of networking was done either through participation in sport or through watching sport. For example, "Because, still a lot's done on the golf course—the old boys' network—very hard to compete with that, as a woman. But you just get on with it" (#3).

Others noted the gender dynamics that arose in some of the partner-client interactions:

> Often, I am the only female going in with maybe five or six of my male partners, into a room of [clients] which traditionally are 99 per cent male, it will take the boys a couple of beers to relax down to then start talking at a real level . . . But I always struggle with that first half an hour in those male events.
>
> (#3)

Both male managing partners and women partners commented that the merit principle is being challenged, but implicitly. In the words of one male managing partner:

> I think women lawyers are regarded as better lawyers on the whole, in the technical sense. There will be clients who only want to work with male partners in an old boys type scenario, I've certainly seen that.
>
> (#11MP)

Within the managing partner group there was some realisation of unconscious bias "a partner may well, given a choice, unconsciously give a job to a bloke because he reminds him of him" (#5MP).

In spite of the clear power differentials and concomitant rewards, a surprising number of the managing partners and female partners professed collegiality and equity as a dominant culture of the firm:

> It's very collegial, we've got a very flat structure so all equity—we're a cooperative so we share our profits . . . So we all succeed if we all succeed, so it's a very collegial firm . . . we have retained the good elements of a focus on individuals, and there's a lot more emphasis on collaboration.
>
> (#34)

The following words of a managing partner summarise the overriding themes evident in the interviews with those "above the partnership line": "The firm is very keen to promote women partners. We have a part-time partner, so we're flexible [but] it doesn't work very well." He went on to explain:

> A partner in the business of law becomes more important than the practice of law . . . it usually requires too much of a woman who is trying to balance her life with other things. And most of the women partners I've met, they've given up a lot . . . they've given up families and that whole part of their life, in other words, they've merely become men.
>
> (#32MP)

Conclusion

Deborah Rhode commented in 1991 that feminism was still to affect law and legal practice (Rhode 1991a). She noted that it had been too easy for the law elite to assert there is "no problem" if measured by the numbers of women joining the law profession (Rhode 1991b, 2220). Twenty-five years later law is numerically a success story, with women integral to this global "capitalist service industry" (Sommerlad 2016, 62). Yet as demonstrated here and elsewhere, archaic attitudes to gender, namely women, persist.

The interaction between law as a gendered profession and the influences of neoliberalism is crucial to the context of our study. This theme, encapsulated in the selected quotes of female partners and male managing partners, is further captured in the following statement: "The evolution of classic professions to businesses practising a profession, and their business imperatives to make profits has created massive change in the way law is practised" (cited in Crawford 2016, 25).[5] It is the heightened value now given to masculine business practices that underpin the structures and cultures of large law firms.

Given this positioning it is not surprising to see credence given to the 'business case' and merit underpinning promotion to partner. Intertwined with this is a stoic belief that there is a 'right' age and stage to 'go up' for partnership. Some women partners did stress a need for change. They also recognised the risks of advocating for change within entrenched masculine structures and cultures. A conundrum now exists: the privileging of law as a 'special' profession requiring extraordinary demands from extraordinary people is neither serving the profession nor the sustainability of its people. Law remains a gendered profession. The question we now ponder is: is it able to embrace the bold changes needed?

Notes

1. A managing partner is a lawyer who has additional responsibilities as a CEO.
2. As at 1 February 2016, men practice law for an average of 21.9 years, women an average of 13.2 years. According to the 2013 census, 88.3 per cent of people who gave their occupation as lawyer or barrister were of European ethnicity.
3. The Gender and Diversity Research Group is an interdisciplinary group based in the Faculty of Business and Law, AUT University, Auckland, New Zealand.
4. This form of coding is to ensure anonymity given the small number of managing partners in the research.
5. Quote is from Dr George Beaton, a senior fellow at Melbourne Law School and a leading authority on professional services industries.

References

Adlam, G. and Jacombs, A. 2016. Snapshot of the Profession. *Law Talk* 883: 17–27. Accessed October 30, 2016. www.lawsociety.org.nz/__data/assets/pdf_file/0006/99078/NZLS-Snapshot-of- the-Profession-2016.pdf.

Baron, P. 2015. "The Elephant in the Room? Lawyer Wellbeing and the Impact of Unethical Behaviours." *Australian Feminist Law Journal* 41(1): 87–119.

Braun, V. and Clarke, V. 2006. Using Thematic Analysis in Psychology. *Qualitative Research in Psychology* 3(2): 77–101.

Brown, C. 2013. "Benjamin, Ethel Rebecca." *Dictionary of New Zealand Biography: Te Ara—the Encyclopaedia of New Zealand*. Accessed May 12, 2016. www.teara.govt.nz/en/biographies/2b18/benjamin-ethel-rebecca.

Callaghan, P. 2009. *Wool to Weta: Transforming New Zealand's Culture and Economy*. New Zealand: Auckland University Press.

Collier, R. 2014. " 'Love Law, Love Life': Neoliberalism, Wellbeing and Gender in the Legal Profession—a Case of Law School." *Legal Ethics* 17(2): 202–230.

Crawford, F. 2016. "Positive Associations." *Acuity* 3(5): 24–26.

Jewson, N. and Mason, D. 1986. "The Theory and Practice of Equal Opportunities Policies: Liberal and Radical Approaches." *Sociological Review* 34(2): 307–334.

Kelsey, J. 2015. *The Fire Economy. New Zealand's Reckoning*. Wellington: Bridget William Books.

Kumra, S. 2015. "Busy Doing Nothing: An Exploration of the Disconnect Between Gender Equity Issues Faced by Large Law Firms in the United Kingdom and the Diversity Management Initiatives Devised to Address Them." *Fordham Law Review* 83(5): 2277–2299.

Lying, S. T. 2010. " 'Mothered' and Othered: (In)visibility of Care Responsibility and Gender in Processes of Excluding Women from Norwegian Law Firms." In *Revealing and Concealing Gender: Issues of Visibility in Organisations*, edited by P. Lewis and R. Simpson, 76–99. London: Palgrave Macmillan.

National Council of Women of New Zealand. 2015. *Enabling Women's Potential: The Social, Economic and Ethical Imperative.* Accessed February 20, 2016. www.ncwnz.org.nz/what-we-do/enabling-womens-potential-the-social-economic-and-ethical-imperative/.

National Council of Women of New Zealand. 2016. "NCWNZ Celebrates 120 Years of Working Toward Gender Equality." Accessed May 12, 2016. www.ncwnz.org.nz/120-years-of-working-toward-gender-equality/.

New South Wales Law Society. 2012. "Flexible Working: A More Flexible, More Diverse Profession at All Levels." www.lawsciety.com.au/cs/groups/public/documents/internetcontent/671890pdf.

New Zealand Law Society. 2015. "By the numbers." *New Zealand Law Society.* Accessed September 19, 2015. www.lawsociety.org.nz/law-society-services/women-in-the-legal-profession/by-the-numbers.

November, J. 2009. *In the Footsteps of Ethel Benjamin.* Wellington: Victoria University Press.

Pinnington, A. H. and Sandberg, J. 2013. "Lawyers Professional Career: Increasing Women's Inclusion in the Partnership of Law Firms." *Gender, Work and Organisation* 20(6): 616–631.

Pringle, J. K., Giddings, L., Harris, C., Jaeger, S., Lin, S., Ravenswood, K. and Ryan, I. 2014. *Women's Career Progression in Auckland Law Firms.* Report produced by the Gender and Diversity Research Group, AUT University for the Auckland Women Lawyers' Association. www.awla.org.nz/wordpress/wp-content/uploads/2013/03/Women-in-Auckland-Law1.pdf.

Rhode, D. L. 1991a. "The 'No-Problem' Problem: Feminist Challenges and Cultural Change." *The Yale Law Review* 100(6): 1731–1793.

Rhode, D. L. 1991b. "Balanced Lives for Lawyers." *Fordham Law Review* 70: 2207–2220.

Rhode, D. L. 2011. "From Platitudes to Priorities: Diversity and Gender Equity in Law Firms." *The Georgetown Journal of Legal Ethics* 24: 1041–1076.

Roper, J., Ganesh, S. and Inkson, K. 2010. "Neoliberalism and Knowledge Interests in Boundaryless Careers Discourse." *Work, Employment and Society* 24(4): 661–679.

Sen, A. 1992. "Equality of What?" In *Inequality Re-Examined*, edited by A. Sen, 12–30. New York: Russel Sage Foundation.

Sinclair, A. 2014. "A Feminist Case for Leadership." In *Diversity in Leadership: Australian Women, Past and Present*, edited by J. Damousi, K. Rubenstein and M. Tornic. Canberra, Australia: The Australian National University.

Smythe, L. 2012. "Discerning Which Qualitative Approach Fits Best." *New Zealand College of Midwives Journal* 46: 5–12.

Sommerlad, H. 2016. " 'A Pit to Put Women in': Professionalism, Work Intensification, Sexualisation and Work-Life Balance in the Legal Profession in England and Wales." *International Journal of the Legal Profession* 23(1): 61–82.

Vaughan, R. 2016. "Raising the Bar." *New Zealand Listener*, April 16–22: 30–36.

Walsh, J. 2012. "Not Worth the Sacrifice? Women's Aspirations and Career Progression in Law Firms." *Gender, Work and Organisation* 19(5): 508–531.

5 Gender, Architecture and Recession in Spain

Elena Navarro-Astor and Valerie Caven

Introduction

Architecture, together with medicine and law, is regarded as an elite profession with a long history, involving lengthy training and with high social status (Roan and Whitehouse 2014). It is an artistic and creative endeavour, in addition to a technical one, a characteristic that separates it from some other professions (Hernández 2014; Matthewson 2015). Furthermore, unlike law and medicine, this profession requires architects in private practice to be entrepreneurial and to seek clients, who might reject the architect's advice (Blau 1984; Matthewson 2015).

Architecture has essential ties to the construction industry, and architects' work is subject to economic cycles and greater changes in demand for their services than other professions (Caven and Diop 2012; Roan and Whitehouse 2014; Roan and Matthewson 2016). Luque (2014) believes that the activities of the architectural profession are 80 per cent related to the building industry. Consequently, its stagnation, or 'building tsunamis or cataclysms', directly affect the functioning of architectural practices and the employment rate in the field (Legény and Spacek 2014). Spain has been one of the European countries hit severely by the economic crisis which resulted from the bursting of the domestic housing bubble in 2008 (Karamessini 2015; Alcañiz and Monteiro 2016; Martinez 2016). This has had serious consequences in the labour market due to the over-reliance of demand on construction. As a result, architects are suffering employment insecurity and very poor working conditions (Rubio and Gómez 2011). But "economic crises are profoundly gendered" (Bettio, Corsi, D'Ippoliti, Lyberaki, Samek and Verashchagina 2013, 57) and when confronting a crisis women and men behave differently.

In Spain, the profession of architecture is rapidly becoming a feminised field of study with 60 per cent of women enrolling in the first year. Women, however, represent only 29 per cent of all registered architects and their career paths remain gendered. The architectural profession in Spain displays both horizontal and vertical segregation, but, to date, equality initiatives have rarely been introduced. This chapter illustrates the difficulties faced by women architects working in this male-dominated profession when there is an insecure working environment resulting from the economic downturn. This study takes an interpretive approach in the qualitative paradigm, and draws on data collected via semi-structured in-depth interviews with Spanish women architects of different ages and employment status (self-employed, unemployed, salaried, public sector) conducted in the middle of the Spanish recession in 2011. We highlight differences in their situations and their extreme vulnerability due to their gender.

The profession of architecture has been researched widely (Adams 2015) but, to date, studies carried out on the status of women architects have focused largely on countries such as Australia, Canada, the UK and the US, which belong to the decentralised Anglo-American model of professionalism (Evetts 2008). Despite trends influencing professions to become transnational (Faulconbridge and Muzio 2012), they emerge in particular national contexts with different regulatory regimes, state relations and institutional forms (Evetts 2011). Hence, there are calls for more studies which examine women architects in different national settings (Stratigakos 2016). In this context, exploring the working experiences of women architects in a country such as Spain fills a research gap.

Research focusing on women architects in Spain is scarce, but it shows that their career paths remain gendered and they are not vertically integrated into the profession. They are not getting posts of responsibility and visibility (Agudo and Sánchez 2011; Caven, Navarro-Astor and Diop 2012; Hernández 2014). A few studies have focused on women architects in Spanish higher education institutions (Basset-Salom, Guardiola-Villora and Serrano-Lanzarote 2009; Sánchez 2010; Gutiérrez and Pérez 2012; Chías 2013; Carreiro 2014), while others have highlighted the work of Spanish women architects (Durán, Escudero, Nunez and Regodon 2013) which reveal gender discrimination and inequality in the practice of architecture (Agudo and Sánchez 2011; Hernández 2014; Matesanz 2015). Denial of gender discrimination is prevalent and, as Gutiérrez and Pérez (2012) point out, there is both a refusal to acknowledge the 'problem' coupled with a belief that 'it' has already been solved.

A number of authors have analysed the impact of the Spanish crisis on gender inequality and precariousness (Congregado, Carmona, Golpe and Van Stel 2014; González and Segalés 2014; Alcañiz 2015; Addabbo, Rodriguez-Modrono and Galvez 2015; Castaño 2015; Rubery 2015; Tobío and Fernández 2015) and, in general, they conclude that women have been more affected than men by the precariousness caused by the downturn. They argue that since women and men occupy different positions and have biased and unequal access to economic resources, employment and positions of power (Gálvez-Muñoz, Rodriguez-Modrono and Addabbo 2013; González and Segales 2014), they are differently affected by political and economic circumstances such as the current recession. As a result, economic crises can either emphasise or modify previous gender imbalances (Addabbo and Rodríguez-Modroño 2015; Castaño 2015).

There is no research that has specifically analysed the working experiences of women architects during the Spanish economic crisis. How are they faring while confronting a landscape of recession, job destruction and precariousness? What are the challenges they confront? In which ways are their personal and work experiences affected by these difficult economic circumstances? Do these experiences differ according to women's occupational status? The objective of this chapter is to explore Spanish women architects' working experiences during a period of economic crisis, with a focus on precariousness and gender roles through the lens of inequality.

This chapter reviews the Spanish context in respect to economic and gender equality, then describes the situation of women architects in the context of higher education and in the profession. Next, we outline the research methods and discuss the empirical findings relating to the vulnerability of women architects when confronting the consequences of the economic downturn. Finally, we conclude with the key insights generated by the study.

The Spanish Context: The Economic Downturn and Gender Equality

Spain ranks third in Europe for the number of its architects (54,000), and its "density" of architects is above the European average (Rubio and Gómez 2011; Mirza and Nacey 2016). Between 2002 and 2007 it was one of the most dynamic economies of the Euro zone with a high sustained growth rate caused by the expansion of the construction industry, which was responsible for 25 per cent of all jobs created between 1998 and 2007, and accounted for 10 per cent of gross domestic product in 2007 (Eurofound 2010; Martínez 2016). Sixteen per cent of the new jobs for women were in the real estate sector (González and Segales 2014). In 2008 the overblown domestic real estate bubble exploded and Spain entered a recession of unprecedented depth and length (OECD 2010; Karamessini 2015; Martínez 2016). While the size of output contraction was broadly similar to that of other European economies, it generated a trend of employment destruction that only stopped in 2014. From 2007 to 2013, the unemployment rate increased from 8.2 per cent to 26.1 per cent (Eurofound 2015) and the number of people out of work rose to 5.7 million, the highest number ever in Spanish history (Congregado et al. 2014). Spain, together with Greece, showed the highest levels of reported unemployment amongst architects in Europe (Mirza and Nacey 2015).

The gender effects of the recession depend on its influence on economic performance, the institutions and societal arrangements extant prior to 2008 (González and Segales 2014). The rapid increase of female workers in the Spanish workforce started during the democratic transition after the Franco era (1939–1975), more recently than many other countries (Alcañiz 2015). This means that the change from the breadwinner model to the dual-earner household has taken place in a shorter period, which may be the cause of more inter-generation and gender-role conflicts (Poelmans, Chinchilla and Cardona 2003; Brullet 2010). In addition, Spain still has a traditional social model based on a gendered division of roles where women do double work as they are expected to perform family and household duties (Fernández-Crehuet 2016). While women's average daily time spent on unpaid work is 258 minutes, it is only 154 minutes for men (World Economic Forum 2015).

Although Spanish society and institutions have evolved, the welfare model is still a Mediterranean regime known as 'familialistic' (González and Segales 2014; Alcañiz 2015; Fernández-Crehuet 2016; Alcañiz and Monteiro 2016). This model views caring responsibilities as a private duty, and families play an important role in dependents' care (Poelmans et al. 2003; Brullet 2010; Tobío and Fernández 2015). The assumption of a broad, supportive family network is embedded in social regulations and the functioning of public services such as health and childcare. In fact, approximately 30 per cent of grandparents in Spain provide care, compared to 2 per cent in Denmark and Sweden (ILO 2016).

Spanish idiosyncratic working hours (from 9 a.m. till 7/8 p.m., with a very long lunch break) increase work-family conflict because there is a two- to three-hour gap between school and office hours (Poelmans et al. 2003). On account of this, the public sector has played a prominent role in the creation of female employees, with women representing the majority of public employment (55 per cent in 2012) and the public sector constituting 31 per cent of total female employment (Gálvez-Muñoz et al. 2013; Addabbo et al. 2015). It offers job security and good working hours, and is governed by principles of equality and merit, with access and promotion based on curriculum requirements and objective tests (Rubery 2015; Fernández-Crehuet 2016).

The first phase of the global economic crisis (2008–2009) struck male-dominated sectors such as construction and manufacturing, causing a faster rise in male unemployment rates and narrowing unemployment gender gaps (Gálvez-Muñoz et al. 2013; González and Segales 2014; Addabbo et al. 2015; ILO 2016). But during the second phase (2010–2012) the adoption of gender-blind austerity measures froze or cut public sector jobs which are female-dominated, affecting women more heavily than men (González and Segales 2014; Rubery 2015; Castaño 2015; Alcañiz and Monteiro 2016). Spanish women have suffered particularly from the damaging political responses and government expenditure reduction. They continue to be worse off regarding the main labour market indicators: employment rate for women aged 25–49 went down from 67.6 per cent in 2012 to 61.3 in 2013 (Tobío and Fernández 2015). Their parlous position is also shown by the fall in Spain's ranking in the World Economic Forum Gender Equality Index, from 10 in 2007 to 30 in 2013 (World Economic Forum 2015).

Qualifications as Architects

Enrollment in architecture degrees at the Universitat Politécnica de Madrid (UPM]), the largest higher education institution in Spain providing architectural education, shows an increase in women. In the 1978–1979 academic year during the country's political transition, women's enrolment at UPM approached 15 per cent. Since then numbers have grown steadily until 2007, when women's enrolment exceeded 50 per cent in the first year (Laquidáin and Molina 2009; Sánchez 2010). A recent report indicates that 60 per cent of first-year students, 55 per cent of graduates and 53 per cent of PhD students are women (Sánchez 2014). This corresponds with figures from four other Spanish schools of architecture: Universidad de La Coruña (Carreiro 2014), Alcalá (Chías 2013), Alicante (Gutiérrez and Pérez 2012) and Universitat Politècnica de València (Basset-Salom et al. 2009).

These numbers do not indicate that the Spanish profession is quickly moving towards greater gender equality. For example, statistics available for academic careers in the Schools of Architecture show clear evidence of vertical segregation (Basset-Salom et al. 2009; Sánchez 2014, 2015; Carreiro 2014). The UPM School of Architecture shows a Glass Ceiling Index over 8, while the average for the whole university is 2.35, and 1.87 for the whole country. This is a clear indicator of the specific difficulties that women confront in architecture. The low percentage of women professors is of concern, especially since this has actually decreased from 5.66 in 2003 to 4.44 in 2013 (Sanchez 2014, 2015).

The Architectural Profession and Women in Spain

There were an estimated 565,000 architects in Europe in 2014, a slight increase since 2012 (Mirza and Nacey 2015). The majority (72 per cent) work in one-person practices and this puts them outside some areas of equity policy (Caven and Navarro-Astor 2013). An understanding of women's participation in the architectural profession is hindered by the challenge of counting architects (Matthewson 2015, 2012). Statistics on registered architects is the usual figure reported, but in Spain registration is not mandatory (CSCAE 2015) and consequently the use of the registration figure understates the number of women in architecture. Luque (2014) analysed the state of the profession through an online survey of 2,520 participants and estimated an approximate population of 65,000 architects in Spain, of which 31 per cent were women. These numbers are similar to data supplied by CSCAE in October 2016 which showed 47,550 registered architects (2,700 less than in 2011).[1] In terms of the gender divide the situation has not improved in the past five years, since women still only represent 29 per cent of registered architects. However, Spain seems to reflect greater equality than other European countries such as Austria, Estonia or the UK, with less than 20 per cent of registered female architects (Mirza and Nacey 2015; Clarke, Michielsens, Snijders, Wall, Dainty, Bagilhole and Barnard 2015). Outside Europe, Spain also fairs well compared to the US where women represent 19 per cent (Stratigakos 2016) and Australia where they represent 21 per cent of architects (Matthewson 2015).

A gender analysis of the third survey of the profession (Matesanz 2015) conducted by Sindicato de Arquitectos de España (SArq), the architects' trade union, shows that the majority of women work as salaried architects (65 per cent), while men are mostly self-employed. This accords with Agudo and Sánchez (2011), who found that female architects concentrate, in a higher percentage than their male colleagues, in the categories of salaried architects, civil servants or teachers, clearly showing horizontal segregation. This situation is related both with difficulties for women's access to work as 'professional liberal' and the search for more stability and security for motherhood.

Hiring terms are worse for women since 62 per cent acknowledge having been hired as "false self-employed" (SArq 2011, 2013; Matesanz 2015). This is an illegal category of workers which covers an employee-employer relationship simulating a commercial relationship between businessperson and client. The architect is not formally hired but has to carry out all kinds of tasks with no social rights, unemployment benefits, sick or maternity leave, while being subject to the employer's will in terms of holidays, working schedule, intellectual property (SArq 2011, 3). It has become a widespread illegal practice among Spanish architectural practices (Matesanz 2015).

Matilde Ucelay was the first woman architect who graduated, in 1936 in Madrid. Yet, during Franco's dictatorship she was disqualified from practicing because women were not supposed to work (Durán et al. 2013). Hence women did not enter the profession until after 1977 with the reintroduction of democracy and the liberalisation of planning laws (Sánchez 2010; Agudo and Sánchez 2011). This implies that around 70 per cent of women architects are younger than 45, an age group characterised by a lack of employment and precariousness (Matesanz 2015).

In the context of a lengthy recession, Spanish women architects have a higher unemployment rate and lower salaries than men. According to the trade union survey the average gross annual salary of male participants was 17,214€, compared to 16,770€ for females (Matesanz 2015), and gender differences were greater in the higher wage bands. Referring to the situation in the US, the pay gap has been described as "the most effective barometer of gender inequality in the profession", and in the US men earn on average 20 per cent more than women among full-time architects (Stratigakos 2016, 28). At a European level the pay gap is even wider, with full-time male architects earning 48 per cent more than full-time women while for part-time architects, men earn 12 per cent more than women (Mirza and Nacey 2016).

Confronted with higher unemployment rates, women architects find other ways to improve their situation: (1) they specialise with further education (29 per cent women undertake postgraduate studies, compared to 23 per cent of men); (2) they emigrate and work abroad (13 per cent women and 10 per cent men); (3) they change profession (14 per cent women and 12 per cent men) (Matesanz 2015). In summary, in architecture the glass ceiling remains, and "gender stubbornly remains a marker of division" (Pickerill 2014, 3).

Methods

The empirical evidence reported here is part of a larger international comparative study focused on the work of architects in Spain, the UK and France (Caven et al. 2012; Caven and Navarro-Astor 2013). Given the exploratory nature of the research questions, we followed an interpretative approach within the qualitative research methodology. Semi-structured interviews were chosen for data collection. Eighteen women architects discussed career and progression issues most salient to them. The main issues discussed were motives for studying architecture, factors that may have helped or hindered their careers, as well as the realities of their working lives, identifying pressures and rewards. The interview guide did not include specific gender equality questions, but when the issue emerged the interviewer tried to explore this in depth, asking for examples and detailed descriptions.

The women architects interviewed were selected via the membership list of the professional regulatory body (Colegio Oficial de Arquitectos) of two Spanish regions: la Comunidad Valenciana and Castilla la Mancha (see Table 5.1). Interviews were conducted face to face by a Spanish native speaker between February and April 2011 and they varied in length between 30 and 100 minutes. The majority were conducted at participants' offices, five at the interviewer's university office and one in a cafeteria. With the permission of the participants, all interviews were recorded, transcribed and analysed through a process of comparative analysis. This involved identifying recurring themes, patterns, similarities and differences (Goulding 2009). No qualitative research software was used.

Interviewees' ages ranged from 27 to 60 (see Table 5.1). Eight were childless, one had four children, two had three, five had two children and two had one child. Most (14) had studied architecture at Universitat Politècnica de València. Participants worked in varied settings: sole self-employed practitioners, self-employed partners, full-time and part-time employees in public sector authorities, 'false self-employed' in architectural practices and university lecturers. The practices involved in this research are small firms with just one staff member, or between two and five architectural staff (including partners, associates, salaried architects and technical staff). Other organisations represented are public schools of architecture and small and medium town councils. Seven interviewees were married to male architects and three of them worked with them as partners in their architectural practices. Reflecting the Spanish economic situation at the time of the interviews, four participants were unemployed.

Findings

All participants were experiencing an unstable economic environment at the time of the interviews, but due to their work situation, age and family situation, their struggles and challenges differed. Results are presented grouping

Table 5.1 Profile of Interviewees

Participants' Pseudonyms	Age	Children	Married to Architect	Employment Status	Length of Service
Nuria	35	0		Full-time "false self-employed"	< 10 years
Celia	42	2		Unemployed	11–20 years
Maria	43	2		Part-time public sector (university lecturer)	11–20 years
Lourdes	36	0		Part-time public sector (town council) and self-employed partner in practice	11–20 years
Sofía	36	2		Unemployed	< 10 years
Aurora	37	2	Yes	Self-employed, partner in practice with husband	< 10 years
Clara	27	0	Yes	Unemployed	< 10 years
Luna	58	4	Yes	Full-time public sector (university professor)	> 21 years
Elena	44	0	Yes	Self-employed, partner in practice with husband	11–20 years
Soledad	39	1		Full-time public sector (town council)	11–20 years
Amparo	43	0		Full-time public sector (town council)	11–20 years
Inés	37	0		Full-time public sector (town council)	11–20 years
Elsa	60	0		Full-time public sector (state owned company)	> 21 years
Carmen	59	3		Self-employed sole practitioner	> 21 years
Eva	34	0	Yes	Unemployed	< 10 years
Alba	36	3	Yes	Part-time public sector (university lecturer)	< 10 years
Gimena	35	2		Part-time public sector (university lecturer) and self-employed sole practitioner	< 10 years
Lucía	42	1	Yes	Self-employed, partner in practice with husband	11–20 years

participants of similar employment status because they tend to depict their experiences in similar ways.

Job Loss and Unemployment

Unemployment is the hardest consequence of the recent recession and four participants were in this precarious situation. Two were receiving unemployment benefits because they had a prior lengthy period of work as salaried employees in the private sector. They had been laid off in 2009 when the firms closed and had been unsuccessful in finding a new job. Both had small children, had experienced career breaks during maternity leave and, due to family responsibilities and the standard work hours established in the organisations employing them, they had returned to work on a part-time basis. This reduction in their working time had negative consequences in their professional lives while they were still employed: "my professional life was completely cut short, there were projects I could not carry out because I wasn't there full time". In addition, their need for flexibility for childcare and their desire to keep working part-time was affecting their employability after dismissal.

> I realised I had a baby and that it was going to be really difficult to find another job where I could balance work and family. Finding a job with an intense continuous working schedule with no long lunch break is very complicated.
>
> (Sofía)

Another unemployed architect found herself in a difficult situation because having worked for two and a half years as "false self-employed" at a small architectural practice, she was not eligible for unemployment benefit. Her working hours (9:00 a.m. to 7:00 p.m. with a two-hour lunch break) had been imposed without negotiation, and she had commuted long distance. Having recently graduated, the youngest interviewee (27 years old) lacked formal working experience. Being married to a young sole practitioner, Clara was aware of the difficulties and challenges of owning an architectural practice and the need to seek clients and commissions that were scarce at the time of the interview. Hence she was practical and very clear about her career options:

> I couldn't work at a practice 8 a.m. to 8 p.m. if I had children, what would I do with them? . . . I have to pass the competitive exams and become a civil servant. It's annoying now since because of the economic situation there are too many applicants . . . It's a permanent post, you don't move around and the schedule is ok for having a family.
>
> (Clara)

Finding it difficult to adjust to the time demands of the private architectural sector, all of them were developing employability strategies for finding a job related to their profession: they were studying hard for competitive civil servant exams, or they were enrolled in a master's degree in order to specialise. Celia, the oldest of this group, was more pessimistic about her situation and conveyed a weaker professional identity. She felt she could not compete with the younger generation, who accepted casualised working conditions.

> Sometimes I think I might have to change career, change my life. But I don't know where to focus . . . I might devote myself to something different. It's difficult because of my age and because there're lots of people behind a lot younger and I've seen them being really exploited.
>
> (Celia)

Precariousness and Instability of the Self-Employed

The 'real' self-employed participants owned their practice either as sole practitioners or as partners with their husbands and/or colleagues. With their income dependent on the profits made at the practice, they faced financial uncertainty, commercial inactivity and a high degree of risk due to the poor economic situation and the lack of commissions. They complained about how difficult it had become to win public tenders, since competition had increased and 80 to 100 architects were bidding for each. They also confronted the unforeseen difficulty of managing their small business with all the different tasks involved in addition to designing projects: talking to clients, making sure the town civil service issued planning permissions, calling for payments and paying taxes and the expensive insurance on civil responsibility, among others. This meant they had very little time for doing what they really liked, which is architecture and designing: "it's just one third of your job's load" (Elena). Aurora elaborated, saying that

> It's probably the same for most self-employed architects, you live under instability and you say "I still have to work for 30 more years, how am I going to survive". . . . You have to put aside the technical side of your job and think on the business side, that spoils the beauty of this profession.
>
> (Aurora)

Some sole practitioners had been protected from the loss of clients because they had specialised in types of work related to a niche market with few competitors:

> I carry out the jobs that nobody wants. I haven't worked for posh architects, I've worked for architects with little money. This means I've worked a lot and I've charged little. Nobody wants public health works

because they are extremely complex projects and involve horrible site management.

(Carmen)

Nuria, who was 'false self-employed', bore precariousness and perceived few opportunities for regular employment. She had accepted this form of casualised work because she had no choice, and she was starting to consider these insecure conditions as normal. She could not ask for a standard contract that would give her rights such as maternity benefit, unemployment benefit, sick leave or paid holidays. If she did not agree with the contingent terms, others from the pool of unemployed young architects would.

Despite doubts and challenges, these self-employed women showed strong professional identities and some pursued career-sustaining strategies in the form of further education to expand their job opportunities. Others had added to their professional work and were able to work part-time as teachers at the university or were trying to do so:

> The problem is that both of us are family unit and we work in the same architectural office, we don't have anything else. It would be good if we could diversify . . ., if one of us could do some teaching and have something more.

(Elena)

The Public Sector: A Comfortable Bastion of Stability and Flexibility, But Few Intrinsic Rewards

Women architects employed in the public sector as tenured civil servants or temporary employees found this decent work and a secure refuge from the vulnerability and concerns caused by the recession. Being well aware of the high unemployment rates among colleagues and the closing of numerous architectural practices, they felt fortunate keeping their jobs, even if they were earning less than in the private sector. Furthermore, their workers' rights were protected and working hours were flexible and regular. This explains the attractiveness of this career option, especially for women who needed to manage their home/work commitments: "We have to work 37.5 hours a week, and fixed office hours are 9:00 to 14:00. The rest is flexible, you organise it as you wish. You may stay until late one evening, or you can start at 7:00" (Soledad).

Working in the public sector, however, meant that they felt forced to betray their aesthetic, and sometimes their ethical ideals (Legény and Spacek 2014). Hence disillusionment and lack of motivation occurred, especially when daily work routines and tasks were monotonous. Amparo outlined these concerns:

> I'm not an architect whose work is going to get published in architectural journals, I'm not bad, but just one more of the bunch, so when

having to choose I thought "if I'm never going to be in the journals and I'm not going to be exceptional in doing buildings since my clients are very small . . . " I decided to stay in the municipality.

Inés discussed the comparison between university studies and the actual work:

> You do have good things such as the working schedule, but in reality what's important is work content and it's a disaster and it's sad. In any work team at university you did things that were a lot better than the ones I'm going to do here. It doesn't make sense that you study a degree, that there are many things to do and all you do here is "moving paper". . . . When you realise that no matter what you do or think decisions are already made, that you can't contribute with anything, it's hard.

Conclusions

Women's experiences vary substantially depending on their occupation and the sector they work in, their age, their education and whether they are mothers and/or carers (Healy and Bergfeld 2016). Approaches to work also differ for professionals working in the public sector compared to the private sector (Adams 2015). Additionally, since they hold different positions and have unequal access to resources and power, women and men are affected differently by economic circumstances (González and Segales 2014).

In the context of a lengthy recession such as the Spanish one, women architects have been severely affected and they are worse off regarding labour market indicators, salaries and working conditions. In general terms the crisis initially hit men harder than women, because employment loss was concentrated in the construction industry. But since architects' work is closely tied to construction, Spanish women architects were negatively affected from the start. The second phase of the recession brought austerity measures including cuts in feminised public sector jobs such as architects in town and city councils.

In short, high qualification levels have not protected women architects from low pay and insecure and unpredictable contexts. In fact, Sindicato de Arquitectos de España (SArq) has denounced their casualisation in the form of an illegal category known as 'false self-employed' (SArq 2011, 2013; Matesanz 2015). It is important and disturbing to note that the architectural profession might be absorbing and considering as normal the nature of this employment contract, especially when it confronts an oversupply of young architects.

In accordance with architectural work in the UK and Australia (Caven 2006; Matthewson 2015) part-time work is not generally seen as adequate, so that those who do it (mostly women reconciling motherhood and work) are perceived as "less of an architect". Hence, in order to belong, they are forced to conform to the norms of the male definition of the profession.

Architecture is supposed to provide emotional satisfaction, pleasure and intrinsic rewards (Chappel and Willis 2010; Navarro-Astor and Caven 2012; Caven and Diop 2012) and our interviewees had experienced these both during their study years and in previous employment. But they were unable to derive the fullest pleasure in their occupations at the time of the interviews. While the self-employed were focused on the business side and sacrificed design, those in the public sector complained about a lack of opportunities and little autonomy.

Despite everything, these women architects appeared resilient, they showed a strong professional identity and held profession-consistent learning goals that translated into focused career strategies. Following Simosi, Rousseau and Daskalaki (2015), they were not 'shifters' but 'sustainers', in the sense that they gave the impression of being able to resist and maintain their career aspirations regardless of the difficult situation.

Note

1. Consejo Superior de los Colegios de Arquitectos de España (CSCAE), an umbrella organisation for the architecture professional bodies in Spain, provided the authors with numbers of registered architects in 2011 and 2016.

References

Adams, T. 2015. "Sociology of Professions: International Divergences and Research Directions." *Work, Employment and Society* 29(1): 154–165.

Addabbo, T., Rodríguez-Modroño P. and Gálvez, L. 2015. "Gender Differences in Labor Force Participation Rates in Spain and Italy Under the Great Recession." *Revista de economía mundial* 41: 21–42.

Agudo, Y. and Sánchez, I. 2011. "Construyendo un Lugar en la Profesión: Trayectorias de las Arquitectas Españolas." *Feminismo/s* 17: 155–181.

Alcañiz, M. 2015. "Crisis, Precariousness and Gender Inequality in Spain and Italy." *OBETS: Revista de Ciencias Sociales* 10(1): 97–125.

Alcañiz, M. and Monteiro, R. 2016. "She-Austerity: Women's Precariousness and Labor Inequality in Southern Europe." *Convergencia Revista de Ciencias Sociales* 72: 39–68. Accessed November 15, 2016. http://convergencia.uaemex.mx/article/view/4089.

Basset-Salom, L., Guardiola-Víllora, A. and Serrano-Lanzarote B. 2009. "20 Años de Presencia Femenina en la Escuela Técnica Superior de Arquitectura de Valencia y en el Departamento de Estructuras." Paper presented at Jornadas Internacionales de Arquitectura y Urbanismo desde la perspectiva de las arquitectas, Madrid, Instituto Juan de Herrera, December 11–12, 2008.

Bettio, F., Corsi, M., D'Ippoliti, C., Lyberaki, A., Samek, M. and Verashchagina, A. 2013. *The Impact of the Economic Crisis on the Situation of Women and Men and on Gender Equality Policies.* Luxemburg: European Commission. Accessed November 18,

2016. http://ec.europa.eu/justice/gender-equality/files/documents/130410_crisis_report_en.pdf.

Blau, J. 1984. *Architects and Firms: A Sociological Perspective on Architectural Practice.* Cambridge, MA and London: MIT Press.

Brullet, C. 2010. "Cambios Familiares y Nuevas Políticas Sociales en España y Cataluña: El cuidado de la Vida Cotidiana a lo Largo del Ciclo de Vida." *Educar* 45: 51–79. www.raco.cat/index.php/Educar/article/view/214608/284900.

Carreiro, M. 2014. *Las Mujeres Arquitectas de Galicia: su Papel en la Profesión y en la Enseñanza de la Profesión (el Ejercicio de la Arquitectura en Galicia desde una Perspectiva de Género).* Universidad de La Coruña. Accessed November 11, 2016. http://igualdade.xunta.gal/sites/default/files/files/documentos/as_mulleres_arquitectas_en_galicia.pdf.

Castaño, C. 2015. "Introducción." In *Las Mujeres en la Gran Recesión,* edited by C. Castaño, 7–49. Cátedra: Universidad de Valéncia.

Caven, V. 2006. "Career Building: Women and Non-Standard Employment in Architecture." *Construction Management and Economics* 24(5): 457–464.

Caven, V. and Diop, M. 2012. "Architecture: A 'Rewarding' Career? An Anglo-French Comparative Study of Intrinsic Rewards in the Architecture Profession." *Construction Management and Economics* 30(7): 513–523.

Caven, V. and Navarro-Astor, E. 2013. "The Potential for Gender Equality in Architecture: An Anglo-Spanish Comparison." *Construction Management and Economics* 31(8): 874–882.

Caven,V., Navarro-Astor, E. and Diop, M. 2012. "A Cross-National Study of Accommodating and 'Usurpatory' Practices by Women Architects in the UK, Spain and France." *Architectural Theory Review* 17(2/3): 365–377.

Chappell, D. and Willis, A. 2010. *The Architect in Practice.* 10th ed. Chichester: Wiley-Blackwell.

Chías, P. 2013. "Estudiantes y Profesionales de la Arquitectura: ¿un Ambito de Igualdad?" In *Arquitectas y Otras Profesionales: Perspectivas Transdisciplinares,* edited by Grupo de Investigación MAGA, 53–61. A Coruña: Universidad de La Coruña.

Clarke, L., Michielsens, E., Snijders, S., Wall, C., Dainty, A., Bagilhole, B. and Barnard, S. 2015. *'No More Softly, Softly': Review of Women in the Construction Workforce.* Working paper. University of Westminster.

Congregado, E., Carmona, M., Golpe, A. and Van Stel, A. 2014. "Unemployment, Gender and Labor Force Participation in Spain: Future Trends in Labor Markets." *Romanian Journal of Economic Forecasting* 17(1): 53–66.

CSCAE. 2015. *El Ejercicio de la Profesión de Arquitecto en España.* Madrid: Consejo Superior de Colegios de Arquitectos de España.

Durán, M., Escudero, A., Núñez, J. and Regodón, E. 2013. "Matilde Ucelay: The First Spanish Woman Architect in History." *Cuaderno de Notas: Journal of the Department of Composition of ETSAM* 14: 1–18. Accessed November 11, 2016. http://polired.upm.es/index.php/cuadernodenotas/article/view/2083.

Eurofound. 2010. *Spain: A Country Profile.*

Eurofound. 2015. *Spain: Working Life Country Profile.*

Evetts, J. 2008. "Introduction: Professional Work in Europe." *European Societies* 10(4): 525–544.

Evetts, J. 2011. "A New Professionalism? Challenges and Opportunities." *Current Sociology* 59(4): 406–422.

Faulconbridge, J. and Muzio, D. 2012. "Professions in a Globalizing World: Towards a Transnational Sociology of the Professions." *International Sociology* 27(1): 136–152.

Fernández-Crehuet, J. 2016. *La Conciliación de la Vida Profesional, Familiar y Personal. España en el Contexto Europeo*. Madrid: Pirámide.

Gálvez-Muñoz, L., Rodríguez-Modroño, P. and Addabbo, T. 2013. *The Impact of European Austerity Policy of Women's Work in Southern Europe*. Módena: DEMB Working papers series 18. Accessed November 16, 2016. http://155.185.68.2/campusone/web_dep/CappPaper/Capp_p108.pdf.

González, E. and Segales, M. 2014. "Women, Gender Equality and the Economic Crisis in Spain." In *Women and Austerity: The Economic Crisis and the Future for Gender Equality*, edited by M. Karamessini and J. Rubery, 228–247. Croydon: Routledge.

Goulding, C. 2009. "Grounded Theory Perspectives in Organizational Research." In *Handbook of Organizational Research Methods*, edited by D. Buchanan and A. Bryman, 381–394. London: Sage.

Gutiérrez, M. and Pérez, R. 2012. "Docencia y Género: Primeros Pasos de la Universidad de Alicante (España) en la Carrera de Arquitectura." *Arquitectura y Urbanismo* XXXIII(3): 52–69.

Healy, G. and Bergfeld, M. 2016. *The Organising Challenges Presented by the Increased Casualisation of Women's Work*. London: Centre for Research in Equality and Diversity, School of Business Management, Queen Mary University of London. Accessed November 11, 2016. www.tuc.org.uk/sites/default/files/casualisation ofwomenswork.pdf.

Hernández, C. 2014. "Architectures and Women Looking for Names: The Architects Against 'Double Hiding'." *Arenal: Revista de Historia de las Mujeres* 21(1): 69–95. Accessed November 11, 2016. http://revistaseug.ugr.es/index.php/arenal/article/view/2261.

ILO. 2016. *Women at Work Trends 2016*. Geneva: International Labour Office.

IMF. 2012. *World Economic Outlook: Coping with High Debt and Sluggish Growth*. Washington, DC: International Monetary Fund.

Karamessini, M. 2015. "Introduction: Women's Vulnerability to Recession and Austerity." In *Women and Austerity: The Economic Crisis and the Future for Gender Equality*, edited by M. Karamessini and J. Rubery, 3–36. Croydon: Routledge.

Laquidáin, B. and Molina, P. 2009. "Arquitectura y Género." *Arquitectos: Información del Consejo Superior de los Colegios de Arquitectos de España* 187: 30–31.

Legény, J. and Špac?ek, R. 2014. "Trapped by Crisis: The 2009, 30–31 Plight of Architects in Europe." *Global Journal of Engineering Education* 16(1): 20–26. Accessed November 11, 2016. www.wiete.com.au/journals/GJEE/Publish/vol16no1/03-Legeny-J.pdf.

Luque, E. 2014. *Encuesta On-Line Arquitectos 2014*. Barcelona: Fundación Arquia. Accessed November 11, 2016. http://fundacion.arquia.es/media/encuestas/down loads/informes/informe_encuesta_profesionales_2014.pdf.

Martínez, J. 2016. "Etnografía de Una 'Burbuja'. Una Aproximación al Auge y Declive del Sector de la Construcción en el sur de la Provincia de Alicante." *Revista de Antropología Experimental* 16: 137–164. Accessed November 15, 2016. http://revistaselectronicas.ujaen.es/index.php/rae/article/view/3133.

Matesanz, A. 2015. "Arquitectas Precarias." In *Arquitectas, Redefiniendo la Profesión*, edited by N. Alvarez Lombardero, 49–61. Sevilla: Recolectores urbanos.

Matthewson, G. 2012. "Nothing Else Will Do": The Call for Gender Equality in Architecture in Britain." *Architectural Theory Review* 17(2/3): 245–259.

Matthewson, G. 2015. "Dimensions of Gender: Women's Careers in the Australian Architecture Profession." PhD thesis, University of Queensland, School of Architecture. Accessed November 11, 2016. https://espace.library.uq.edu.au/view/UQ:373190/s42738134_phd_submission.pdf.

Mirza & Nacey Research Ltd. 2015. The Architectural Profession in Europe 2014: A Sector Study. Brussels: Architects' Council of Europe. Accessed November 11, 2016. www.ace-cae.eu/fileadmin/New_Upload/7._Publications/Sector_Study/2014/EN/2014_EN_FULL.pdf.

Mirza & Nacey Research Ltd. 2016. *The Architectural Profession in Europe 2015: A Sector Study*. Brussels: Architects' Council of Europe. Accessed February 1, 2017. www.ace-cae.eu/fileadmin/New_Upload/7._Publications/Sector_Study/2016/2016_EN_FN_180117.pdf.

Navarro-Astor, E. and Caven, V. 2012. "Architects in Spain: A Profession Under Risk." In *Proceedings of the 28th Annual ARCOM Conference*, edited by S. Smith, 577–587. Association of Researchers in Construction Management. Accessed November 11, 2016. www.arcom.ac.uk/-docs/proceedings/ar2012-0577-0587_Navarro-Astor_Caven.pdf.

OECD. 2010. *OECD Economic Surveys: Spain*. OECD, December 2010. Accessed November 11, 2016. www.oecd.org/eco/46654901.pdf.

Pickerill, J. 2014. "Bodies, Building and Bricks: Women Architects and Builders in Eight Eco-Communities in Argentina, Britain, Spain, Thailand and USA." *Gender, Place & Culture: A Journal of Feminist Geography* 22(7): 901–919.

Poelmans, S., Chinchilla, N. and Cardona, P. 2003. "The Adoption of Family-Friendly HRM Policies: Competing for Scarce Resources in the Labour Market." *International Journal of Manpower* 24(2): 128–147.

Roan, A. and Matthewson, G. 2016. "Challenges and Change in the Architecture Profession: Demonstrating Uncertain Futures Through the Struggle for Gender Equity." In *Perspectives on Contemporary Professional Work: Challenges and Experiences*, edited by A. Wilkinson, D. Hislop and C. Coupland, 211–231. UK: Edward Elgar.

Roan, A. and Whitehouse, G. 2014. "Australian Architecture in Comparative Perspective: A Snapshot of Gendered Participation." *Architecture Australia* 103(5): 66–66.

Rubery, J. 2015. "From 'Women and Recession' to 'Women and Austerity'." In *Las Mujeres en la Gran Recesión*, edited by C. Castaño, 17–36. Cátedra: Universidad de Valéncia.

Rubio, J. and Gómez, C. 2011. *Arquitectos en la Encrucijada: ¿Qué Puede Hacer un Arquitecto en la Situación Actual?* Madrid: Alianza.

Sánchez, I. 2010. "Women in Architecture: The Spanish Case." *Urban Research & Practice* 3(2): 203–218.

Sánchez, I. 2014. *Women at UPM: Gender Statistics at Universidad Politécnica de Madrid*. UPM. Accessed November 11, 2016. https://triggerprojectupm.files.wordpress.com/2015/01/d5-1_womenatupm_2015-01-26_low.pdf.

Sánchez, I. 2015. "Arquitectas. Estado de la Cuestión." In *Arquitectas, Redefiniendo la Profesión*, edited by N. Alvarez Lombardero, 37–47. Sevilla: Recolectores urbanos.

SArq. 2011. *II Estudio Sobre el Sector de la Arquitectura*. Sindicato de Arquitectos. Accessed November 11, 2016. https://sindicatarquitectes.wordpress.com/2011/12/14/ii-estudio-sobre-el-sector-de-la-arquitectura-noviembre-de-2011.

SArq. 2013. "III Encuesta del Sindicato de Arquitectos: Sindicato de Arquitectos." Accessed November 11, 2016. www.sindicatoarquitectos.es/descargas/iii-estudio-laboral-arquitectura-sarq-2013.pdf.

Simosi, M., Rousseau, D. and Daskalaki, M. 2015. "When Careers Paths Cease to Exist: A Qualitative Study of Career Behavior in a Crisis Economy." *Journal of Vocational Behavior* 91: 134–146.

Stratigakos, D. 2016. *Where Are the Women Architects?* Princeton: Princeton University Press.

Tobío, C. and Fernández, J. 2015. "El Déficit de Cuidado ante la Crisis." In *Las mujeres en la Gran Recesión*, edited by C. Castaño, 201–238. Cátedra: Universidad de Valencia.

World Economic Forum. 2015. *The Global Gender Gap Report 2015*. Geneva: World Economic Forum.

6 Academics at the Intersection of Age and Gender

A Ghanaian Experience

Cynthia Forson, Moira Calveley, Steven Shelley and Christeen George

Introduction

The chapter takes an intersectional approach examining the effect of age on the career and workplace experiences of young women and men academics in a Ghanaian university (hereafter referred to as "The University"). African universities were historically designed and developed as male spaces and the philosophy of African higher education (HE) has traditionally had a "malestream" agenda, mirroring colonial antecedents in tradition and reform (Tsikata 2007). There have been changes to the African academy and there are now higher numbers of female students and staff than there has ever been (Barnes 2007), although in examining the University of Ghana, Tsikata (2007) argues that change has been slow. Feminist writers on African HE have tended to focus on gender as the overriding factor of inequality. Similarly, with few exceptions (see Snape and Redman 2003; Garstka, Schmitt, Branscombe and Hummert 2004) research in industrialised countries has centred on the disadvantages experienced by older workers. However, in the context of a culture that reveres age maturity, this chapter argues that youth is a strong determining factor in the disadvantage experienced by *younger* women *and* men in Ghanaian workplaces. The chapter employs Evett's (2000) multi-dimensional analytical framework on the cultural, structural and action dimensions of women's career progress to examine the work experiences of young male and female academics. Quantitative and qualitative data collected in a Ghanaian HE institution in 2011 forms the basis of the discussion.

Previous research has highlighted the disadvantage and discrimination that women academics characteristically experience in higher education institutions globally. Women in higher education across the world face disadvantage with regards to participation, progression and pay (Morley and Crossouard 2014; AAUP 2014; UCU 2016). In terms of outputs of higher education, i.e. the number of graduates produced, the global picture shows a near balance between men and women who obtain bachelor's degrees. The ratio of women to men who get bachelor's degrees is 56:48. But, men outstrip women in almost all countries at the doctoral (56 per cent) and researcher (71 per cent) levels (UNESCO 2010).

In terms of progression, organising processes of the academy privilege masculinity (Özbilgin and Healy 2004; Healy, Özbilgin and Aliefendioğlu 2005; Strachan, Broadbent, Whitehouse, Peetz and Bailey 2011; Seierstad and Healy 2012) and the typical academic has been conceptualised in terms of the 'lonely hero at the top' which reflects hegemonic positioning of males within the academy (Benschop and Brouns 2003). The disadvantages outlined above are reflected in even more stark terms in higher education in Sub-Saharan Africa where a male hegemonic society dominates and prevails (Amadi and Amadi 2015) albeit the level of disadvantage for women differs between African countries.

Conceptualising Gender Disadvantage in the 'African Academy'

Although globally women have reached, and in some cases exceeded, parity with men in terms of participation in higher education, they face significant barriers in poorer countries such as many of those located in Sub-Saharan Africa (UNESCO 2010; World Bank 2012). Women's disadvantage in higher education in Africa is a function of wider gender inequalities in society. However, educational institutions themselves are socialising spaces in which gender is 'done', albeit covertly (Mama 2003) and in which gendered cultural dynamics are produced, internalised, reproduced and reinforced (Barnes 2007). A range of social, cultural and political factors combine to limit girls' and women's participation in education both as learners and teachers (World Bank 2012). Indeed Reskin and Padavic (1994) conceptualise women's disadvantage in terms of a multi-layered, multi-dimensional phenomenon that has at its heart the interlocking structures of gender ideology, employer's actions and workers' preferences.

Africa is behind the developed world in terms of political and institutional recognition of the disadvantage that women face in organisations (World Bank 2012; Amadi and Amadi 2015). Writers on gender issues in the African academy have highlighted the difficulties that female academics face in raising awareness of gender disadvantage (Tsikata 2007). As such there is a justified focus on gender issues in higher education institutions in Sub-Saharan Africa in spite of the salience of other strands of inequality in cultural dynamics. Indeed at the intersection of gender and other social and demographic factors such as poverty, ethnicity, social space, disability and age, the chances of being excluded from participation in higher education increase (UNESCO 2010; World Bank 2012). For example, in Ghanaian society, seniority and ethnicity are important dimensions through which inequality can be experienced (Apt 1996; Aboderin 2004). As such there is a need for a multi-layered intersectional analysis of women's experiences in the context of a society stratified by age seniority and where age maturity is revered rather than despised (Ogwumike and Aboderin 2005).

An intersectional approach relates to the way in which different strands of disadvantage link together in a complex dynamic to result in a multiple burden. Bradley (2007) delineates the value of using an intersectional approach in terms of three advantages: firstly it avoids the reductionist approach that focuses on a single aspect of disadvantage and enables the unveiling of other forms of oppression; secondly different social dynamics are in operation within any given social interaction; and finally some of the most extreme forms of disadvantage, produced by an intersection of differences, can be seen. Similarly, Healy (2015) points to the importance of an awareness of history, society and biography when we are considering inequality and how the intersection of the varying strands of these can limit individual choice. Such a reminder is imperative when we are considering equality in any context as the impact of cultural traditions dominates societal and workplace practices.

In order to consider the dynamic and complex interrelationship between age, gender, culture and structure we draw primarily upon the work of Evetts (2000), who has developed a framework to explore women's career trajectories through three distinct but interrelated dimensions. Her framework is particularly useful in that it allows us to remove boundaries between culture, structure and action and to recognise the overlapping nature of these. Drawing upon the work of Bourdieu and Wacquant (1992), Evetts points out that "structure and culture arise out of actions and actions are influenced by structure and culture" (2000, 64).

In her cultural dimension Evetts argues that "cultural belief systems influence and control behaviour by means of common-sense notions of what is 'natural' as well as through moral precepts of what is right and appropriate" (2000, 59). Respecting age maturity is a cultural tradition that permeates Ghanaian society. Age groupings are socially constructed and socially determined (Bradley 1999, 2015) with societal pressures placed on individuals to conform to their age 'norm'. Age discrimination, certainly in 'western' cultural contexts, often focuses on the alienation of the more mature worker where 'older' workers can be viewed as no longer adding value to the workplace or indeed society in general. The social construction of age in other cultural contexts, such as those in many Sub-Saharan African countries, is different. Within these contexts, 'older' people are generally seen as providing voices of wisdom; their views are sought and their maturity is respected. Relating back to Healy's (2015) point above, history, society and biography become intertwined within these societies and provide the background to the cultural mosaics in which individuals live and work.

These cultural dimensions overlap and interlink with the structural dimensions that also help determine career trajectories. The latter Evetts identifies as "the institutional and organisational forms and patterns in both the family and the work organisation" (2000, 61). She goes on to explain how structural dimensions include division of both domestic and workplace labour and also 'promotion ladders and career paths'; these structures provide the contextual domain in which men and women—as actors—make their career choices and decisions. This leads us to Evetts's (2000) final dimension, that of action, which she defines as the individual choices and strategies that mediate the impact of culture and structure. The argument here is that people actively strategise in order to develop their careers within environments that have been generated and sustained by the broader cultural and structural influences.

In this chapter, we draw upon these three dimensions in order to consider the multi-layered and multi-dimensional nature of women's disadvantage in academia in Ghana. Within a Ghanaian cultural context, where age maturity is revered and the respect of elders is seen as both 'natural' and 'right and appropriate', we ask: what is the effect of age (im)maturity on the career and workplace experiences of young men and women? Further, we consider how, at the intersection of age and gender, combined with patriarchal and culturally defined organisational structures, women face a double disadvantage vis-a-vis the experiences of their male colleagues.

The Research

This chapter draws upon qualitative data gathered for a larger project, which was a comparative exploration of the psychological contract of academics in two higher education institutions, one in the UK and one in Ghana. The data for the project were collected between November 2010 and July 2011 using a mixed methods approach. We initially conducted an online survey of 200 academics from both countries, which provided both quantitative and qualitative data. Following the survey, we undertook a total of 43 semi-structured in-depth interviews. The interviewees were both male and female and drawn from a variety of positions in the universities. Both management (up to and including deans and heads of schools) and staff (including some teaching assistants) were represented as well as research-active and non-research-active academics. The interviewees were from different age groups and with varying lengths of service. Some participants also kept diarised accounts of their feelings over a three-month period and we also reviewed HR documents at the Ghanaian institution. All the interviews were recorded and fully transcribed.

The research set out to explore the impact of culture, history and change on the psychological contract of academics in a developed (UK) and developing (Ghana) country context. It aimed to uncover both similarities and differences between the psychological contract of academics in these countries with particular regards to the historical influence, if any, of colonialism in Ghana. In order to do this we explored multi-level issues and expectations with regards to: leadership, communication, trust, security, equity and fairness, career development, culture, trade union engagement, change, collegiality. The qualitative data in particular has provided some rich and valuable insights, including data on the intersectionality of age and gender. For this chapter, we draw upon interviews with 28 Ghanaian male and female academics, all of whom remain anonymous. Their gender, positions and age groups are outlined in Tables 6.1, 6.2 and 6.3.

Table 6.1 Profile of Participants by Age and Gender

Gender	<30 years	30–39 years	40–49 years	50–59 years	60+ years	Total
Male	5	1	7	4	3	20
Female	2	3	0	2	1	8
Total	7	4	7	6	4	28

Table 6.2 Profile of Participants by Position and Gender

Gender	Managers	Employees	Total
Male	8	12	20
Female	4	4	8
Total	12	16	28

Table 6.3 Profile of Participants by Rank and Gender

Gender	Professor/ Associate Professor	Senior Lecturer	Lecturer	Assistant Lecturer	Teaching Assistant	Total
Male	8	5	2	0	5	20
Female	2	2	1	2	1	8
Total	10	7	3	2	6	28

National and Institutional Context

The Western, Anglo-American societal, institutional and organisational context is often viewed as a 'norm' by academics and others when considering areas of employment practices, including issues of equality and diversity. In order to appreciate the complexities of the 'developing economy'/Sub-Saharan Africa context, it is important to begin by outlining the national and institutional contexts within which the research for this study was undertaken.

National Context

There are 54 countries in Africa and, with the exceptions of Ethiopia and Liberia, all of these have a history of colonisation. It is the second most populous continent, with approximately 1.1 billion people. Ghana is situated in West Africa and in 1957 was the first Sub-Saharan country to gain independence from British colonisation. Although characterised by political turmoil in the ensuing decades, Ghana now boasts a relatively stable governmental infrastructure (World Bank 2016). Ghana is rich in natural resources, most notably oil, but still has a high proportion of poverty in some of the more rural areas. With a heterogeneous population of around 25 million there are around 20 ethnolinguistic groups, demonstrating the diversity of the country.

As in many countries, women in Ghana take on more of the domestic caring and household duties (as much as 80 per cent of this), even when they are the sole contributor to the family income (World Bank 2012). In spite of resource challenges, most children attend school and there is a fairly equal balance between boys and girls. However, as in most societies, it is the children from the more affluent families who benefit from higher education, and indeed better non-tertiary education. This often results with them moving outside the country (Europe and the US) for their further education experiences.

Institutional Context

Ghanaian universities were inaugurated following the British model of university, but the resource constraints and demand for student places in Ghana (Abukari and Corner 2010; Tetteh and Ofori 2010) depicts a relatively poorer context for academic work than the UK. With a historical focus on primary and secondary education, African governments have persistently under-funded tertiary institutions (Teferra and Altbach 2004). In their study of the University of Development Studies in Northern Ghana, Abukari and Corner (2010) found resource shortages in some areas of staffing, equipment, buildings and other infrastructure. Since 2005 the quality assurance regime previously applied to polytechnics and private higher education institutions has been extended to include the public universities (Abukari and Corner 2010), putting further pressure on staff and management. Despite the low proportion of the population who attend university, compared to other West African countries (Abukari and Corner 2010), there has been enormous growth, with enrolments increasing by 1,800 per cent over 22 years from 11,867 in 1991–1992 (Tetteh and Ofori 2010) to 213,688 in 2013–2014 (National Council on Tertiary Education 2015). Demand far exceeds capacity. Approximately only a third of qualified applicants are admitted to the Ghanaian university system each year (Abukari and Corner 2010; Tetteh and Ofori 2010). This causes motivational pressure on staff to provide education to meet this demand and such high student volumes and workloads may lead to pressures and compromises.

The university in this study is one of over 180 tertiary institutions in the country, including 10 public and 66 private universities (National Accreditation Board 2016) coping with increasing demand for places fuelled by population growth and increasing numbers in primary and secondary education levels (Tetteh and Ofori 2010). At the time there were about 950 full-time contracted academic staff in the University, a relatively small number when compared to a student population of over 35,000. It was within this context of a staff-student ratio of about 1:36 that we explored the experiences of young academic staff.

Findings and Discussion

Our findings indicate that although gender is a significant factor in the dis-advantage faced by women academics at the University, at the intersection of age and gender, based on cultural attitudes, participation and informal expectations and obligations, older women seem to be advantaged in their employment experiences compared to younger women and, to some extent, younger men. Further, there is a convergence in many of the experiences of young women and men.

At the time of data collection there was much re-organising of financial resources and tightening of financial management practices taking place in higher education institutions across the country, including this University. The staff were expected to cut back on financial and other resources, but without this impacting upon the quality of the education provided. In recent times a performance-driven culture had been introduced, which was some-times at variance with the public sector ethos of the staff. The management of the University had embarked upon a more consumer-focused orientation and there was a very active program of marketing taking place.

These managerialist policies and practices need to be considered within the Global South context of limited government resources. The University was being under-funded and was receiving only 30 per cent of the monies required to sustain it. The reality of this in the workplace context was that staff were overworked and frequently went without pay. High student num-bers (around 35,000) meant very high teaching loads with staff teaching between five and six modules per semester. There was a huge lack of physi-cal resources, including IT equipment, books and teaching space. Nonethe-less, staff that participated in this research wanted to stay in their jobs and saw academia as a worthy career.

Career progress, however, was based on getting 'tenure', that is, a full-time permanent position at the University. There was much emphasis on the attainment of doctoral qualifications, for which the University provided funding as part of academic contracts. PhDs from American and European institutions carried higher value and were more favoured as was publishing in European and American academic journals. However, study leave for PhDs and sabbaticals for publishing purposes were usually at the discretion of managers. Many of the staff we spoke to were on temporary contracts, pending their promotion to tenured positions. Although generally given the title of Assistant Lecturer, and paid a commensurate sum for that lower position, they were usually carrying a full academic load. The quid pro quo for working at this 'lowly' position was the opportunity to gain a PhD.

Table 6.4 University Academic Members by Age and Gender

Gender	<30 years	30–39 years	40–49 years	50–59 years	60+ years	Total
Male	10	133	214	239	118	714
Female	10	72	63	66	22	233
Total	20	205	277	305	140	947

Table 6.5 University Academic Members by Rank and Gender

Gender	Professor	Associate Professor	Senior Lecturer	Lecturer	Assistant Lecturer	Total
Male	70	97	162	360	25	714
Female	8	22	55	123	25	233
Total	78	119	217	483	50	947

The University reflected the typical structure of an organisation based in a patriarchal society in most countries: the ratio of men to women academics increases as one goes up the organisational hierarchy, as well as the age structure (see Tables 6.4 and 6.5).

Regardless of the historical reasons for the more recent participation of women in higher education, these structures set the scene for higher numbers of women to experience disadvantage in the organisation compared to men, based on the fact of the intersection of gender and age. In Ghana, where age immaturity is undervalued, being younger in age and lower down in the organisational hierarchy compounds disadvantage.

Controlling Notions of Femininity and Youth

Internationally, the higher levels of the academic hierarchy are male-dominated, and the academic culture to be such that 'maleness' is valued. In African academic institutions, the colonial antecedents of gender attitudes have often remained and been emulated. Interlocked with these already entrenched institutional structures is the cultural convention of deferring to age.

One issue that the young academics, both female and male, identified was how they sometimes struggled to gain credibility as academics with students. The 'mature man' was the stereotypical 'professor': "There are certain statements they [students] can't make to an elderly person but they would do that to a young person like me" (Male teaching assistant, 20–29 years).

If you tell [MBA] students to study there are times they take offence, just because of who you are. This "young" [woman], to tell an elderly person who manages his business to study! But the Head of Department says things and because he is elderly and a man all of them will listen to it.

(Female assistant lecturer, 20–29 years)

In an organisational environment characterised by performance management practices, student feedback was an unofficial, but nonetheless recognised, mechanism of asserting pressure on staff, particularly with regards to career development. In order to progress within the University system of tenure, teaching staff needed to demonstrate their ability to generate a positive learning environment. For some staff cultural norms and behaviours, outside their control, impacted upon their ability to facilitate the desired learning environment:

> The Ghanaian culture is sometimes . . . you would not be able to put a finger on it sometimes, but we know it. So even with your interaction with students, especially the older ones . . . For instance I was just accused last week of talking to them like kids—these are managers and executives on the [MBA] program. It was the vice dean who drew my attention to it. This is a typical Ghanaian situation. It is a culture situation. These are persons who probably see me and think they are older than me, and I am telling them "no". They can't fit themselves into it [and] that is the most current issue I am trying to figure out, how do I manage it? So the Ghanaian culture seriously influences relationships with students and with colleagues.
>
> (Female assistant lecturer, 20–29 years)

There is a complexity here for this woman who is rooted in a culture that she recognises and respects, but one which frustrates her ability to perform her academic work. Her own educational achievement is diminished and delegitimised when it is linked to her personal profile of 'young woman'. The "institutional and organisational forms and patterns" (Evetts 2000, 61) within which she is being evaluated are such that they privilege the more mature, male, academic.

It is not only with students that younger members of staff have to gain credibility, they also have to do so with their peers and the age issue is further exacerbated when it comes to taking on the position of line manager. Age seniority impacts managerial practices to the extent that cultural and corporatist practices become entwined and it is difficult to extrapolate one from the other, as these two male managers explain:

> In one of the departments, should I say two departments, most of the Senior Members . . . taught the Head of Departments (HoDs) . . . they [HoDs] were their students and sometimes the Heads . . . they find it very difficult to manage the department because of them . . . because

of their egos and things like that. It is a problem. It's that Ghanaian problem.

(Male manager, 40–49 years)

An interesting incident occurred during the interview that produced the quote below. This young academic manager had called an important departmental meeting and left instructions with administrative staff not to allow the booking of any rooms for other meetings during that time slot. This was to ensure that all staff attended the meeting. While we were speaking to him and he was relaying this information to us (as an indication of his authority), an older academic walked into his office and demanded to know why he had been denied a room for a meeting at the same time. Our interviewee made an initial attempt at 'pulling rank', however, when his colleague challenged his managerial authority, he capitulated and agreed that the colleague could come to the departmental meeting later. Even so, after the colleague had left he was very concerned about how the interaction would be perceived by this older academic:

For instance this man is older than me, he taught me so he expects that when he does something—[because] in our culture, an elderly man is usually right, yes? And you can't talk to him in a certain way. I am sure he will later come back to me and say I didn't talk to him well . . . why do I question what he's doing and all that? It is in our system. It pervades our system . . . It's like the young one hasn't got any sense. So the culture plays a heavy role in managing because in decision making you are there but your contribution to the decision-making is low . . . it's low.

(Male manager, 40–49 years)

In a patriarchal society and an institutional context where seniority is the domain of men (Tsikata 2007), the impact of such cultural values and norms are intensified for younger women taking up managerial positions. Having broken through a 'glass ceiling' to progress to managerial level, the female manager talks of the frustrations of returning to a culture that she simultaneously respects and finds exasperating:

I had a conflict at first with one of the [male, older] staff members where—[my] expectations were too high; I was expecting something to be done by a certain time and it did not happen. So there was some confrontation. Then . . . it came to the attention of the Dean. And the Dean was trying to explain to me that people do things differently, that it is possible that this person sees you in a certain light—you know [me] younger, female (laughter) . . . . I am [Ghanaian], but I spent a lot of years outside Ghana. I spent too many years outside Ghana. I have been accused of not behaving like a Ghanaian. I have been accused of that but sometimes I have to remember the context.

(Female manager, 30–39 years)

This quote highlights a two-pronged tension: firstly a tension within herself and secondly, between her own notions of managerial authority and that of her colleagues and her manager. In the first, her identity as a Ghanaian woman and a 'western' academic is brought into stark relief. Whilst she appreciates the former she regrets the loss of the latter. Moving back to Ghana has emphasised the cultural and structural constraints that she had moved away from. The second paradox is reflected in the friction between her on the one hand, and her colleague and her manager on the other. She sees management from a 'western' perspective, where authority is vested in the 'office' irrespective of age, yet her colleague and manager expect her to conform to Ghanaian standards of respect for age and seniority, regardless of 'office'. This conflict is so severe that it leads to the internal and external questioning of her identity as a Ghanaian.

Although she is clearly aware that her actions are limited by cultural influences, this woman does not appear to challenge these but is resigned to them. She has 'returned' to societal values that constrain her actions but she also respects these as the underlying context of her home country. This is understandable, but nonetheless, in doing so, she is perpetuating the privileging of age maturity within her organisational environment, a context that young women following her will also have to deal with.

Academic Freedom and Societal Culture

Academic spaces do not sit in isolation from the societies in which they are embedded. Indeed as Mama (2003) has argued, apart from reflecting the societal culture the academy also actively produces and reinforces societal notions of gender. In fulfilling their duties with the commitment that would otherwise be seen as normal in an older man, some young female academics felt that their dedication was seen as 'overstepping their boundaries'—confirming Tsikata's (2007) suggestion that in the culture of the Ghanaian academy real academics are apparently male, and in this case, older men. Young women's hard work was viewed with suspicion, and they were perceived as having ulterior motives. Further, the next narrative demonstrates how the coping mechanisms of an overloaded young unmarried woman can be misconstrued in the context of a culture that devalues youth and women:

The kind of suspicion people could have here . . . if they find a young woman busily doing work they assume because you are a woman—and they think that is not supposed to be done by you—you are doing a lot more just to rub shoulders with your *older* male counterparts which is not so! There are times it is just the love of the job and the fact that yes, maybe you have to do a lot more than others who have been in the field for all these years.

(Female assistant lecturer, 20–29 years)

Compounded with single marital status, the triple intersection of these strands in the life of young, single female lecturers can exacerbate their already difficult work lives as junior academics:

If they look at an elderly person they wouldn't say these things but just because of the age and the sex and they look at you as a woman and the fact that you don't even . . . they can't see any ring so they think all of those things means you are quite 'small'.

(Female lecturer, 30–39 years)

Despite the fact that hard work is necessary in order to progress in their careers, these women are caught in a culture-structure-action trap. The mature male societal and institutional culture dominates the organisational structures, which asks for long hours and commitment, but if a young woman attempts to follow this 'norm' then her actions are dismissed and derided by those helping to perpetuate the norm. If the women above, and their female colleagues, do not work hard they will not progress, but if they follow what is seen as a typical male career path then they are seen as acting in a way that is contrary to the notions of their society. As mentioned, in Ghanaian culture being younger in age and lower down in the organisational hierarchy compounds an employee's disadvantage. Indeed this is reflected in the narratives below where we explore voice and workload.

Silencing Young Voices

Millward et al. (2000) define employee voice as the enabling of employees to influence employer actions and Calveley et al. (2014) argue that such voice is vital in maintaining a balance within the employment relationship. Our findings show that in Ghana, both young male and young female staff felt that they had limited voice in the organisation. The culture of respect for one's elders effectively silences younger workers and bars them from the decision-making process. It was clear in the participants' narratives that age was the overriding factor in their experience, as opposed to gender:

Because we are young, we cannot challenge lecturers and we cannot make our concerns known. Challenging the lecturers is understood in terms of a personal challenge of the lecturer's ability rather than an intellectual debate.

(Male teaching assistant, 20–29 years)

As a young person we are not consulted on any issues regarding work or work conditions.

(Female teaching assistant, 20–29 years)

These young academics are having their views obstructed by cultural belief systems which are embodied within the organisational processes and practices. Of course, these practices work to the benefit of the more mature faculty, who no doubt went through the same processes themselves, but who are able to avoid confrontation with their younger colleagues. In the light of Robinson and Rousseau's (1994) findings that suggest that perceptions of psychological contract breach are prevalent among highly skilled new entrants into organisations, the lack of input into decision-making or the lack of opportunity to articulate grievances among this group can pose a challenge to the University. Interestingly, although there is demand for academic staff in Ghana, exit was not considered as being a solution to this situation, perhaps because these young people are aware that this deeply embedded culture is likely to persist wherever they go to work.

Workload—Expectations and Obligations

High teaching workloads, which is a problem across many universities, was a recurring theme for all, but particularly so for the younger faculty:

There are people who are on retirement contracts who don't want to do much at all and the younger faculty who need time and space to do their research and so on, actually find themselves teaching the larger classes, the classes that have a thousand students and that kind of thing, so I think the workload is a huge challenge.

(Female manager, 40–49 years)

Some staff identified this to be a form of discrimination and linked it to the intersection of gender and age: "Discrimination working here . . . there are certain things you won't be asked to do because maybe you are a woman and you are young (Female assistant lecturer, 20–29 years). Further, there were expectations that younger and newer staff would take on more than their share of the workload in exchange for funding for staff development despite the latter being their entitlement. In the next narrative managers used their power, both as people in authority but also as older members of the faculty, to 'force' younger members to take on extra workload, on the threat of withdrawing funding for a PhD:

[He] complained that he had been given too many courses to teach and we said "we all know that you are going to leave and do your PhD. Who do you think is going to teach your courses while you are away?

So you've got to carry the load now and then while you're away, some-body else carries the load". Then within three months after the alloca-tions had been made he came and put his papers down that he had got a school and that I should sign his papers to release him and I looked at him and I said "I am not signing".

(Male manager, 40–49 years)

Both male and female managers wielded this power. The experiences of the staff emerged through the interaction of managerial discretion and work-place ageism, in which a line manager operates with strong notions of what sort of reciprocal obligations will be exacted from younger staff in exchange for staff development. As the staff members referred to in the narratives above and below did not conform with their line managers' perceptions of the workplace conduct of a younger subordinate, this led to threatening behaviour by the managers:

I mentioned to them that the fact that you are due to go for PhD studies doesn't mean that you should go right away; what if you come back and there is no department to come back to because it's collapsed? So you have to sacrifice. I have asked them to sacrifice so I suppose . . . that's why . . . my voice is very unpopular.

(Female manager, 30–39 years)

For the younger women, the workload issue was double-edged. Some of these women were juggling work and family commitments, again, a usual phenomenon for female workers and not unique to Ghana. Many of the women were either young parents or considering becoming parents. This caused extra anxiety and sometimes resulted in taking on the responsibility for the whole of their gender, as demonstrated in this quote:

For the workload, [there was] the time I had to do the five courses . . . one of my colleagues went on maternity leave just at the time we entered. I felt if the person goes on maternity leave and they had to get a part-timer to come and take the person's place, in the near future maybe the department could think if they would have lots of young people . . . childbearing [age] and those things could interfere with their work. Maybe they'd decide not to pick a lot more very young people and maybe pick the elderly and we think it wouldn't be good. We thought it wouldn't be good so I decided to stand in for the person and that was what I did.

(Female assistant lecturer, 20–29 years)

Although this quote seems to reflect concern with the experiences of young people in the department in general, in particular it reveals the greater bur-den that young women face at the intersection of gender, age and seniority.

What it also reveals is the potential for underlying tensions to develop between young women and young men, tensions that undermine their ability to portray a united front to challenge some of the inequalities they face. Evetts (2000) argues that actors who find themselves in structural and cultural constraints utilise their own agency to navigate their career paths and experiences, in order to mediate the impact of culture and structure. This means that it was important for the academics to develop coping and resistance strategies to steer their way through the constraints they encountered; however, they did so with varying success.

Negotiation, Adaptation and Confrontation

The young academics we spoke to found ways of adapting themselves and their lifestyles to cope with the extra pressures they were under, but this was sometimes to the detriment of career progress:

> I didn't find a good structure to balance teaching and research so it became teaching, teaching, teaching . . . and now I am trying to see some line [*colloquialism meaning 'a way through'*] to apportion some time to each [teaching and research] but teaching gets heavier and heavier as programs get introduced.
>
> (Female assistant lecturer, 20–29 years)

Given the University's insistence on the acquisition of a PhD and/or publications as a condition of tenure, time to do research, or indeed engage in scholarly activity was clearly important. However these adaptation strategies seem to lead to extra workload, which undermined staff intentions and ability to progress their careers. Several younger staff we spoke to had put their doctoral intentions on hold in order to maintain and cope with existing workloads. Clearly this would be exacerbated in the lives of women with young families who carried a double burden of both domestic and work responsibilities as demonstrated by one young female academic who decided to confront her manager with the problem and seek his advice. Unfortunately, the advice that was given to them was stereotypically male:

> I have talked to the head of department under whom I was hired and he is trying to give me a sense of what he does. He is a male so when he tells me some of the things [that] work for him it doesn't seem to be working for me like: "Work long hours". Who would pick up my kids? Who would take care of them at home? After school yes, and then working at home then what would happen to the kids?
>
> (Female assistant lecturer, 30–39 years)

This advice might be appropriate for the younger men trying to progress their careers, but less so for women. In a traditional and patriarchal society like Ghana, where, unfairly, a woman's caring responsibilities include husbands, children, elderly parents or parents-in-law, being advised to work even longer hours fails to recognise the staff member's issue in context. For young parents like this woman, the intensity of her work-life conflict is deepened by her manager's ambivalence and assumption of a gender-neutral organisation. The need to be professional and the pressure from family and friends to be a 'good' mother and/or wife can intensify the guilt associated with a perceived inability to balance work and life. The irony of the manager's response is that academia has historically portrayed itself as an egalitarian liberal space where knowledge is created and equality is valued—as such, a safe space for women.

Conclusions

This chapter has considered how the focus on gender alone in research on the African university tells a partial story of the workplace discrimination faced by women. Within the complex Sub-Saharan context of Ghana, in order to get a more comprehensive understanding of policies, processes and practices it is necessary to take a deeper and broader, multi-level view. In order to do this, we drew upon Evetts's (2000) use of culture, structure and action dimensions to develop a conceptual framework, which helps us to explore the academic career paths of young women and men.

From our empirical research, we identified how the ability of younger academics to manage their work and careers is influenced by cultural notions of youth. In a society that reveres age maturity and correlates this with seniority and respect, it is difficult for young people to find a voice. This is not just the case for the more 'junior' academics, nor is it the case for women only. Both men and women who are appointed to managerial positions are faced with resistance by more mature colleagues who see age as a license to act independently, and they have to navigate a path which treads a fine line between managerial authority and disrespect. For women, employed within institutions heavily influenced by a patriarchal culture, at the intersection of femininity and youth they are faced with a double disadvantage, this often being exacerbated by their more junior position in the academic hierarchy. With managers holding all the cards vis-a-vis career progression, it is often the case that young academics are doubly taken advantage of, firstly by the exploitative management practices which extract high volumes of work from them, and secondly by themselves as they see the ultimate goal of tenure and career development as being worth the sacrifice of long hours and low pay.

As the cultural and structural processes that shape the young women's and men's experiences with respect to work interactions are embedded in the practices of the society and institution, they become resilient and are therefore reproduced over time. Of course, as Evetts (2000) suggests, these young academics have agency and are able to strategise in order to develop their careers, but for them, the notion of privilege following age maturity is 'natural' and is 'right and appropriate' (Evetts 2000, 59). Nonetheless, the more these cultural and institutional norms are adhered to, the more they persist. This does not bode well for young Ghanaian academics of the future.

Our research found that there was frustration amongst the young academics, both male and female, as they struggled to carve out a place for themselves within the academy. It also identified how in such a patriarchal society young women, at the intersection of age and gender, found this more difficult on three fronts. Firstly, women—as women—are viewed as having less power, both as tutors (by students) and managers (by colleagues). Secondly, their youth delegitimises their authority in the classroom and in the academic community. Finally, they are expected to take on the undervalued responsibilities of home-related caring, which compounds the struggle to achieve respect and recognition in the academic community. Indeed managers failed, or perhaps refused, to see that this was a societal issue that inhibited the progression of young women in the workplace. To get on in academia in Ghana, it would appear that one has to be willing to follow the mature male cultural 'norm' regardless of your gender or age.

As Healy (2015) reminds us, it is important to have an awareness of how history, society and biography intersect when considering diversity, whilst Evetts (2000) points out how people's behaviour is influenced and even controlled by cultural belief systems. Our research has demonstrated that in Ghanaian society characterised by a deep reverence towards age maturity, to pay respect, honour and give privilege to elders is a time-honoured convention. These attitudes are so embedded within workplaces that not to act in this way would almost be deemed as deviant behaviour. This intersection of cultural beliefs and attitudes impacts the approach taken to age and gender in the workplace, even in the 'enlightened' sphere of academia.

References

Aboderin, I. 2004. "Intergenerational Family Support and Old Age Economic Security in Sub-Saharan Africa: The Importance of Understanding Shifts, Processes and Expectations. An Example from Ghana." In *Living Longer: Ageing, Development and Social Protection*, edited by Peter Lloyd-Sherlock, 163–176. London: UNRISD, Zed Books.

Abukari, A. and Corner, T. 2010. "Delivering Higher Education to Meet Local Needs in a Developing Context: The Quality Dilemmas?" *Quality Assurance in Education* 18(3): 191–208.

Amadi, L. and Amadi, C. 2015. "Towards Institutionalizing Gender Equality in Africa: How Effective Are the Global Gender Summits and Convention? A Critique." *African Journal of Political Science and International Relations* 9(1): 12.

Apt, N. A. 1996. *Coping with Old Age in a Changing Africa*. Aldershot: Avebury.

Barnes, T. 2007. "Politics of the Mind and Body: Gender and Institutional Culture in African Universities." *Feminist Africa* 8: 8–25.

Benschop, Y. W. M. and Brouns, M. 2003. "Crumbling Ivory Towers: Academic Organizing and Its Gender Effects." *Gender, Work and Organization* 10(2): 194–212.

Bourdieu, P. and Wacquant, L. 1992. *An Invitation to Reflexive Sociology*. Cambridge: Polity Press.

Bradley, H. 1999. *Gender and Power in the Workplace: Analysing the Impact of Economic Change*. Basingstoke: Palgrave Macmillan.

Bradley, H. 2007. *Gender*. Oxford: Polity Press.

Bradley, H. 2015. *Fractured Identities: The Changing Patterns of Inequality*. Oxford: Polity Press.

Calveley, M., Allsop, D. and Lawton, N. R. 2014. "Managing the Employment Relationship." In *Strategic Human Resource Management: An International Perspective*, edited by G. Rees and P. Smith, 267–301. London: Sage.

Curtis, J. W. and Thornton, S. 2014. *Losing Focus: The Annual Report on the Economic Status of the Profession, 2013–2014*. American Association of University Professors. Accessed August 20, 2016. https://www.aaup.org/sites/default/files/files/2014%20salary%20report/zreport_0.pdf.

Evetts, J. 2000. "Analysing Career Change in Women's Careers: Culture, Structure and Action Dimensions." *Gender Work and Organization* 7(1): 57–67.

Garstka, T. A., Schmitt, M. T., Branscombe, N. R. and Hummert, M. L. 2004. "How Young and Older Adults Differ in Their Responses to Perceived Age Discrimination." *Psychology and Aging* 9(2): 326–335.

Healy, G. 2015. *The Politics of Equality and Diversity: History, Society, and Biography*. Oxford: Oxford University Press.

Healy, G., Ozbilgin, M. and Aliefendioğlu, H. 2005. "Academic Employment and Gender: A Turkish Challenge to Vertical Sex Segregation." *European Journal of Industrial Relations* 11(2): 247–264.

Mama, A. 2003. "Restore, Reform But Do Not Transform: The Gender Politics of Higher Education in Africa." *Journal of Higher Education in Africa* 1(1): 101–125.

Millward, N., Bryson, A. and Forth, J. 2000/2002. *All Change at Work? British Employment Relations 1980–1998, Portrayed by the Workplace Industrial Relations Survey Series*. 1st ed. London: Routledge.

Morley, L. and Crossouard, B. 2014. *Women in Higher Education Leadership in South Asia: Rejection, Refusal, Reluctance, Revisioning*. University of Sussex, Centre for Higher Education & Equity Research.

National Accreditation Board. 2016. "Private Tertiary Institutions Offering Degree Programmes." Accessed October 4, 2016. www.nab.gov.gh/private-tertiary-institutions-offering-degree-programmes.

National Council on Tertiary Education. 2015. "Education Sector Performance Report 2015." Accessed October 4, 2016. www.moe.gov.gh/site/reports.

Ogwumike, F. O. and Aboderin, I. 2005. "Exploring the Links Between Old Age and Poverty in Anglophone West Africa: Evidence from Nigeria and Ghana." *Generations Review* 15(2): 7–15.

Özbilgin, M. and Healy, G. 2004. "The Gendered Nature of Career Development of University Professors: The Case of Turkey." *Journal of Vocational Behavior* 64(2): 358–371.

Reskin, B. F. and Padavic, I. 1994. *Women and Men at Work*. 1st ed. London: Pine Forge Press.

Robinson, S. L. and Rousseau, D. M. 1994. "Violating the Psychological Contract: Not the Exception But the Norm." *Journal of Organisational Behaviour* 15(3): 245–259.

Seierstad, C. and Healy, G. 2012. "Women's Equality in the Scandinavian Academy: A Distant Dream?" *Work, Employment and Society* 26(2): 296–313.

Snape, E. and Redman, T. 2003. "Too Old or Too Young? The Impact of Perceived Age Discrimination." *Human Resource Management Journal* 13(1): 78–89.

Strachan, G. J., Broadbent, K., Whitehouse, G., Peetz, D. R. and Bailey, J. M. 2011. "Looking for Women in Australian Universities." In *Research and Development in Higher Education: Reshaping Higher Education*, edited by K. L. Krause, M. Buckridge, C. Grimmer and S. Purbrick-Illek, 308–319. Australia: HERDSA.

Teferra, D. and Altbach, P. G. 2004. "African Higher Education: Challenges for the 21st Century." *Higher Education* 47(1): 21–50.

Tetteh, E. N. and Ofori, D. F. 2010. "An Exploratory and Comparative Assessment of the Governance Arrangements of Universities in Ghana." *Corporate Governance: The International Journal of Business in Society* 10(3): 234–248.

Tsikata, D. 2007. "Gender, Institutional Cultures and the Career Trajectories of Faculty of the University of Ghana." *Feminist Africa* 8: 26–41.

UCU. 2016. *Holding Down Women's Pay: Report for International Women's Day.* London: Universities and Colleges Union.

UNESCO. 2010. *Global Education Digest 2010: Comparing Education Statistics Across the World.* Paris: UNESCO Institute for Statistics: Special Focus on Gender.

World Bank. 2012. "World Development Report 2012." Accessed 28 September, 2016. http://econ.worldbank.org/WBSITE/EXTERNAL/EXTDEC/EXTRESEARCH/EXTWDRS/EXTWDR2012/0,contentMDK:22999750~menuPK:8154981~pagePK:64167689~piPK:64167673~theSitePK:7778063,00.html.

World Bank. 2016. "Ghana Overview." Accessed September 28, 2016. www.worldbank.org/en/country/ghana/overview.

7 Gender and Migration

The Experiences of Skilled Professional Women

Susan Ressia, Glenda Strachan and Janis Bailey

Introduction

Why do individuals migrate? Many refugees do so for reasons relating to persecution or discrimination, but a major reason for much migration is economic benefit (Bartram 2010; Dean and Manzoni 2012) or 'upward mobility' by achieving higher-level employment (Pedraza 1991; Glaesser and Cooper 2014). But what are the gender implications of migration and, in particular, how do professional women fare? Such women are migrating in ever-increasing numbers. In fact, they are overtaking men as primary applicants (Docquier, Lowell and Marfouk 2009; Syed and Murray 2009; IOM 2010a). However, we understand little about these women's experiences and outcomes (Cooke, Zhang and Wang 2013; Kofman 2013; Ressia 2014; Phan, Banerjee, Deacon and Taraky 2015), including how they progress professionally (Al Ariss 2010; González-Ferrer 2011; Pio and Essers 2014). This chapter concentrates on three issues: What happens when women migrants do not achieve expected outcomes of equivalent professional employment? Why does this occur and is there a relationship to gender and family responsibilities? What strategies do women migrants use to access employment? The experiences of 16 skilled professional women who migrated from various non-English-speaking-background (NESB) countries to Australia are considered to illustrate these arguments.

Skilled Migration and Gender: An Overview

Skilled migration programs are now the major pathway for migrants entering traditional settler societies such as Australia, Canada, New Zealand and, more recently, the United Kingdom (Ressia, Strachan and Bailey 2016). Such programs are intended to attract and select immigrants based on their human capital, that is, their skill, education, occupational experience, language levels and age (Anderson 2010; Boucher and Cerna 2014). Skilled migration programs are aimed at fulfilling (higher) skill shortfalls in local labour markets, and curb the impact of ageing populations and declining birthrates in such societies (Phan et al. 2015). Earlier programs focused on those in unskilled and semi-skilled jobs (Taksa and Groutsis 2010), so recent government policies represent a major change in direction.

Historically, men were the primary applicants in the migration process (Alcorso 1991; Cobb-Clark, Connolly and Worswick 2001; Raghuram 2004; Mushaben 2009). Thus men's rather than women's experience of migration was highlighted (Kofman 2004; Raghuram 2004; Iredale 2005; Syed and Murray 2009). Women were seen as mere dependents, as "family migrants", trailing spouses or "tied movers" (Zlotnik 1995; Kofman 2004; Raghuram 2004; Smith 2004; Cooke 2007; Docquier et al. 2009; González-Ferrer 2011; Zaiceva 2010). Women migrants, in other words, attend to family needs, rather than being economic actors in their own right (Cooke 2007; Riaño and Baghdadi 2007; González-Ferrer 2011; Cliff, Grün, Ville and Dolnicar 2015). Thus female migrants have often been rendered 'invisible' in historical accounts of the migration process (Riaño and Baghdadi 2007; Ryan 2008; Mushaben 2009).

This view is now very outdated. In 2014 women were nearly half the world's migrants (IOM 2014), and the figure is growing (Docquier et al. 2009; UN 2013). Many of these women are independent skilled migrants (Zlotnik 1995; Syed and Murray 2009; Cooke et al. 2013). Further, many highly qualified migrant women—with employment and economic objectives of their own—migrate as spouses of male primary applicants (Kofman 2004; Kofman and Raghuram 2006). Consequently, migrants—both men and women—seek appropriate work. Little is known, however, about the job-seeking experiences and outcomes of skilled migrant women, in contrast to our extensive understanding of men's experiences (Pedraza 1991; Raghuram 2004; Boucher 2007; Cooke et al. 2013; Kofman 2013; Shinozaki 2014; Phan et al. 2015). Therefore, how do such women navigate unfamiliar labour markets (Pio and Essers 2014; González Ramos and Martín-Palomino 2015)?

Complex gender norms clearly influence this process (O'Dwyer and Colic-Peisker 2016). Migrant women face challenges due to spousal, societal and cultural expectations of a woman's role, and lack practical support in areas like childcare (Kofman 2004; Ressia 2014). Research over the last 25 years (Pedraza 1991; Pessar 1999; Boyd and Grieco 2003; Mahler and Pessar 2006; Raghuram 2008; Herrera 2013, 473) has shown how gender plays out in the migration experience. At a theoretical level, intersectionality has been adopted as a useful lens (Crenshaw 1989; Anthias 2012a) contesting essentialist views on gender (Lutz, Vivar and Supik 2011; Herrera 2013, 476). Intersectional approaches consider gender, class and ethnicity (as well as many others) (Bürkner 2012) within the context of economic, political and broader social systems (Pessar and Mahler 2003; Anthias 2012a, 2012b; Smith and King 2012). Thus, intersectionality enables the examination of characteristics of difference between people and groups within a wide range of contexts and locations, and recognises that people of all backgrounds experience discrimination from their own unique standpoint.

This then provides a more nuanced way of understanding the migration experiences of individuals and the differences in outcomes between women and men.

Navigating the Labour Market in a New Country

A number of empirical studies have highlighted the challenges facing women migrants. Cooke et al. (2013), for example, explore the many complex factors affecting Chinese professional women's progress as they attempt to re-build careers in Australia. Language, skill and qualification recognition, and lack of networks, local knowledge and understanding of the job search process are often cited in the academic literature (Al Ariss 2010; Docquier et al. 2009; Dyer, McDowell and Batnitzky 2010; Liversage 2009; O'Dwyer and Colic-Peisker 2016). Confidence and capacity building is required to help women develop strategies to increase their chances of securing employment (Cooke et al. 2013, 2637). Cooke et al. (2013) argue that migrant women face the loss of human and social capital, with discrimination by employers a part of the problem. There is a lack of support for such migrants in terms of helping them adapt to a new labour market (Cooke et al. 2013; Ressia 2014). So finding jobs in the first place is difficult.

In addition, migrants, both women and men, frequently face downward occupational mobility, meaning that their jobs are at lower skill and pay levels than those held prior to migration (Chiswick, Lee and Miller 2003; Ho 2004; Ho and Alcorso 2004; O'Dwyer and Colic-Peisker 2016; Zorlu 2016). Gender segregation in new labour markets means that women fight for work within even more unfavourable labour market segments than men encounter. Care occupations are a particular example of 'reproductive' forms of work into which skilled professional women drift. In England, for instance, migrants—most of them women—comprise 18 per cent of care workers (IOM 2010b), who are poorly remunerated and have little chance of progression. Many are qualified and highly skilled medical or health care professionals. While their skills are used, they suffer occupational downgrading by their employers (IOM 2010a), enduring poor working conditions and pay, and lacking promotional opportunities. As highlighted in one report, "rarely are their degrees and qualifications mentioned as contributing factors for the high quality of care that the elderly receive from them" (IOM 2010b, 10). One empirical study shows that Lebanese women in France are relegated to lower level jobs by a combination of gender, race and the regulatory environment, and lack of recognition of their human capital (Al Ariss 2010). A study of Latin American women migrants to Switzerland (Riaño and Baghdadi 2007) found four main strategies were used: first, to 're-skill', meaning working on language skills, repeating former tertiary studies or enrolling in postgraduate degrees; second, to work below skills, to create their own employment or to do volunteer work; third, to postpone, limit or decide to have no children to enable time for further study and increase human capital; and fourth, to completely withdraw from the labour market, and either work within the domestic sphere, or return to their home country (Riaño and Baghdadi 2007; Fossland 2012). These devices are used to circumvent, manage or work around the barriers to obtaining equivalent employment.

Segregation of women into feminised, lower-paid occupations acts as a trap. Once skilled professional women take these jobs as 'stop-gaps', they are unlikely to move out of them. Women migrants also lack social support networks around childcare, which may force them to revert to traditional domestic roles. Women migrants to Israel of Asian and African descent are a case in point (Raijman and Semyonov 1997; Remennick 2005). Combined, these factors mean that downward occupational mobility is more likely for women than men.

Experiences of Women Migrants in Australia

How to flesh out these issues, and demonstrate the experiences of migrating professional women? This section examines the experiences of female migrants from a range of countries settling in Brisbane, Australia, within the past five years. The participants were sourced mainly through migrant support services and state and local government bodies. Each woman was interviewed twice during the research—12 months apart. The women were all non-English-speaking background (NESB) professionals arriving on a variety of visa arrangements. Three women arrived as primary independent skilled migrants, two arrived on humanitarian visas and the rest migrated as secondary migrants (on spouse visas), as their husbands were the primary applicant. Most had children. The research was designed to tease out women's expectations and actual experiences, and to analyse the findings using the research literature summarised above.

Expectations

Women expected they would find good job opportunities resulting in better economic outcomes for themselves and their families. But a range of issues thwarted their expectations: lack of local work experience, and problems of language and qualifications equivalency. These are common themes highlighted in the migrant literature (see Docquier et al. 2009; Liversage 2009; Al Ariss 2010; Broadbent, Bailey, Strachan, and Ressia 2010; Dyer et al. 2010; O'Dwyer and Colic-Peisker 2016; Ressia et al. 2016). For example, one woman, a highly qualified accountant, had migrated from China as the primary migrant. She had brought her husband and young child, and she had come to Australia seeking economic opportunity and a better lifestyle. However, she experienced problems with securing work. She felt that this was caused by her language skills and lack of work experience, a common issue amongst interviewees. She felt that potential employers were not recognising her extensive experience (as noted in a recent UK study by

Papadopoulos [2016]). She remarked that her experience of seeking work left her 'depressed' and disappointed'.

Similarly, a woman emigrating from war-torn Iraq on a humanitarian visa encountered problems with seeking employment. With 15 years' experience in the field of civil engineering she believed that moving to Australia would give her the opportunity to increase her skills and secure her family's future. She actively began looking for work on arrival in Australia, but found that her skills and work experience were not enough to acquire work. She indicated that local job experience was a big problem, and she was keen to find an opportunity to get a 'foot in the door'.

These experiences were echoed by all the women in the study. Further issues affected some. Teachers needed to meet additional accreditation requirements, for example. This set them back time-wise and also economically due the unexpected costs of extra study (Ressia 2014). These women sought alternate employment as their partners were also struggling to find work. One female teacher who was trying to complete accreditation requirements while her husband was in a low-paying job said:

> It is very difficult to undergo all that training . . . if I want to get a job, he then [my husband] may undergo training [in his field] because we won't go at the same time . . . because we need money to survive here.

These experiences bring to light the struggles that these migrants face, showing that while they have the human capital that should enable a smooth(ish) transition into employment, the experience is not straightforward, as their skills are unrecognised and undervalued (Riaño and Baghdadi 2007; O'Dwyer and Colic-Peisker 2016).

Employment Outcomes

Research participants did not find the employment that they had expected prior to migration, even though they had the skills needed to satisfy immigration requirements. Prior to migration, women felt their job search would be relatively easy and they would find employment quite quickly, and so would continue to develop their professional careers. However, outcomes did not match expectations (see Table 7.1).

Almost all participants suffered downward occupational mobility even though they were actively seeking work in their field. At the first interview, all participants were working below their skill level, if indeed they had found work. For example, a woman from India changed occupation from primary school teacher to food services assistant. A woman from Spain was only able to secure part-time work in her field. A female civil engineer with 15 years' experience could only find work as a casual childcare assistant, highlighting the 'disadvantage' these women face in relation to 'professional success post-migration' (O'Dwyer and Colic-Peisker 2016, 60).

Table 7.1 Employment Outcomes

Country of Origin	Time Since Arrival	Married/ Children	Job Prior to Migration	Job at First Interview	Job at Second Interview
Iraq	6 mths	Yes/2	Civil engineer	Unemployed	Unemployed
India	9 mths	Yes/2	Primary school teacher	Casual food service	Unemployed
Spain	1 yr	Yes/No	Social worker	P/T social worker	P/T social worker
China	1 yr	Yes/1	Accountant	Work placement	F/T Payroll officer —temporary
Iraq	1 yr	Yes/2	Civil engineer	Unemployed	Casual childcare worker
Indonesia	1 yr	Yes/3	Accountant	Unemployed	Unemployed
Sri Lanka	1 yr 4 mths	Yes/3	Paralegal	Work placement	Returned to Sri Lanka
Bangladesh	2 yrs	Yes/1	Accounting/Admin	Unemployed	Unemployed
Ethiopia	2 yrs	Yes/1	Office admin commercial TV	Work placement	Administrative assistant— temporary
Colombia	2 yrs 4 mths	Yes/No	Lawyer	Unemployed	Unemployed/volunteer
India	2 yrs 8 mths	Yes/1	Primary school teacher	Housekeeper	F/T Housekeeper
China	2 yrs 9 mths	Yes/No	Primary school teacher	Work placement	Started own business
Russia	2 yrs 9 mths	Yes/1	Economist	Work placement	Payroll officer —temporary
Brazil	3 yrs	Yes/No	Marketing	Community services officer	F/T Manager/marketing
Vietnam	3 yrs	Yes/No	Teacher trainer	Work placement	P/T Assistant librarian
South Africa	5 yrs	Yes/2	Primary school teacher	Supply teacher	Primary school teacher— contract

Lack of employment and fear of the deterioration of their skills often led to the loss of occupational identity. One of the women from Iraq explained that being out of work meant that she was not keeping up to date with changes in her industry, and in particular the difficulty of keeping up with the changes in technology. She said:

> I'm not happy, no. It's a very difficult life, it's not easy . . . I lost all my skills. I'm not sure what happened around me? I can't work on computers because I stay at home . . . [and] I didn't know what happened, what's the new thing [technology]?

Gender and Caring Responsibilities

What role do women's family and caring responsibilities play? Many women raised issues regarding settling family into a new home and finding suitable schooling. The inability to access childcare hindered women's access to employment, especially for those with young children. Women felt it was their responsibility to take care of their children, affecting their labour market mobility (Ressia et al. 2016). Having husbands who were working away from home or studying to increase their qualifications generally meant that childcare responsibilities fell to these women. Hence gender and family responsibilities hindered access to employment. In particular, women with younger children were clearly constrained by mothering and the intensity of care giving. Women with older children were less disadvantaged than those with younger children. Overall, however, these trends led women to prioritising family over their own careers (Cooke 2007; Raghuram 2008; Boyle, Feng and Gayle 2009; Liversage 2009).

Strategies for Finding Employment

What was most interesting was the variety of strategies used to gain employment. English language studies were a high priority, as inability to find work dented these women's confidence. Undertaking further study in their occupation was also a priority. This was especially important for those requiring accreditation. This strategy provided women with the opportunity to update their career skills while looking after children. Part-time and/or online enrolment enabled women to juggle studies and family demands.

Some women, however, decided to switch from high-skilled careers to feminised jobs such as childcare. Another strategy was to find any type of work in the hope of gaining much needed local work experience, and improving language skills. This was also seen as providing an opportunity to develop their personal networks for future job search (Cooke 2007).

The Intersection of Gender, Race and Family

The study explored the experience of migrant women with professional skills and experience in a new country, and the difficulties experienced by them as a result of gender, race and family responsibility. It is very difficult for skilled migrant women to secure employment in an occupation equivalent to a position held in their originating country when they first arrive, and for some time after. Those who find employment mostly do so in lower-level occupations (Ho 2006; Cooke 2007; Connell and Burgess 2009). Hence women experience downward occupational mobility.

The gendered expectations of caring for the family, together with problems of skill and qualification recognition, mean that women are less likely than men to experience 'economic betterment' as a result of the migration process (Hardill 2004). Skilled migrant women often find themselves in lower-skilled employment (Adib and Guerrier 2003) in traditionally feminised occupations (Dyer et al. 2010) of childcare, cleaning, cashier/sales, housekeeping and food services (Table 7.1). Women lose out in terms of career re-establishment post migration (Raghuram 2004; Smith 2004; Boyle et al. 2009), receiving low returns on qualifications and skills (Dyer et al. 2010; Hopkins 2012).

The challenges in finding commensurate employment and the difficulty of managing family significantly affect women's success. They actively strategise by studying English and/or pursuing further studies in their field to 're-skill' and further develop their human capital (Riaño and Baghdadi 2007; Cooke et al. 2013), especially where accreditation is necessary. A number actively pursue a change in career, as a job in any field helps pay bills and develops networks in the local labour market, while others consider a complete withdrawal (Riaño and Baghdadi 2007; Fossland 2012).

Intersectionality theory explains the interplay of gender and racial inequalities. As noted by Herrera (2013, 475), "migration is . . . a set of complex networks of inequality that need to be disentangled". The operation of gender, race and family illustrates how the lives of the 16 women in our study are shaped leading to poorer labour market outcomes than they each expected. Thus we see first-hand how inequality is produced and maintained in the labour market (McDowell 2008).

Conclusion

Highly skilled migrants—and in particular women—represent an increasingly large component of global migration (Iredale 2001). The chapter has highlighted the difficulties experienced by female migrants in Australia within the broader international context. The research raises important issues concerning the effective management of migration, particularly the responsibilities of policy makers and practitioners (OECD 2011). While policy is necessary to manage migration intakes and attract female migrants, it needs to be expanded to assist skilled migrants to integrate more effectively into labour markets and provide targeted support for women migrants. Because of the small sample size and the particular context, we cannot over-generalise our findings, but they do indicate where further research is needed. For example, a better understanding of organisational perspective is required to fully understand NESB women migrants' failure to secure good jobs (Cooke et al. 2013).

It is important to note that not all professionally skilled women experience adverse outcomes, especially those who arrive through sponsored forms of migration (and thus already have a guaranteed job) or those who are from Anglophone countries. However, we must not lose sight of those who are more likely to be disadvantaged and struggle to achieve economic security and career advancement.

References

Adib, A. and Guerrier, Y. 2003. "The Interlocking of Gender with Nationality, Race, Ethnicity and Class: The Narratives of Women in Hotel Work." *Gender, Work and Organization* 10(4): 413–432.

Al Ariss, A. 2010. "Models of Engagement: Migration, Self-Initiated Expatriation, and Career Development." *Career Development International* 15(4): 338–358.

Alcorso, C. 1991. *Non-English Speaking Background Immigrant Women in the Workforce*, Working Papers in Multiculturalism No. 4. Wollongong: Centre for Multicultural Studies, University of Wollongong: 133.

Anderson, B. 2010. "Migration, Immigration Controls and the Fashioning of Precarious Workers." *Work, Employment and Society* 24(2): 300–317.

Anthias, F. 2012a. "Transnational Mobilities, Migration Research and Intersectionality." *Nordic Journal of Migration Research* 2(2): 102–110.

Anthias, F. 2012b. "Intersectional What? Social Divisions, Intersectionality and Levels of Analysis." *Ethnicities* 13(1): 3–19.

Bartram, D. 2010. "The Normative Foundations of 'Policy Implications': Reflections on International Labour Migration." *Work, Employment and Society* 24(2): 355–365.

Boucher, A. 2007. "Skill, Migration and Gender in Australia and Canada: The Case of Gender-Based Analysis." *Australian Journal of Political Science* 42(3): 383–401.

Boucher, A. and Cerna, L. 2014. "Current Policy Trends in Skilled Immigration Policy." *International Migration* 52(3): 21–25.

Boyd, M. and Grieco, E. 2003. "Women and Migration: Incorporating Gender into International Migration Theory." *Migration Information Source* 1: 1–7.

Boyle, P., Feng, Z. and Gayle, V. 2009. "A New Look at Family Migration and Women's Employment Status." *Journal of Marriage and Family* 71: 417–431.

Broadbent, K., Bailey, J., Strachan, G. and Ressia, S. 2010. *"Reaching out:" Enhancing the Accessibility of the Queensland Working Women's Service (QWWS) for Migrant Women*. Report written for the Queensland Working Women's Service (QWWS). Brisbane: Griffith University.

Bürkner, H. 2012. "Intersectionality: How Gender Studies Might Inspire the Analysis of Social Inequality Among Migrants." *Population, Space and Place* 18(2): 181–195.

Chiswick, B. R., Lee, Y. L. and Miller, P. W. 2003. "Patterns of Immigrant Occupational Attainment in a Longitudinal Survey." *International Migration* 41(4): 47–48.

Cliff, K., Grün, B., Ville, S. and Dolnicar, S. 2015. "A Conceptual Framework of Skilled Female Migrant Retention." *Economic Papers* 34(3): 118–127.

Connell, J. and Burgess, J. 2009. "Migrant Workers, Migrant Work, Public Policy and Human Resource Management." *International Journal of Manpower* 30(5): 412–421.

Cobb-Clark, D., Connolly, M. D. and Worswick, C. 2001. *The Job Search and Education Investments of Immigrant Families.* Discussion papers, Centre for Economic Policy Research. Canberra: Australian National University.

Cooke, F. L. 2007. "'Husband's Career First': Renegotiating Career and Family Commitment Among Migrant Chinese Academic Couples in Britain." *Work, Employment and Society* 21(1): 47–65.

Cooke, F. L., Zhang, J. and Wang, J. 2013. "Chinese Professional Immigrants in Australia: A Gendered Pattern in (Re)building Their Careers." *The International Journal of Human Resource Management* 24(14): 2628–2645.

Crenshaw, K. 1989. "Demarginalizing the Intersection of Race and Sex: A Black Feminist Critique of Antidiscrimination Doctrine, Feminist Theory and Antiracist Politics." *University of Chicago Legal Forum* Issue 1:138–167.

Dean, L. and Manzoni, A. 2012. *International Migration as Occupational Mobility.* SOEP Papers on Multidisciplinary Panel Data Research No. 498. Berlin: DIW.

Docquier, F., Lowell, B. L. and Marfouk, A. 2009. "A Gendered Assessment of Highly Skilled Emigration." *Population and Development Review* 35(2): 297–321.

Dyer, S., McDowell, L. and Batnitzky, A. 2010. "The Impact of Migration on the Gendering of Service Work: The Case of a West London Hotel." *Gender, Work and Organization* 17(6): 635–657.

Fossland, T. 2012. "Negotiating Future Careers: A Relationship Perspective on Skilled Migrants" Labour Market Participation." *Journal of Management Development* 32(2): 193–203.

Glaesser, J. and Cooper, B. 2014. "Using Rational Action Theory and Bourdieu's Habitus Theory Together to Account for Educational Decision-Making in England and Germany." *Sociology* 48(3): 463–481.

González-Ferrer, A. 2011. "Explaining the Labour Performance of Immigrant Women in Spain: The Interplay Between Family, Migration and Legal Trajectories." *International Journal of Comparative Sociology* 52(1–2): 63–78.

González Ramos, A. M. and Martín-Palomino, E. T. 2015. "Addressing Women's Agency on International Mobility." *Women's International Studies Forum* 49: 1–11.

Hardill, I. 2004. "Transnational Living and Moving Experiences: Intensified Mobility and Dual-Career Households." *Population, Space and Place* 10(5): 375–389.

Herrera, G. 2013. "Gender and International Migration: Contributions and Cross-Fertilizations." *Annual Review of Sociology* 39: 471–489.

Ho, C. 2004. "Migration as Feminisation: Chinese Women's Experiences of Work and Family in Contemporary Australia." PhD thesis, University of Sydney.

Ho, C. 2006. "Migration as Feminisation? Chinese Women's Experiences of Work and Family in Australia." *Journal of Ethics and Migration Studies* 32(3): 497–514.

Ho, C. and Alcorso, C. 2004. "Migrants and Employment: Challenging the Success Story." *Journal of Sociology* 40(3): 237–259.

Hopkins, B. 2012. "Inclusion of a Diverse Workforce in the UK: The Case of the EU Expansion." *Equality, Diversity and Inclusion: An International Journal* 31(4): 379–330.

IOM. 2010a. *IOM Gender and Migration News: Issue 34 April 2010.* Geneva: IOM. Accessed November 2, 2013. http://publications.iom.int/bookstore/free/gender_bulletin_apr10.pdf.

IOM. 2010b. *IOM Gender and Migration News: Issue 35 July 2010.* Geneva: IOM. Accessed November 2, 2013. http://publications.iom.int/bookstore/free/gender_bulletin_jul10.pdf.

International Organization for Migration (IOM). 2014. *International Women's Day— IOM Director General Swing: "Integrate Migrant Women into Development Agenda."* Geneva: IOM. Accessed July 19, 2016. www.iom.int/statements/international-womens-day-iom-director-general-swing-integrate-migrant-women-development.

Iredale, R. 2001. "The Migration of Professionals: Theories and Typologies." *International Migration* 39(5): 7–26.

Iredale, R. 2005. "Gender, Immigration Policies and Accreditation: Valuing the Skills of Professional Women Migrants." *Geoforum* 36(2): 155–166.

Kofman, E. 2004. "Gendered Global Migrations." *International Feminist Journal of Politics* 6(4): 643–665.

Kofman, E. 2013. "Towards a Gendered Evaluation of (Highly) Skilled Immigration Policies in Europe." *International Migration* 52(3): 116–128.

Kofman, E. and Raghuram, P. 2006. "Editorial." *Geoforum* 36: 149–154.

Liversage, A. 2009. "Vital Conjunctures, Shifting Horizons: High-Skilled Female Immigrants Looking for Work." *Work, Employment and Society* 23(1): 120–141.

Lutz, H., Vivar, M. T. H. and Supik, L. 2011. "Framing Intersectionality: An Introduction." In *Framing Intersectionality: Debates on a Multi-Faceted Concept in Gender Studies*, edited by H. Lutz, M. T. H. Vivar and L. Supik, 1–24. Surrey: Ashgate Publishing.

Mahler, S. J. and Pessar, P. R. 2006. "Gender Matters: Ethnographers Bring Gender from the Periphery Toward the Core of Migration Studies." *The International Migration Review* 40(1): 27–63.

McCall, L. 2005. "The Complexity of Intersectionality." *Signs* 30(3): 1771–1800.

McDowell, L. 2008. "Thinking Through Work: Complex Inequalities, Constructions of Difference and Trans-National Migrants." *Progress in Human Geography* 32(4): 491–507.

Mushaben, J. 2009. "Up the Down Staircase: Redefining Gender Identities Through Migration and Ethnic Employment in Germany." *Journal of Ethnic and Migration Studies* 35(8): 1249–1274.

O'Dwyer, M. and Colic-Peisker, V. 2016. "Facilitating the Professional Transition of Migrants in Australia: Does Gender Matter?" *Australian Journal of Social Issues* 51(1): 47–66.

OECD. 2011. *International Migration Outlook: SOEPMI 2011.* Geneva: International Organization for Migration.

Papadopoulos, A. 2016. "Migrating Qualifications: The Ethics of Recognition." *British Journal of Social Work* 47(1): 219–237.

Pedraza, S. 1991. "Women and Migration: The Social Consequences of Gender." *Review of Sociology* 17: 303–325.

Pessar, P. R. 1999. "Engendering Migration Studies." *The American Behavioural Scientist* 42(4): 577–600.

Pessar, P. R. and Mahler, S. J. 2003. "Transnational Migration: Bringing Gender In." *International Migration Review* 37(3): 812–846.

Phan, M. B., Banerjee, R., Deacon, L. and Taraky, L. 2015. "Family Dynamics and the Integration of Professional Immigrants in Canada." *Journal of Ethnic and Migration Studies* 41(13): 2061–2080.

Pio, E. and Essers, C. 2014. "Professional Migrant Women Decentering Otherness: A Transnational Perspective." *British Journal of Management* 25: 252–265.

Raghuram, P. 2004. "The Difference that Skills Make: Gender, Family Migration Strategies and Regulated Labour Markets." *Journal of Ethnic and Migration Studies* 30(2): 303–321.

Raghuram, P. 2008. "Migrant Women in Male-Dominated Sectors of the Labour Market: A Research Agenda." *Population, Space and Place* 14(1): 43–57.

Raijman, R. and Semyonov, M. 1997. "Gender, Ethnicity, and Immigration: Double Disadvantage and Triple Disadvantage among Recent Immigrant Women in the Israeli Labor Market." *Gender and Society* 11(1): 108–125.

Remennick, L. 2005. "Immigration, Gender, and Psychosocial Adjustment: A Study of 150 Immigrant Couples in Israel." *Sex Roles* 53(11/12): 847–863.

Ressia, S. 2014. "Skilled Migrant Women and Men Seeking Employment: Expectations, Experiences and Outcomes." PhD thesis, Griffith University.

Ressia, S., Strachan, G. and Bailey, J. 2016. "Going Up or Going Down? Occupational Mobility Outcomes of Skilled Migrants in Australia." *Asia Pacific Journal of Human Resources* 55(1): 64–85.

Riaño, Y. and Baghdadi, N. 2007. "Understanding the Labour Market Participation of Skilled Immigrant Women in Switzerland: The Interplay of Class, Ethnicity, and Gender." *International Migration and Integration* 8: 163–183.

Ryan, L. 2008. " 'I Had a Sister in England': Family-Led Migration, Social Networks and Irish Nurses." *Journal of Ethnic and Migration Studies* 34(3): 453–470.

Shinozaki, K. 2014. "Career Strategies and Spatial Mobility Among Skilled Migrants in Germany: The Role of Gender in the Work-Family Interaction." *Tijdschrift voor Economische en Sociale Geografie* 105(5): 526–541.

Smith, D. P. 2004. "An 'Untied' Research Agenda for Family Migration: Loosening the 'Shackles' of the Past." *Journal of Ethnic and Migration Studies* 30(2): 263–282.

Smith, D. P. and King, R. 2012. "Editorial Introduction: Re-Making Migration Theory." *Population, Space and Place* 18: 127–133.

Syed, J. and Murray, P. 2009. "Combating the English Language Deficit: The Labour Market Experiences of Migrant Women in Australia." *Human Resource Management Journal* 19(4): 413–432.

Taksa, L. and Groutsis, D. 2010. "Managing Diverse Commodities? From Factory Fodder to Business Asset." *Economic and Labour Relations Review* 20(2): 77–98.

United Nations. 2013. "International Migration 2013: Age and Sex Distribution." Population Facts No. 2013/14. Accessed November 10, 2015. http://esa.un.org/unmigration/documents/PF_age_migration_FINAL_10.09.2013.pdf.

Zaiceva, A. 2010. "East-West Migration and Gender: Is There a Differential Effect for Migrant Women?" *Labour Economics* 17(2): 443–454.

Zlotnik, H. 1995. "Migration and the Family: The Female Perspective." *Asian and Pacific Migration Journal* 4(2–3): 253–271.

Zorlu, A. 2016. "Immigrants" Occupational Mobility-Down and Back Up Again." *IZA World of Labor*, September: 1–12.

8   Clergywomen in the UK

Implications of Professional Calling

Anne-marie Greene

Geraldine.	Hello, I'm Geraldine, I believe you're expecting me.
David.	No. I'm expecting our new vicar, unless of course you are the new vicar and they've landed us with a woman, as some sort of insane joke.
Geraldine.	Oh dear . . .
David.	Oh my God.
Geraldine.	You were expecting a bloke. Beard, bible, bad breath?
David.	Yes, that sort of thing.
Geraldine.	Yeah, instead you've got a babe with a bob cut and a magnificent bosom.
David.	So I see.

Vicar of Dibley, Episode One, first broadcast
10 November 1994, BBC1

Introduction

Ordained clergy are interesting to look at as a professional group because religious calling lies at the core of their work. It is not often that the place of God within the employment relationship and professional life is considered (see Styhre 2014), and I have become fascinated with understanding the impact that calling has on the ways that work is experienced. It is also interesting to explore the experiences of clergywomen in particular, because there are now a number of writers, myself included, who have clearly established the gendered nature of clergy work, particularly within the established Christian denominations in the UK (of which here I consider two of the most prominent—the Church of England [CofE] and the Methodist Church). The quote that opens this chapter is from the first episode of the long running British Broadcasting Company (BBC) comedy series *The Vicar of Dibley*, where a newly ordained female vicar is appointed to a village parish in the English countryside. What is clear is that the implicit (and often explicit) prejudice against clergywomen and expectations of a religious minister as being situated in a male body still resonates very strongly some 20 years later. I have therefore been interested in exploring the impact that religious calling has on the ability of clergywomen to have voice and challenge the discriminatory treatment they experience. This chapter reflects on research conducted over the last five years involving clergywomen in the CofE and Methodist Church in the UK. While some of the work on CofE clergywomen has been published (Greene and Robbins 2015; Dean and Greene, 2017; Robbins and Greene, 2017), the Methodist research remains as yet largely unpublished and therefore the empirical material discussed will focus largely on the latter as a point of comparison.

Ordained Clergy as Professionals and Workers

The Church is often claimed to be the site of the one of the first professions, along with law and medicine, indeed this is noted within the introduction to this book. However, despite this, whether clergy can be categorised as professionals is not uncontested, and indeed there is some discussion about whether clergy are even workers. My concern is with *ordained* clergy, i.e. those individuals on whom the churches have conferred holy orders and who then undertake responsibilities as ritual or spiritual leaders (in the case of CofE-parish priests, in the case of Methodists-presbyters). This distinguishes them from the 'laity' who may undertake certain duties and responsibilities within the churches but who are not ordained. While there are many individuals who work unpaid for church organisations, including ordained clergy, I focus on clergy receiving a stipend, because they represent the closest situation to being in an employment relationship.

Clergy work is arguably set apart from other professional work because it has a religious calling at its core. Ministers in the CofE and Methodist Church undertake ordination vows which bind them to God and religious service: what Peyton and Gatrell refer to as the *sacrificial embrace*—"the embracing of personal sacrifice, and the governance of body and soul . . . underpinned by a theological and ministerial rationale, and ultimately an eternal dimension" (2013, 86). Ministers answer to something external to social organisation—their religious calling and their belief in God (Styhre 2014, 309); however, the notion of calling is not exclusive to clergy. Rosso, Dekas and Wrzesniewski (2010) categorise calling in two different forms, with both sharing a perspective that the work is 'an end in itself' and usually done in the conviction that it is contributing in some positive way to wider society (2010, 98). The forms differ in that the first is seen as developing *post* entry to the job, in parallel with doing it: for example, that exhibited by domiciliary and residential care workers. The second form applies more clearly to clergy and involves a religious or secular vocation to do the specific job: "a meaningful beckoning toward activities that are morally, socially, and personally significant" (Wrzesniewski, Dekas and Rosso 2009). However, calling is only part of the picture of clergy work, leading McDuff and Mueller (2002) to assert that the parish setting, in the US context at least, is a professional labour market. However, it is a labour context that is difficult to classify and which seems to stand on the outside of conventional typologies.

The work of clergy possesses some characteristics of what might be termed a standard employment relationship (Vosko 2010), for example, receiving a salary (stipend), and undergoing rigorous recruitment and selection processes. They also undergo lengthy training; indeed, clergy are highly educated, ordination training leading to the receipt of at least the equivalent of a university degree–level qualification. In both the CofE and Methodist Church, extensive policies and procedures exist including around discipline and grievance. Clergy in the UK are also organised by a trade union, namely Unite, within the 'faith organisations' sub-sector of the 'community, youth workers and not-for-profit' sector.[1] Therefore, some of the credentialising and closure processes which characterise an occupation denoted as a profession exist. For Styhre (2014), ordained clergy occupy a professional domain of jurisdiction that excludes other professional and occupational groups within the church as the "principal professional category with expertise in core activities" (2014, 314). Styhre (2014), uses older typologies of professions (Brint 1994; Friedson 2001) to denote religious ministers as a mix between 'social trustee' and 'civic' professionalism, although he notes that the place of God means that ministers stand apart from others in this category such as doctors who are also viewed as demonstrating social trustee professionalism.

However, clergy do not meet some of the characteristics of the standard employment relationship. This includes the unusual relationship to remuneration (see Greene and Robbins 2015) but most importantly, that the appointment of clergy has traditionally been held as a spiritual matter, as office holding for God, with no intention to create legal relations and thus no employment rights (Cranmer 2012). Decades of ambiguity around whether or not clergy in the UK should be viewed as employees has been officially resolved by a number of legal rulings establishing them as officeholders and not as employees (including most recently President of the Methodist Conference v Preston 2013 UKSC 29 (Supreme Court, 2013)). Therefore, in the UK at least, clergy are currently not considered as employees and are not covered by either the protections of the Employment Relations Act or the Equality Act 2010.[2]

Clergy Work as Gendered Work

The fact that clergy are not covered by the Equality Act 2010 is more significant given research which has established the discriminatory nature of church contexts, particularly that of the CofE (for example, Bagilhole 2003; 2006; Page 2011; 2012; Greene and Robbins 2015; and Dean and Greene, 2017). Unequal access to work, vertical segregation, lower pay and overt and active sex discrimination are the common experiences of clergywomen (Greene and Robbins, 2015; Robbins and Greene, 2017). Recent debates around the ordination of women bishops encapsulates divisions within the CofE regarding women, continuing to support the salience of the 'doctrine of taint' where women priests are viewed as 'untouchable' and 'polluting' by those who hold a theological opposition (Bagilhole 2006, 364). Page's analysis highlights how "women are negotiating a discriminatory terrain at many different levels" (Page 2012, 1), and she explores the negotiation of the clergywomen's sacred roles as 'profane' bodies within Christian theology (2011), the effects of motherhood on priestly identity and liturgical practice (2011; 2012) and women's embodiment issues particularly involving clerical dress as an exclusionary mechanism (2014). While there is now arguably much less overt and direct sex discrimination in many organisations, Greene and Robbins (2015) argue that the CofE provides an example of a contemporary 'inequality regime' (Acker 2006, 443) involving gendered practices, processes, actions and meanings. As will be argued later, while there are less examples of overt sex discrimination experienced by Methodist clergywomen, they still experience many of the negative effects of a 'man-made' (Tutchell and Edmonds 2015) church.

Clergywomen in the CofE and Methodist Contexts

Women were admitted as ordained Methodist clergy in 1974, and in the CofE as late as 1994. Progression has changed very recently in the CofE and, as with Methodists, women are now finally eligible to apply or be recommended for senior roles: the consecration and appointment of the first woman bishop in January 2015 ended a long battle for formal gender equality (see discussion in Greene and Robbins 2015). While there has been a steady increase in the numbers of women since they were allowed to be ordained, women still account for only 23 per cent of those ordained as full-time stipendiary CofE clergy and 11 per cent of senior positions, such as archdeacons and cathedral canons (Archbishops Council 2013). Moreover, they hold more than half of unpaid clergy posts. Methodist women's progression is better established institutionally, although this context is also male-dominated: women account for 39 per cent of presbyters, and in senior positions for 30 per cent of district chairs and 25 per cent of superintendents (Methodist Church House 2015). Remuneration in both church contexts includes provision of a house while in post and payment of a centrally set average 'stipend' of between £22,600 (Methodists) and £24,000 (CofE) per annum. While this is not technically low pay, it is low for a graduate-level job and, importantly, the stipends do not increase beyond cost of living rises unless through appointment to more senior posts which, as noted, significantly fewer women hold. Overall, women continue to be disproportionately represented in unpaid, part-time and low-status jobs in both Churches.

Researching Clergywomen

Academic research on clergywomen in the UK outside of theological studies has been limited to a couple of notable survey studies (Bagilhole 2003; 2006; Robbins 2008) and two examples of qualitative work discussed earlier, notably Peyton and Gatrell (2013) and Page (2011; 2012; 2014).

The research work I have been engaged with has crossovers with this body of work, but has some features which differentiate it, it being focused on women and based within an employment relations paradigm. Bagilhole's (2002; 2003) research has the closest affinities, exploring clergywomen as professional workers within a male-dominated environment. However, her research was based on survey data of a small number of CofE clergywomen, and was not designed to yield the level of qualitative detail that has been possible in the empirical research discussed in this chapter. Furthermore, Bagilhole's sample comprised women in senior roles, rather than those at parish minister level (at the 'coal face' of clergy work). Finally, I know of no research to date in the employment relations field looking at the experiences of Methodist clergywomen.

This chapter draws on interviews undertaken between 2011 and 2015 with 38 stipendiary women ministers in the UK (21 parish priests in the CofE and 17 presbyters in the Methodist Church). In addition, the national officer and a lay representative of the Faithworkers Branch of the trade union Unite were interviewed. Some of the CofE clergywomen were contacted by an initial email approach from the union and snowballing on from that, and others by random selection from lists of ministers, the latter being the sole method of access for the Methodist clergywomen. The eventual sample included a good spread over rural and urban parishes/congregations, and also geographically across the UK. The age range of sample was between late 20s and late 60s years, in proportion to the overall population of clergywomen and all but one interviewee were white, reflecting the fact that 97 per cent of stipendiary clergy are white (Archbishops Council 2013). Two thirds of our interviewees had dependent children under 18 years old at some point during their ministry, and 10 of these were single parents.

The interviews ranged in length from an hour and a half to three hours, and were recorded and transcribed. Interviewees were asked to think specifically about being a minister from the perspective of work and the employment relationship and explored a variety of issues including: their calling, previous work experiences, selection and training experiences, reflections on work-life balance, job satisfaction, relationships with employment relations actors such as trade unions and those acting in 'management' roles within the Church and experiences of gender discrimination. In line with the approach taken by Martin (2001), conversations were deliberately started as general enquiries into the life histories of the women, and their perspectives on their clergy work, without specifically utilising gender as a construct in order to avoid focusing from the start on the problems they faced. However, there was also an intention to try and assess the extent of their experiences of differential treatment as women or of sex discrimination and therefore if perspectives/opinions on these issues were not raised spontaneously by the interviewees, they were pressed later in the interviews on this point.

Thematic analysis of the interviews was conducted manually with general categories developed initially from the interview agendas themselves, which were then expanded upon and subdivided. While being aware of highlighting exceptions, the existence of shared meanings or "interpretive repertoires" (Potter 1996) among the views of the interviewees have been looked for. The intention was not to provide research that could be generalised across the whole population of clergywomen, or even across the two denominations. There are also no interviews with clergymen with which to directly compare the interview data that might offer some perspective on whether the women's views are gender-specific. However, given the lack of research on clergywomen, it is important to capture the experiences of the women as a separate group. This reflects Martin's premise of feminist standpoint theory that "accounts of the less powerful offer knowledge of the more powerful" (2003, 593). In providing an exceptional case, the interview data is also useful to analyses of other male-dominated professional contexts, providing insight into processes and mechanisms that may not be as easily discernible under more moderate conditions (Eisenhardt 1989 cited in Creed, DeJordy and Lok 2010).

Exploring the Views of Clergywomen

Calling and Personal Recovery

There can be no doubt that calling is at the centre of these women's work and lives. The majority of interviewees from either denomination had first felt the calling to be ordained early on in their lives, commonly between the ages of 14 and 21. However, for a variety of reasons, including the fact that ordained ministry was not allowed for women at the time, they were not able to live out this calling, and therefore for all but four of the interview group, ordained ministry was a fairly late development for them, with a variety of different jobs being held before. Moreover, their eventual ordination had often come at a critical time in their lives, often coinciding with other 'crisis' points. For more than a third of the interview group, the move to ordination came within three years after marriage breakdown, divorce, death of their spouse and even a suicide attempt. For many, they felt that being able to be ordained had finally allowed them to live out their calling, and therefore represented the end to significant life struggle over many years. One important side of the story for these women, therefore, is an immense feeling of relief that they were now doing what they were supposed to do with their lives and all but one interviewee was adamant that they found their ministry work satisfying. The other side of the story is that this satisfaction with their ministry is despite a number of negative experiences, which the next sections go on to discuss in more detail.

Overt Hostility and Discrimination

What emerged clearly from our interviews was the ubiquity of sex discrimination as a *key feature* of their work. Without exception, they had all either personally experienced, or had been witness to, disadvantageous treatment of, and/or hostility and opposition to, them as clergywomen. Examples include direct refusal to accept communion and other duties such as presiding over funerals and marriages from a clergywoman, verbal and physical attacks, unwanted sexual advances and inappropriate touching, threatening emails and letters, sexist jokes and banter, belittling and undermining of women in meetings and decision-making. Greene and Robbins (2015) paint a picture of discrimination in the CofE that indicates very little progress on from Bagilhole's (2003) study over a decade earlier.

The experience of Methodist clergywomen was generally more positive, with less incidences of overt hostility and direct discrimination. Many of the interviewees commented on their experience as Methodist ministers in direct comparison to the CofE, for example:

> I think having journeyed ecumenically through training and kept in touch with some Anglican colleagues and hearing their experiences I'm so grateful I'm in the Methodist church, not the Church of England . . . I've never come across anything like that at all.
>
> (BB, Methodist)

There was an overall feeling that the culture of the Methodist Church militated against such overt views and behaviours. Part of this related to the longer length of time that women have been ordained in the Methodist Church: "I think the problems are ecumenical than within the Methodist family really. I think we've had women ministers since the early seventies, I think most people have experienced one now" (JC, Methodist). This is not to say that clergywomen within the Methodist Church did not face difficulties as women. Over half of interviewees related incidents of congregation members resisting their ministry such as refusing to take communion. This must be placed in the context whereby Methodist congregations have significantly more power than their CofE counterparts in the appointment (stationing) of ministers and perhaps more importantly, whether a minister's fixed-term post is extended. Congregational dissatisfaction with aspects of their ministry was often seen as being directly attributed to their gender: "You still hear 'we shan't have another woman minister' . . . I don't think anybody ever says 'we shan't have another man' " (CP, Methodist).

Family and Work-Life Balance

Greene and Robbins (2015) explore the prominence and expectation among congregations and some clergymen of the stereotype of the male vicar who has a full-time wife. This is supported by other research in the CofE, such as Page (2008), who in her study of male clergy spouses, traces how the entry of ordained women disrupts the traditional model because the male spouse refuses to accept this identity. She indicates that the work that is usually done by the 'wife' is expected to be taken on by the clergywoman in a way it is not expected of clergymen, as one of the Methodist interviewees explained:

> they wanted a Methodist minister but they also wanted a minister's wife. So, there was an expectation that they would come here to a meeting and there would be cake and there would be homemade biscuits and I'm like 'so when am I going to have time to make those?'
>
> (RW, Methodist)

Overall, family-life-work clashes, maternity and childcare issues and lack of understanding of the demands of motherhood were highlighted as serious problems for most of the interviewees in both denominations. Interestingly, this was emphasised to an extent that did not have the same prominence in research with gender-mixed samples of clergy such as Peyton and Gatrell (2013). It should also be noted that despite the longstanding entry of ordained women within the Methodist Church, here too the dominance of the male 'breadwinner' model was found to be equally problematic for interviewees, and their experience was very similar to that of their CofE counterparts. One interviewee noted the antagonism to her first appointment:

> people said 'oh, you're not going to be able to do that because you've got a young child' . . . I had three small children . . . two of them still in a pushchair and [one] running along beside and that wasn't people's normal picture of a minister.
>
> (HW, Methodist)

> It is still a bit of a shock when, you know, my little girl . . . was only eighteen months and she was having a tantrum in the middle of Asda [supermarket] and you think 'I cannot shout at her because there could be members of the congregation walking around'.
>
> (GM, Methodist)

The fact that clergy work is so intricately tied up with their lives has also been identified as differentiating it from other professions such as teaching or medicine (Finch 1980, 851). For clergywomen with the main responsibility for childcare, the demands of the job become even more difficult to balance, as one interviewee related:

> Twelve months ago, I could just disappear out of the house leaving a note by the kettle saying I've gone out to see Mrs So-and-So . . . but I can't do that now. If my child is at home I have to wait for my husband to come back and there's this kind of . . . 'but no, you're our minister, we want you now.
>
> (RW, Methodist)

How Women Have Changed the Church

All of our interviewees indicated that they thought that the Church had changed positively as a consequence of the ordination of women. The CofE women in Bagilhole's study (2006; 2003), a decade or so ago all felt that they were making change in the Church—to the nature of priesthood, the use of language and symbolism, the style or working and acceptance of women in the hierarchy (Bagilhole 2006, 121). In accordance with Bagilhole's findings and despite continuing experiences of discrimination, most of our interviewees also felt that their Church was now more diverse, representative and egalitarian, and they welcomed the fact that women were now more accepted by both male clergy and congregations, and that there were now more opportunities for women, providing role models and spaces to fulfil vocational conviction for girls and women within the lay membership. For example:

> We've had a lot of growth; a lot of new people have come in. It feels, they tell me it feels quite different . . . I don't get the feeling that we've got as many people coming in and putting on a Sunday face . . . it does feel more relaxed, there are more children around.
>
> (ALB, CofE)

However, many of the interviewees were also acutely aware of the need to address concerns about the possible feminisation of clergy and of congregations. Some indicated that they needed to make deliberate efforts to avoid an over-feminisation of their own services and to avoid what one interviewee called a "petticoat ministry". One interviewee reflected on the practice of her own Sunday services:

> I'm always concerned . . . that we should try to get some kind of balance between male and female so that everyone can relate to what's happening and it's relevant. I think you have to be careful that . . . it's [not] all women at the front.
>
> (HW, Methodist)

Another interviewee felt the need to make liturgy that was relevant and interesting to men, and particularly to boys, which she felt was not improved by the increase in the number of women clergy. There was a common view that men and women brought different skills to their ministry, many of these based around stereotypes of female/feminine skills.

> I do think there are some traditional men who are a bit surprised that women can do things competently . . . I think they think that, that they're all going to be like the Vicar of Dibley, a bit dizzy and . . . they're

a bit surprised that actually women are quite capable and can lead liturgy with dignity and so on. And we can preach. As well and as badly as men . . . And I also think that there is this, this whole thing about the fact that, that women tend to work for peace and tend to want to be mediators and negotiators and, you know, diplomatic.

(KC, Methodist)

They were able to identify advantages that came to them as a consequence of being a woman, for example, being able to get easier access to schools, hospitals and conducting children and youth activities. While a couple of interviewees were adamant that they wanted to be viewed in a gender-neutral way and not as a clergy*woman*, the majority were acutely aware of their difference, both positive and negative, and the need to either play this down, compensate for it, or emphasise its effects.

Acceptance and Silence

A key finding of Peyton and Gatrell (2013) is that clergy are less likely to resist the demands of their job because of the centrality of their vocational commitment—that acceptance of 'sacrifice'. Similarly, we found that while interviewees indicated deep sadness about the things that happened to them, and they were concerned about the effects on their families and especially children, these were not seen as issues that could easily be challenged. There was general acceptance of frequent discriminatory behaviour as part of their work, with even directly abusive behaviour going largely unchallenged and unreported. Reported feelings of isolation by most interviewees also reflects the lack of support they felt they could draw on from senior clergy, and most felt that the only choice they had was to personally resolve or ignore issues, or to resign: "I don't think the church deals effectively with any conflict to be honest. My experience is that they avoid it by moving somebody on" (DY, Methodist).

Elsewhere we have explained this apparent silence in the face of discriminatory treatment as being specifically related to their religious calling (Greene and Robbins 2015; Dean and Greene, 2017). What we have called the "ideology of God" (Dean and Greene, 2017) enables them to make sense of and thus redirect elements of dissatisfaction. Most claimed that in order to act in accordance with their calling, people opposed to women's ordination should be accepted and accommodated rather than challenged. The view here was typical:

there needs to be some provision within the Church for those people who do not accept women priests . . . I don't share their views but can respect that they hold them, and for the Church to just abandon them . . . is not being a loving sister or brother in Christ.

(VB, CofE)

Christian conviction therefore mitigates negative experiences by producing a desire to accommodate and accept working conditions:

> So, God is very much there in my work . . . it's like in a state of grace . . . a bit tiring really but it's not a bad thing because I think that's part of Christianity really, to sort of go out of one's way to be friendly to people really regardless.
>
> (F, Methodist)

> a lot of my work . . . is . . . making allowances for people . . . my calling in a sense . . . we're there to show an alternative way.
>
> (K, CofE)

This can be linked to what Peyton and Gatrell describe as the "personal vocational professionalism" (2013, 92) of ordained clergy relating to a theology of professional responsibility, a personal integrity that "what clergy do is governed by who they are" (2013, 97).

Furthermore, this unwillingness to challenge or speak up also has to be seen within the context of the lack of unionate, feminist or 'radical' attitudes amongst our interviewees (Greene and Robbins 2015). This means that possible alternative sources of help and support, for example, the trade union or women's campaign groups within the churches are largely not available to them or have relatively little power and influence (Greene and Robbins 2015; Dean and Greene, 2017).

Reflections on the Professional Lives of Clergywomen

Ordained clergy are an unusual professional group, and within that, clergywomen are even more unusual compared to their male counterparts. Their story is one of surprising levels of discrimination and unequal treatment on the basis of the fact that they are women. Despite women being ordained for a considerable length of time now, both of these contexts could still be described as highly gendered. A large body of literature now exists around women in male-dominated occupations and many of the experiences of our interviewees would accord with the experiences cited in this wider research. A lot our interviewees described experiences which are "citational of the gender order" (Butler 1993) in terms of expected ways of behaving, modes of action, attitudes, beliefs and form of body. In 2003, Bagilhole set out three recommendations for the CofE emerging from her research including the introduction of family-friendly policies and strong codes of practice that prohibit unacceptable behaviour towards women. It seems that more than a decade on both the CofE and Methodist contexts still have a long way to go to address such concerns.

Perhaps what is most interesting theme to emerge from my research has been the level of acceptance of the discriminatory treatment faced by the clergywomen themselves and lack of challenge within the Churches generally. Indeed, this makes clergywomen somewhat unique in the context of this book, where for others, the notion of being a professional leads to enhanced space for challenge. Overall, the advantages of their work largely outweigh the disadvantages, in that their ministry work is deemed to be satisfying and represents a life recovery for them. In addition, they are positive about the changes that have been wrought within the Churches as a consequence of the ordination of women. However, the sense of calling, and the associated professional ethics that are connected to this, are centrally important in determining their ability to voice dissatisfaction and challenge the treatment they face. An exclusive focus on clergywomen thus places the gendered consequences of Peyton and Gatrell's (2013) 'sacrificial embrace' in stark relief, particularly in terms of limited space for resistance or challenge (Greene and Robbins 2015). In Dean and Greene (2017) we place the analysis of the clergywomen's acceptance of poor treatment in comparison to women actors, who also simultaneously indicate both recognition of poor conditions and satisfaction with aspects of their work. In that article, we argue that the notion of occupational ideology in relation to Hirschman's (1970) concept of loyalty as special attachment thus penalty for exit has explanatory purchase in relation to the acceptance of disadvantage in both occupations. Actors and clergy have a pre-entry calling orientation to their occupation and the ideologies associated with each calling, respectively 'God' and 'Art', were shown to be mediating factors in encouraging silence around these issues.

In terms of future research, the case of clergywomen exposes difficulties in the application of conventional strategies for women coping with working in male-dominated occupations, for example, the strategies that women use in order to 'cope with' or 'change' the unequal situation they find themselves in (see summary in Powell et al. 2009), the ability of these women to act as change agents (Bagilhole 2002) and to 'undo' gender (Butler 2004) and aspects of gender performance they engage in. The clergy context is interesting in that, at least in the Christian denominations, where the CofE and Methodist Churches are no exceptions, the situation is one of declining congregation numbers and overall declining clergy numbers (Church of England 2015; Methodist Church House 2015). Institutional recovery of the Churches was arguably at the heart of the debates leading up to the first ordinations of women in both Churches, with proponents of women's ordination having used arguments of renewal, revitalisation and modernisation. However, while the number of women being ordained has increased, this has not reversed the overall pattern of decline (Roberts et al. 2006). Clergy are having to work over multiple parishes and congregations and with less overall finances as attendance declines and churches close. It will be interesting see what impact such factors have on policy and behaviour regarding women and women's concerns within the Church.

The experiences of clergywomen could usefully be compared with women in other occupations where a sense of calling, vocation or mission is required, to explore how the particular nature of that calling, played out in the particular organisational/occupational context, impacts upon their work experiences and access to conventional mechanisms of employee voice and support. Future analysis could also explore the identity work (Creed et al. 2010) undertaken by, the possibilities for challenge utilized by and the change agent role of clergywomen. Additionally, the role and organising strategies of trade unions and other social movement organisations within other work contexts where vocation and calling are relevant would be of interest.

Acknowledgements

I would like to thank the Susana Wesley Foundation, Roehampton University for partly funding this research and for the invaluable assistance of Sue Miller in research access.

Notes

1. Originally the Clergy and Church Workers Branch of the trade union Manufacturing Science Finance (MSF) set up in 1994.
2. It should be noted that clergy who work in hospitals, prisons and schools, for example, are covered by employment law within these contexts, leading to a strange situation where the same office holder such as a parish vicar with chaplaincy responsibilities can have different legal rights depending on their location of work that day.

References

Acker, J. 2006. "Inequality Regimes: Gender, Class, and Race in Organizations." *Gender & Society* 20(4): 441–464.
Archbishops Council. 2013. *Statistics for Mission 2012: Ministry*. London: Archbishops' Council, Research and Statistics, Central Secretariat.
Bagilhole, B. 2002. *Women in Non-Traditional Occupations: Challenging Men.* London: Palgrave Macmillan.
Bagilhole, B. 2003. "Not a Glass Ceiling More a Lead Roof: Experiences of Pioneer Women Priests in the Church of England." *Equal Opportunities International* 25(2): 109–125.
Bagilhole, B. 2006. "Prospects for Change? Structural, Cultural and Action Dimensions of the Careers of Pioneer Women Priests in the Church of England." *Gender Work and Organisation* 10(3): 361–377.
Brint, S. 1994. *In the Age of Experts: The Changing Role of Professionals in Politics and Public Life.* Princeton: Princeton University Press.
Butler, J. 1993. *Bodies that Matter: On the Discursive Limits of Sex.* New York: Routledge.

Butler, J. 2004. *Undoing Gender*. New York: Routledge.

Church of England. 2015. "Ministry Statistics 2012–2015." https://churchof england.org/media/2521560/ministry_statistics_2012_to_2015.pdf.

Cranmer, F. 2012. *Case Law on Church Employment*. Churches' Legislative Advisory Service. London: Church House.

Creed, D., DeJordy, R. and Lok, J. 2010. "Being the Change: Resolving Institutional Contradiction Through Identity Work." *Academy of Management Journal* 53(6): 1336–1364.

Dean, D. and Greene, A-M. 2017. "How Do We Understand Worker Silence Despite Poor Conditions—as the Actress Said to the Woman Bishop." *Human Relations*. DOI: https://doi.org/10.1177/0018726717694371.

Eisenhardt, K. M. 1989. "Building Theories from Case Study Research." *Academy of Management Review* 14: 532–550.

Finch, J. 1980. "Devising Conventional Performances: The Case of Clergymen's Wives." *Sociological Review* 28(4): 851–870.

Freidson, E. 2001. *Professionalism: The Third Logic*. Chicago: Chicago University Press.

Greene, A. and Robbins, M. 2015. "The Cost of a Calling? Clergywomen and Work in the Church of England." *Gender, Work and Organization* 22: 405–420.

Hirschman, A. O. 1970. *Exit, Voice, and Loyalty. Responses to Decline in Firms, Organizations and States*. Cambridge, MA: Harvard University Press.

Martin, P. Y. 2001. "Mobilizing Masculinities: Women's Experiences of Men at Work." *Organization* 8(4): 587–618.

Martin, P. Y. 2003. " 'Said and Done' Versus 'Saying and Doing': Gendering Practices, Practicing Gender at Work." *Gender & Society* 17(3): 342–366.

McDuff, E. and Mueller, C. 2002. "Gender Differences in the Professional Orientations of Protestant Clergy." *Sociological Forum* 17(3): 465–491.

Methodist Church House. 2015. *Statistical Data from the Connexional Team*. Accessed April 15, 2016. http://www.methodist.org.uk/mission/statistics-for-mission.

Page, S. J. 2008. "The Construction of Masculinities and Femininities in the Church of England: The Case of the Male Clergy Spouse." *Feminist Theology* 17(1): 31–42.

Page, S. J. 2011. "Negotiating Sacred Roles: A Sociological Exploration of Priests Who Are Mothers." *Feminist Review* 97: 92–109.

Page, S. J. 2012. "Femmes, Méres at Prêtres dans l'Église D'Angleterre: Quels Sacerdoces." *Travail, Genre et Sociétés* 27: 55–71.

Page, S. J. 2014. "The Scrutinized Priest: Women in the Church of England Negotiating Professional and Sacred Clothing Regimes." *Gender, Work & Organization* 21: 295–307.

Peyton, N. and Gatrell, C. 2013. *Managing Clergy Lives: Obedience, Sacrifice, Intimacy*. London: Bloomsbury.

Potter, J. 1996. *Representing Reality: Discourse, Rhetoric and Social Construction*. London: Sage.

Powell, A., Bagilhole, B. and Dainty, A. 2009. "How Women Engineers Do and Undo Gender: Consequences for Gender Equality." *Gender, Work and Organization* 16(4): 411–429.

President of the Methodist Conference v Preston. 2013. "United Kingdom Supreme Court 29." http://www.supremecourt.gov.uk/decided-cases/docs/UKSC_2012_0015_Judgment.pdf.

Robbins, M. 2008. *Clergywomen in the Church of England: A Psychological Study*. New York: Edwin Mellen.

Robbins, M. and Greene, A. M. 2017. "Clergywomen's Experience of Ministry in the Church of England." *Journal of Gender Studies*. DOI: 10.1080/09589236. 2017.1340153.

Roberts, C., Robbins, M., Francis, L. J. and Hills, P. 2006. "The Ordination of Women and the Church of England Today: Two Integrities But One Pattern of Decline in Membership Statistics." *Journal of Anglican Studies* 4(2): 201–218.

Rosso, B. D., Dekas, K. H. and Wrzesniewski, A. 2010. "On the Meaning of Work: A Theoretical Integration and Review." *Research in Organizational Behavior* 30: 91–127.

Stewart-Thomas, M. 2009. "Gendered Congregations, Gendered Service: The Impact of Clergy Gender on Congregational Social Service Participation." *Gender Work and Organization* 17(4): 406–432.

Styhre, A. 2014. "In the Service of God and the Parish: Professional Ideologies and Managerial Control in the Church of Sweden." *Culture and Organization* 20(4): 307–329.

Supreme Court. 2013. "Press Summary - The President of the Methodist Conference (Appellant) v Preston (Respondent) [2013] UKSC 29." https://www.supreme court.uk/cases/docs/uksc-2012-0015-press-summary.pdf.

Tutchell, E. and Edmonds, J. 2015. *Man-Made: Why So Few Women Are in Positions of Power*. Farnham: Gower Publishing, Ltd.

Vosko, L. 2010. *Managing the Margins: Gender, Citizenship, and the International Regulation of Precarious Employment*. Oxford: Oxford University Press.

Wrzesniewski, A., Dekas, K. and Rosso, B. 2009. "Calling." In *The Encyclopedia of Positive Psychology*, edited by S. J. Lopez and A. Beauchamp, 115–118. Oxford: Blackwell Publishing.

Women in Information Technology
in Sri Lanka
Careers and Challenges

Arosha Adikaram and Pavithra Kailasapathy

Background

Information Technology (IT) is an important industry for many countries, including Sri Lanka. Export revenue from the IT/Business Processing Organisation (BPO) sector has grown from USD 108 million in 2003 to an estimated USD 720 million in 2013, with an increase in the number of companies from 170 in 2007 to over 220 in 2013 (SLASSCOM 2014). In 2014, the IT industry in Sri Lanka employed 82,824 professionals, an increase from 15,586 in 2003 (ICTA 2013). The country's vision is to achieve USD 5 billion in exports by 2022 from IT and IT-enabled knowledge services, while also generating 200,000 jobs and creating 1,000 start-ups in this process (SLASSCOM 2014).

Women form 35.1 per cent of the total workforce of 8,193,266, and have an unemployment rate of 7.3 per cent compared to 3.1 per cent for men (Department of Census and Statistics 2016). Yet women's participation in most academic disciplines is higher than men, especially in law, medicine and agriculture (Department of Census and Statistics 2014). In 2014, only 29 per cent of women held managerial, senior official and legislator positions and only 5.8 per cent were members of parliament (Department of Census and Statistics 2014).

Women are a vital part of the IT workforce and represent almost half the undergraduates in computer science courses at national universities:[1] 44.5 per cent were women in the academic year 2014/2015 (UGC 2016) and 49 per cent in 2012/2013 (UGC 2014); however, the proportion of women is lower in external and post-graduate degrees.[2] The limited research on women's participation in the IT industry has focused on the augmented demand for IT professionals around the globe and the labour shortage. In addition to helping the demand shortage and thereby the growth of the sector, increasing women's participation in the field is seen to bring additional talent and perspectives into this workforce (Sauter 2012; Balcita et al. 2002 cited in Draus et al. 2014): "[w]ith fewer women, IT is deprived of a workforce component that can contribute alternate perspectives on systems design, development, and utilization" (Adya 2008, 602).

Scholars, practitioners and policy makers highlight the need to promote women's entry and retention in the sector, however increasing women's participation is a challenge (Ahuja 2002; Lemons and Parzinger 2007). The reasons for this are numerous: few women choose IT as their area of study (Cheryan, Plaut, Handron, and Hudson 2013), women face discrimination and differential treatment even when they have good educational qualifications (Bhardwaj 2013) and women face many difficulties in climbing the career ladder and hence they are underrepresented in senior managerial positions (Michie and Nelson 2006; Lemons and Parzinger 2007). In addition, there is role stress for women (Aziz 2004), emotional costs (Aaltio and Huang 2007) and resultant work-family conflicts (Aaltio and Huang 2007; Bhardwaj 2013).

Given these issues, there is a need to understand the factors hindering women's choice of, and advancement in, the IT sector. How do women enter the field of IT? How do they progress? What challenges do they face as the minority in a male-dominated field? We explore the career experiences of professional IT women in Sri Lanka. An IT professional is defined as someone engaged in producing information technology–related output as their primary job function. It comprises the following types of work: programming/software engineering, systems and network administration, business analysis and system integration, digital media and animation, database administration and development, IT research and development, solutions and technical architect, management information systems/IT management, web development, technical writing, IT sales and marketing, software quality assurance and project and program management (ICTA 2013).

These issues are examined using the Social Cognitive Career Theory (SCCT) of Lent, Brown and Hackett (1994; 2000). Specifically, we examine how career-relevant interest towards IT was formed among these IT professionals and how these women selected IT as an academic field and then as their career. The chapter discusses their experience of work, the challenges they face in their career and their performance as women in this male-dominated industry.

Women in IT

Women represent approximately one-quarter of the Sri Lankan IT workforce. The proportion of women has increased from 21 per cent in 2009 to 29.7 per cent in 2013 (see Table 9.1 below) (ICTA 2013). There are various theories, at macro and micro levels, which attempt to explain the underrepresentation and inequalities of women in IT. These include neoclassical, labour market and feminist theories (Adya 2008); essentialist, socio-cultural (social constructivist) theories (Trauth 2002; Michie and Nelson 2006; Adya 2008); individual differences perspective (Trauth 2002; Adya 2008; Quesenberry and Trauth 2012) and structural theories (Ahuja 2002). The essentialist perspective highlights the masculine nature of IT and

Table 9.1 Female Participation in ICT Workforce (%)

	Females	Males
Total	29.7	70.3
BPO-Other	48.3	51.7
BPO-IT	33.6	66.4
Government	39.2	60.8
Non-ICT	18.8	81.2
ICT	28.1	71.9

Source: ICTA (2013), 40

the psychological and biological characteristics that are believed to make men inherently more suitable for IT. Women are said to lack, or perceived to lack, aptitude and passion for the field (Michie and Nelson 2006) and hence do not select disciplines such as IT.

Another key explanation, socio-cultural theory, explores societal views and beliefs about women and their roles in society and workplace (Ahuja 2002; Michie and Nelson 2006). Women are expected to be feminine, giving priority to families and households (Bhardwaj 2013), as a result of which masculine and technology-oriented industries such as IT are considered unsuitable for women. Stereotypes of the IT industry and associated academic disciplines influence who participates in these fields, so that women who hold these traditional stereotypes about the IT field do not select it for academic study (Cheryan, Plaut, Handron and Hudson 2013). These social and cultural beliefs lead to different expectations for women who self-select occupations which conform to cultural expectations. This situation is more prominent for women during certain life stages when they have to assume multiple gender roles such as wife, mother and caretaker (Ahuja 2002), which can happen during specific periods of women's careers (Ragins and Sundstrom 1989 cited in Ahuja 2002). The difficulty of women in IT to balance work and family, due to societal and family expectations and pressure to give priority to family and engage in household work and child rearing has been detailed (Aziz 2004; Bhardwaj 2013). The long or extended working hours, traveling time and additional assignments or jobs can add to guilt of not being able to take care of self, family and elders at home (Bharathi and Bhattacharya 2015).

Structural factors such as long hours on the job, the need to travel, the need to constantly update skills which adds to longer hours of work and lack of mentors and role models are discussed as reasons for lack of entry, retention and advancement of women into the IT sector (Ahuja 2002). In a similar vein, the complex nature of the processes of the field which privilege male workers and their competencies rather than those of women (Woodfield 2002) are discussed as structural factors (Ahuja 2002).

The individual differences perspective highlights "individual ways that individual women experience the social shaping of both gender and IT" (Trauth 2002, 115), focusing on similarities among women and men as individuals and disparities between genders with regard to IT skills and propensity to enter the IT field (Trauth 2002). Explanations are presented by scholars for the underrepresentation and inequality women face such as gender schemas (Lemons and Parzinger 2007), hostile and unfriendly work cultures (Roldan et al. 2004), role stress due to workplace resource inadequacy, role overload and personal inadequacy (Aziz 2004), lack of career progression opportunities and gender discrimination at work. Another issue is women's own self-perception of low self-efficacy related to subjects such as IT, science and engineering, even though, compared to men, they do not show any difference in academic ability (Hackett and Betz 1981). Against this backdrop, the need for organisational interventions to increase the representation of women in the IT profession has been promoted (Quesenberry and Trauth 2012).

There is a dearth of research into why women select IT as a profession. According to Turner, Bernt and Pecora (2002), the influence of male friends or colleagues is the main reason women choose this field. Adya (2008) has identified how parents, family and encouragement of teachers significantly influence a woman's selection of IT as a career choice. Many women who select the field have not majored in traditional technological fields as undergraduates (Turner, Bernt, and Pecora 2002). Furthering this understanding on why women select IT, the current study explores in detail how career-relevant interest towards IT was formed among women IT professionals, as well as how they experience work and perceive their performance.

Social Cognitive Career Theory (SCCT)

Based on social cognitive theory (Bandura 1986), Lent, Brown and Hackett (1994; 2000; 2002) developed SCCT, which is used extensively to explore academic and career choices and performance of professionals. SCCT emphasises and elaborates the "process through which people form interests, make choices, and achieve varying levels of success in educational and occupational pursuits" (Lent, Brown and Hackett 2000, 36) through the interplay of personal, environmental and behavioural variables (Lent, Lopez, Lopez and Sheu 2008). According to SCCT, self-efficacy, the belief one has about their ability to perform a certain behaviour/course of action successfully, promotes favourable outcome expectations which will lead to development of interest for a certain academic or career stream. In turn, self-efficacy, outcome expectation and interest will result in choice of goals which are affected by various contextual factors and the relative absence of barriers. At the same time, these contextual factors and various barriers may either promote or weaken self-efficacy, indirectly affecting the choices (Lent et al. 1994, 2000; Lent et al. 2008).

Numerous studies using SCCT have attempted to explore students' interest, choices and performance in computer or information technology fields and careers (e.g. Lent et al. 2008; Smith 2002). We build on these prior studies by exploring how women form interest, select and perform in the field of IT, within an Asian context amid contextual facts and various cultural and social barriers.

Methodology

To gain insight and engage in a richer exploration of the experiences of women IT professionals, this study employs a qualitative research approach. Three focus groups (five to six participants each) with a total of 16 women from three IT companies were conducted in early 2016 (see Table 9.2). Individual, in-depth interviews with the three human resources (HR) personnel of these IT companies were undertaken as well and this facilitated triangulation of data. The focus group discussions and individual interviews were conducted in English (the main mode of communication of these professionals) and transcribed verbatim. A meticulous process of coding and categorising was conducted starting from the first focus group, using SCCT as the theoretical lens. The main categories identified were refined through further data collection with HR personnel and focus groups.

The three companies (two Sri Lankan and one international) in which the focus groups were conducted are leading IT solutions providers catering to the international market. The two Sri Lankan companies have 150–200 employees while the international company has approximately 750 employees. Interviews with HR personnel of the three companies revealed women represent only 15–20 per cent of the total workforce in their companies while in the international company women represented 36 per cent of its workforce in Sri Lanka despite their focus being 40 per cent women.

Selecting a Career in IT

Both the focus group respondents and the HR personnel interviewed indicated that women's participation in the field of IT is increasing, but there are still more opportunities women could take up in the field. In exploring the themes which emerged from the interviews, we use the key theoretical constructs of SCCT: self-efficacy, outcome expectations, interests, goal choices and contextual factors (Lent et al. 2000).

According to SCCT, interest for a particular study area or career forms through a person's self-efficacy and outcome expectations. This interest then transpires to goal choices and subsequent selection (and retention) of a career with the influence of various contextual influences such as work and life circumstances (for example, birth of a child, job layoff, support system, amount of barriers) (Lent et al. 1994, 2000). There were a variety of situations and reasons leading respondents to develop an interest in and then

Table 9.2 Respondents of Focus Groups (FG)

Company	Name	Designation	Unit/Area of Expertise	Highest Educational Qualifications	Age	Marital Status & No. of Children	No. of Years of Experience in IT Field (total)
Sri Lankan Company 1	Sanduni	QA Engineer	QA (software)	B.Sc (Hons) in IT	25	S	3.5
	Thara	Trainee Software Engineer	QA (software)	Undergraduate student	24	S	4
	Amila	Associate Project Manager	Project management (software)	B.Sc (Hons) in Digital Technology and Information Systems	33	M 1	11
	Dilum	Tech Lead	Software development	B.Sc (Hons) in Computer Science	32	M 1	9.5
	Chathu	Associate Tech Lead	Software development	B.Sc in Computer Science	31	M 0	6
Sri Lankan Company 2	Imani	QA Lead/ Info Designer	Testing/ documentation	B.Sc in Information Systems	43	S	19
	Sarala	Software Engineer	Software development	B.Sc (Hons) in IT	26	S	1
	Gameela	Senior Software Engineer	Software development	M.Sc in Technology Management	27	S	4
	Mary	Senior Software Engineer	Software development	B.Sc (Hons) in IT	26	M 0	3
	Eresha	Senior Tech Lead	Software development	B.IT	37	M 2	13
International Company 3	Mala	Product Architect	Software	B.Sc	36	M 1	17
	Lalani	Lead Business Systems Analyst	Accounting/ finance	MBA	33	M 0	10
	Patty	Manager Information Services	Management	MBA in Finance	33	M 0	8
	Rupika	Software Engineer Supply Chain	Software	B.Sc	26	M 0	2
	Samy	Manager Software Development	Software	B.Sc (Hons)	31	M 1	10
	Kusala	Senior Manager Software Development	Management	M.Sc	39	M 0	14

select a career in IT, including their own interest, exam results, reputation of the field and the success of women IT professionals, and family influence. Mary, a Senior Software Engineer, was influenced by a school subject:

> During our advanced level we had a subject called General IT and that was actually when I learnt anything about IT and I really liked it because I liked logic and stuff, and I did math [as the majoring subject for GCE Advanced Level] . . . so I kind of picked IT because I liked it more than literature.

Gameela, another Senior Software Engineer, went into the IT field as a "second" choice:

> Actually, during my school days, I was aiming to become a doctor and I did my Advanced Levels in Bio science stream. But I did not get enough marks to go to Medical College. . . . Through my relatives, friends and teachers I have heard of some success stories relating to the IT industry. So . . . I thought of applying for IT at . . . [University] and got selected there.

Eresha, a Senior Tech Lead, had a strong parental influence in her choice:

> after school, it's not that I had a passion or anything, it's just that my dad thought that was the best way to go . . . so I didn't have a choice in the matter as such, he said just go in that line so that's how I came into [IT].

Other respondents described how both negative and positive outcomes expectations played a role in their interest in IT. Dilum, Tech Lead, explained how the job opportunities compared to other fields, in the context of high unemployment in Sri Lanka, had influenced her choice:

> During school days and in the University, I was very much interested in mathematics . . . they all [cousins] said if you do mathematics, you can do higher studies, but you can't focus much on the job market. That's why I got interested in IT.

Kusala (Senior Manager, Software Development) stated that she did not like the working conditions in other professions, and this influenced her selection of IT as her major at university:

> sometimes [in other engineering professions] you have to go on site visits to various places, I mean the travelling and the type of work you have to undertake, probably the duration, the hours, the shifts and that type of thing.

For others, the dynamic nature of the industry was the impetus:

> IT was my second choice. . . . But I just moved to IT because . . . I thought there was always something new to learn, there's always something new coming up . . . and like, you will never get bored . . . It keeps revolutionising and the knowledge keeps growing.
>
> (Sanduni, Quality Assurance Engineer)

Self-efficacy is a main theoretical construct of SCCT that leads to interest in a particular career. Research indicates that men report greater interest and self-efficacy in subjects such as maths and science compared to women (Smith 2002) and that women perceive they lack efficacy related to science, technology, engineering, mathematics (STEM) subjects, even when they do not show any difference in academic ability (Hackett and Betz 1981). The participants in this study did not directly indicate high belief about their ability to succeed in IT, even though it was their career. Many respondents had a STEM background in secondary education, and, perhaps unconsciously, believed in their ability to study IT at university. Gameela believed that it is easier for those who have studied STEM subjects to learn IT:

> Very rarely those in the commerce or arts fields join IT. Even if they do join, sometimes it is very hard for them to continue . . . when I started BIT [Bachelor of IT] most of my friends who came from those fields also tried . . . but once they started the programming language and all, they were trying to get out of IT. Most of them couldn't handle it.

These attitudes carry economic implications, where students studying social sciences, arts and humanities, who constitute the majority of the student population in national universities (UGC 2014), develop low self-efficacy towards subjects such as IT and hence do not develop an interest in IT. This even occurs in the context where there is high unemployment among arts graduates and higher labour force demands in the field of IT (Ariyawansa 2008).

It was particularly interesting to note how the respondents, even when they had majored in a STEM subject, had only started believing in their abilities (self-efficacy) after selecting IT for further studies or starting a career in IT. Sarala (Software Engineer) illustrates the sentiment of many respondents:

> While in the university . . . there was a common saying that girls cannot be [software] developers . . . but after coming to the industry and after like spending a few years here I now realise that it is just not right.

This is not surprising as IT had not been part of the educational experience for many of the interviewees as computer science only entered the school curriculum in 2005, so most of them would not know of their ability until they studied IT at post-secondary level. As Lent et al. (2002, 262) highlight, "the experience of success with a given task or performance domain tends to raise self-efficacy, whereas repeated failure lower them".

Even though the participants had started to believe in their ability to perform well in IT, they still had low self-efficacy about more technical jobs or tasks, and they appear to believe that men are better at these jobs:

> In my opinion there are specific jobs that men are really good at, some hardware, even electronics, those kinds of areas . . . when it comes to technology I think it is mostly men [who are more capable]. So they are the ones who build our platforms for us to code.
>
> (Samy, Manager, Software Development)

Gameela stated that she avoided technology-oriented work even at university:

> In our university, we actually had a hardware course, but I did not like it. . . . I think it is something in their [men's] genes . . . where they like to tinker around with these little switches and gadgets, whereas we [women] don't.

With these sentiments, respondents tend to limit themselves to certain jobs within IT such as quality assurance (QA), software and business analysis, which are considered less technical. These appear to be the most popular career choices for women in IT. According to one HR manager, and confirmed by others, when the company advertises for technical jobs such as hardware design and systems analysis, most applicants are men, with only 5 per cent of women applying. The proportion of women increases to 70 per cent when vacancies for software and quality assurance jobs are advertised.

Interviewees' perceptions indicate how contextual factors including cultural beliefs such as gender role stereotyping have influenced self-efficacy and outcome expectations (Lent et al. 2000):

> I think it comes from your childhood where girls like dolls and boys like to play with cars and electronic things, I think that has some influence. They like to always play with electronic equipment or some gadgets but if you take a girl, they always start with a doll. I mean that's the general thing.
>
> (Mala, Product Architect)

Within a cultural context where these gender role stereotypes are very much ingrained, it is unsurprising that participants question their ability to succeed in IT.

With more women entering IT and excelling in the field, women are starting to see more positive outcomes indicating a 'breaking away' from dominant gender stereotypes. More than the conscious evaluation of their ability to succeed in IT, perceived positive consequences of engaging in IT careers have played an important role in respondents' selection of IT careers. They stated how the male-dominated IT field has become more accommodating and accepting of women with positive attitudes towards women. This is a change and a contrast to the past. Imani (QA lead/information designer) reflected on the difficulties she experienced at the start of her career 19 years ago:

> [Women] Developers were at that time very few and far between so you had to . . . compete in a man's world and then they tended to look down on you, at that time. So, ok, so you're a girl and then we don't expect much of you kind of thing. Not exactly outright saying it but there was a kind of a notion.

According to Imani, and echoed by others, these perceptions and attitudes have changed and they feel more accepted and enjoy their careers in IT. Women now believe that they can perform successfully *vis à vis* men.

Mary looked to the future and summarised the situation of women's entry to IT, where it is clear how more robust efficacy expectations and positive outcomes will lead to more women entering the field:

> I think at a university level we need to do something because most of the girls are a bit scared to come into IT . . . . Especially into the [software] development track I guess because of the workload and stress. They think they can't handle it once they get married with children and a family life. But there is growth anyway, there are more girls coming into the field but we can also pass the message and then more girls will join.

Performance, Persistence and Challenges

Having selected IT, respondents were clearly more self-confident about their abilities and performance in the field and hence content in their careers. The participants specifically discussed how the social support they receive is significant for them in remaining in the industry, and also in overcoming various barriers or challenges at work and in the family. Many interviewees appeared to have considered their ability to balance work life in selecting a dynamic field such as IT where long work hours and travelling are part of the job. Yet, with support from families as well as family-friendly organisational policies and practices such as flexi-hours, day care centres and women/family-friendly work arrangements, respondents have been able to translate their interest in IT to a career. Support from family and employers can also been seen as contextual factors (Lent et al. 2000, 2002) influencing the goal choice and performance.

Respondents highlighted the support they receive from family members and how difficult it would be for them to balance work and family without this support, and that without this support they would "be a housewife" (Amila, Associate Project Manager). Samy, similar to many respondents, explained how her husband is very supportive, particularly when she has to travel overseas:

> I was away for two weeks but he is very understanding about it. He does not mind me travelling alone. I think that a lot of people have issues, husbands don't like wives going out, because, say when you go with a group you will get men and women and you would be like travelling together, going to places together. But if your husband does not accept that and if he's like restricting you that would be a major problem. But luckily for me, my husband is not like that.

Some respondents emphasised how receiving support from customers, colleagues and managers helped them to manage work. For example, Mala said:

> If we work in a team it will mostly be guys who are in the team. But they are more understanding. . . . sometimes when you plan events and when you have a woman with kids in the team, they [men in the team] might go for a lunch rather than a dinner. Simple things like that.

Dilum detailed the support and understanding she got from a US-based customer:

> Calls [meetings with customers] started from 6:30 p.m. so it was very hard for me to stay for calls [because I was pregnant]. So then I told that to client. We asked for an early call, but then they said no you don't have to stay, we can manage the call. So that's how I got my freedom.

Organisational support, especially in terms of family-friendly policies and practices, was also a significant factor that determined not only the selection of a company to work for, but also the retention and contentment of professionals in their jobs. Respondents spoke about day care centres, flexible work arrangements, maternity leave, supportive work teams and cultures and working from home as practices assisting them remain, not only with the company, but also in IT. Respondents, whether married or single, preferred companies with family-friendly cultures and policies:

> My brother was always telling me that Company 3 is a really good IT company for a girl to work in, and I heard the same from my friends. So when I was thinking of joining a company, I thought that it would be good if I could get into Company 3.
>
> (Rupika, Software Engineer—Supply Chain)

Dilum described how without the support and understanding of the company, she would consider changing jobs (within the company or moving to another company) or quitting:

> I would try to talk to my manager and see whether I would be able to go home at this particular time. But if it is not working, then probably I would have to change the job or stay at home. I have no other option.

At the same time, change in career direction can occur in conjunction with environmental conditions or life challenges (Lent et al. 2002). Women professionals had to change their career interests when faced with challenging life situations such as birth of children:

> If I think about my scenario, before I got married my situation was like, I go home open my laptop, check mails and do some office work until midnight. And in the morning also I get up, chat with clients and get some points clarified. That was my life before I got married. I think I can't give that much dedication [now] because I am married and have a kid. So what I feel is, if you are in QA or something then you can have a balanced life all the time.
> (Amila)

However, even with the support they get and the heightened self-efficacy about their abilities to excel in IT, the respondents still do not appear to aspire to climb the career ladder. Perceived negative outcomes together with lack of self-confidence about their ability to hold managerial positions appear to hamper their interest in higher positions. This is highlighted by Gibbons and Shoffner (2004, 94) as "a belief of low competency or in negative outcomes will lead people to avoid certain activities".

In all three companies where focus groups were conducted, there were no women in the senior managerial, decision-making level. When it came to middle-level managers, the international company had 29 per cent women, and one Sri Lankan company had only one woman manager and she was the HR manager. The other Sri Lankan company had approximately 5 per cent representation of women in middle management. This underrepresentation at the managerial level is not unique to the IT industry in Sri Lanka (Devi 2002) but is common to many industries.

Respondents did not indicate experiencing any gender discrimination in the workplace related to career progression. Rather, they spoke of their own reservations in terms of low self-efficacy and negative outcome expectations such as concerns about managing their work and life, when deciding their future career path in the field. Amila explained why she changed her career path after starting a family:

> Actually I wanted to [be a] software architect. But what I feel now is I can't give that much dedication because of my kid and my other commitments. So I have changed my career aspiration.

Another major challenge in their career (Aziz 2004) was the need to constantly update their skills. For Eresha, family responsibilities left her little time and effort for additional reading and updating:

> I have two kids at home. One is at school and my husband is . . . not at home all the time and I have a hard time. Because when I go home, I can't spend time with this [updating myself] . . . If I start something, it's after 11 o'clock actually. Even then, I will start working with the customers. So then, I have to make more sacrifices and spend less time updating my skills.

For Amila her need to balance work and life meant she remained in her current position as a Tech Lead without aspiring to the higher position of architect.

> I am not reading much. But they [men] get updated every day, but I am not like that . . . that's another reason I changed my career path a little bit. . . . I cannot give that dedication.

Thara (Trainee Software Engineer) explained that as a result she feels less technically competent compared to her male counterparts. The lack of ability to update skills in a fast-moving industry clearly affects respondents' self-efficacy and, in Amila's case, their career progression.

None of the respondents indicated aspirations to start their own IT companies or to head an IT company. Their career aspirations ended far below senior management positions. There were only four interviewees from two companies (one from a Sri Lankan and three from the international company) out of the 16 participants who were in middle management positions and they also did not indicate any higher management ambition. They had mixed perceptions about their capabilities as managers. They thought in certain instances they were more humane and better at relationships than male managers and in other instances that they were not tough enough to handle people, especially the older men in the team:

> I have been in this role since 2007 . . . there are challenges with the managerial side, because apart from the fact that you are a female, I mean this management side dealing with people, that of course is a challenge. And sometimes I think being a woman we are more understanding and sometimes that has helped me a lot when moving in this field.
>
> (Kusala, Senior Manager Software Development)

Another observed that:

> They are like 45-plus [age] guys in my group under me so that's a huge challenge when it comes to evaluations etc. Even talking as a

manager . . . there was a male who joined my team and he said "I was thinking it was very difficult to work with a woman manager".

(Lalani, Lead Business System Analyst)

As a result, interviewees were inclined to remain in the technical area, citing their disinterest in managing people as a reason for not pursuing a management career: "I don't like to go for the line managerial aspects . . . in this company it is mostly the HR responsibilities that comes with the line management. So that is not my preference" (Rupika). Research indicates women without technical degrees prefer managerial positions, whereas those who are technically trained dislike managerial positions because of their desire to develop their technical expertise and the unappealing nature of managing people (Adya 2008).

Amidst the challenges faced by this group of IT professionals, overall they were content with their jobs and companies, and did not admit to experiencing any gender discrimination in their workplaces. Adya's (2008) research raised these issues concluding that Asian women were rarely found to indicate unequal treatment at workplaces and tolerated or coped passively with the short-term challenges they faced in the workplace compared to US women. It is unclear if respondents in this study are not experiencing significant gender discrimination in their workplaces or are reluctant to admit to such experiences.

Conclusion

Through interviews with women IT professionals, this chapter aimed to understand how career-relevant interest towards IT was formed among women IT professionals and how they selected a career in IT, as well as their experiences at work in this male-dominated industry. Unlike the past, women are entering the field in greater numbers and there appears to be more acceptance of women in what is still a male-dominant field.

Women appear to form an interest in the field of IT due to a variety of reasons where outcome expectations play a more dominant role than self-efficacy. In fact, the respondents did not appear to have strong self-efficacy beliefs when they select a career in IT. However, upon entering the field positive experiences in their jobs have made respondents more confident about their abilities. Yet, this confidence is not robust and tends to falter when it comes to more technical jobs within IT and higher managerial level jobs. Gender role stereotyping beliefs, where women are said to lack, or are perceived to lack, the aptitude and passion for the field (Michie and Nelson 2006), while men are said to have more self-efficacy for IT occupations and greater passion for computers (Michie and Nelson 2006), can be a major reason for this vulnerable self-efficacy beliefs of these women interviewees. With this backdrop, women restrict themselves to certain jobs only within IT such as software development and quality assurance and do not appear to aspire to climb the career ladder. This inevitably hampers their career success (Smith 2002) as they will not seek their full potential nor contribute their fullest to the field.

Effect of contextual and environmental factors such as gender role stereotyping beliefs, social support, employer support (Lent et al. 1994) were seen to play an important role in the formation of interest and goal choice, as well as career performance. Women's inability to update their knowledge due to time/family commitment as well as gender stereotyping beliefs was another major challenge in their career and an influence on their career choices in the IT field. It was specifically noted how, for many participants and especially for married participants, their careers revolved around their families. Their contentment and retention in the field was mainly based on how well they balanced and coped with their family commitments and the social support they received at work from client, manager and peers, and from the family (husband, parents, in-laws). The need to balance work-life significantly affected their work and career decisions ranging from selecting a company to selecting a job within IT, their career advancement and retention within the company.

Notes

1. Includes the Management and Information Technology, Information Technology, Information and Communication Technology, Information Technology and Management, Computation and Management, Business Information Systems, etc.
2. However, the number of women students enrolling in IT-related programs for external degrees is far below that of males, at a rate less than 30 per cent. Women postgraduate students' enrolment in national universities' IT related programs are low (University Grants Commission 2014).

References

Aaltio, I. and Huang, J. 2007. "Women Managers' Careers in Information Technology in China: High Flyers with Emotional Costs?" *Journal of Organizational Change Management* 20(2): 227–244.

Adya, M. P. 2008. "Women at Work: Differences in IT Career Experiences and Perceptions Between South Asian and American Women." *Human Resource Management* 47(3): 601–635.

Ahuja, M. K. 2002. "Women in the Information Technology Profession: A Literature Review, Synthesis and Research Agenda." *European Journal of Information Systems* 11: 20–34.

Ariyawansa, R. G. 2008. "Employability of Graduates of Sri Lankan Universities." *Sri Lankan Journal of Human Resource Management* 2(1): 91–104.

Aziz, M. 2004. "Role Stress Among Women in the Indian Information Technology Sector." *Women in Management* 19(7): 356–363.

Bandura, A. 1986. *Social Foundations of Thought and Action: A Social Cognitive Theory*. Englewood Cliffs, NJ: Prentice Hall.

Bharathi, V. and Bhattacharya, S. 2015. "Work Life Balance of Women Employees in the Information Technology Industry." *Asian Journal of Management Research* 5(3): 324–364.

Bhardwaj, P. 2013. "A Study on the Dual Role of Working Women in the Information Technology Sector in Bangalore." PhD thesis, Christ University.

Cheryan, S., Plaut, V. C., Handron, C. and Hudson, L. 2013. "The Stereotypical Computer Scientist: Gendered Media Representations as a Barrier to Inclusion for Women." *Sex Roles* 69(1–2): 58–71.

Department of Census and Statistics. 2014. *The Sri Lankan Women: Partner in Progress*. Sri Lanka: Department of Census and Statistics.

Department of Census and Statistics. 2016. *Sri Lanka Labour Force Statistics QuarterlyBulletin: Sri Lanka Labour Force Survey 2nd Quarter 2016*. Sri Lanka: Department of Census and Statistics.

Devi, S. U. 2002. "Globalization, Information Technology and Asian Indian Women in US." *Economic and Political Weekly*, October 26: 4421–4428.

Draus, P., Mishra, S., Goreva, N., Caputo, D., Leone, G. and Repack, D. 2014. "A Comprehensive Study of the Perceptions and Support Structures of Women Engaged in IT/IS Careers." *International Journal of Management and Information Systems (Online)* 18(3): 155–160.

Gibbons, M. and Shoffner, M. 2004. "Prospective First-Generation College Students: Meeting Their Needs Through Social Cognitive Career Theory." *Professional School Counseling* 8(1): 91–97.

Hackett, G. and Betz, N. 1981. "A Self-Efficacy Approach to the Career Development of Women." *Journal of Vocational Behavior* 18(3): 326–339.

Information and Communication Technology Agency of Sri Lanka (ICTA). 2013. *NationalICT Workforce Survey 2013*. Colombo: ICTA.

Lemons, M. and Parzinger, M. 2007. "Gender Schemas: A Cognitive Explanation of Discrimination of Women in Technology." *Journal of Business and Psychology* 22(1): 91–98.

Lent, R., Brown, S. and Hackett, G. 1994. "Toward a Unifying Social Cognitive Theory of Career and Academic Interest, Choice, and Performance." *Journal of Vocational Behavior* 45(1): 79–122.

Lent, R., Brown, S. and Hackett, G. 2000. "Contextual Supports and Barriers to Career Choice: A Social Cognitive Analysis." *Journal of Counseling Psychology* 47(1): 36–49.

Lent, R., Brown, S. and Hackett, G. 2002. "Social Cognitive Career Theory." In *Career Choice and Development*, 4th ed., edited by D. Brown and Associates, 255–311. San Francisco, CA: Jossey-Bass.

Lent, R., Lopez, A., Lopez, F. and Sheu, H. 2008. "Social Cognitive Career Theory and the Prediction of Interests and Choice Goals in the Computing Disciplines." *Journal of Vocational Behavior* 73(1): 52–62.

Michie, S. and Nelson, D. 2006. "Barriers Women Face in Information Technology Careers: Self Efficacy, Passion and Gender Biases." *Women in Management Review* 21(1): 10–27.

Quesenberry, J. and Trauth, E. 2012. "The (Dis)Placement of Women in the IT Workforce: An Investigation of Individual Career Values and Organisational Interventions." *Information Systems Journal* 22(6): 457–473. DOI: 10.1111/j.1365–2575.2012.00416.x.

Roldan, M., Soe, L. and Yakura, E. 2004. *Perceptions of Chilly IT Organisational Contexts and Their Effect on the Retention and Promotion of Women IT*. Proceedings of the 2004 ACM SIGMIS Conference, Tucson, April 22–24, 108–113.

Sauter, V. 2012. "The Absence of Gender Differences Among Students in an MIS Program." *Communications of the Association for Information Systems* 31(4). http://aisel.aisnet.org/cais/vol31/iss1/4.

SLAASSCOM. 2014. *Sri Lankan IT/BPM Industry 2014 Review.* Colombo: SLAASSCOM.

Smith, S. 2002. "The Role of Social Cognitive Career Theory in Information Technology Based Academic Performance." *Information Technology, Learning, and Performance Journal* 20(2): 1–10.

Trauth, E. 2002. "Odd Girl Out: An Individual Differences Perspective on Women in the IT Profession." *Information Technology and People* 15(2): 98–118.

Turner, S., Bernt, P. and Pecora, N. 2002. "Why Women Choose Information Technology Careers: Educational, Social, and Familial Influences." Paper presented at the Annual Meeting of the American Educational Research Association, New Orleans, LA, April 1–5, 2002.

University Grants Commission. 2014. "Sri Lanka University Statistics 2013." Accessed November 14, 2006. www.ugc.ac.lk/en/component/content/article/1418-sri-lanka-universitystatistics-2013.html.

University Grants Commission. 2016. "Sri Lanka University Statistics 2015." Accessed November 14, 2016. http://ugc.ac.lk/en/component/content/article/1709-sri-lanka-university-statistics-2015.html.

Woodfield, R. 2002. "Woman and Information Systems Development: Not Just a Pretty (Inter)Face?" *Information Technology & People* 15(2): 119–138.

10 Multiplicity of 'I's'

STEM-Professional Women in the Canadian Space Industry

Stefanie Ruel

Introduction

This chapter presents empirical research focused on why there are so few science, technology, engineering and mathematics (STEM)-trained women managers in the Canadian space industry. I examine the gendered discourses and the impact of these discourses in order to reveal this exclusionary social reality. The following questions guided the study: What is the range of anchor points associated with STEM-professional women within the Canadian space industry? How do gendered discourses shape the interaction between STEM-professional women and men? By applying the critical sensemaking framework (CSM) (Helms Mills, Thurlow and Mills 2010) to data collected from unstructured interviews and supporting organisational documentation, the study reveals these gendered discourses. This chapter showcases two women, their anchor points and a sample of the gendered discourses surrounding them in the workplace.

The Canadian space industry includes a diversity of gendered men, gendered women and transgendered women/men[1] fulfilling various occupational roles. In 2012, the industry employed 7,993 people, including 2,932 highly qualified professionals (HQPs) (engineers, scientists and technicians) and 671 managers (CSA 2013a). In 2013, less than 20 per cent of STEM management positions were occupied by HQP women (CSA 2012a; Catalyst 2013). White, military-trained and/or engineering-trained men predominantly occupy the STEM management/executive positions, while HQP women are relegated into supporting technical and administrative/corporate roles.

Research focused on gender and diversity in the engineering and science professions is extensive (see Jorgenson 2002; Chu 2006; Faulkner 2007; Hanappi-Egger 2013). I chose to focus on gendered discourses, and the impact of these discourses on the identities of professional women, in order to reveal the lived, ordered experience of these HQP women. An individual's identity is represented in this study by self-identity and social identity. Self-identity is the "notion of who he/she is becoming" (Corlett and Mavin 2014, 262). Social identity, on the other hand, consists of 'inputs' into this self-identity (Watson 2008). These inputs are socially constructed and manifested in discourses via interactions with others. The majority of engineering and science positivist and postpositivist studies focus on self-identity alone. Social identity has been hinted at, for example in Chu (2006), but is not prevalent in the literature.

The social order, that is, the paucity of HQP women managers in this industry, requires an examination of the notion of intersecting identities. Intersecting identities—whether self or social or a combination of both—are defined as identity categories such as gender, race, ethnicity, etc. that are interdependent and that constitute each other (Crenshaw 1989, 1991). These intersecting identities are non-additive and ephemeral, changing through time and through interactions—reflective of power relations—with others. Empirical research by authors such as Crenshaw (1989) and Hill Collins (2000) demonstrate that these complex identity intersections can position individuals in society, creating an order.

The challenge is how to investigate these intersecting identities and the creation of an order. By investigating the discursive manifestation of intersecting identities along with the power relations among individuals and their sensemaking processes, the concept of identity anchor points is needed (Ruel, Mills, and Thomas 2015). Discourses are defined here as sets of statements and practices that bring an object or set of objects into being (Parker 1992). Power relations are used in the Foucauldian sense, where they exist locally in day-to-day interactions, are continuous, productive and are "capillary" (Fraser 1989, 22). Sensemaking works hand in hand with power relations,

> unfold(ing) as a sequence in which people concerned with identity in the social context of other actors engage [in] ongoing circumstances from which they extract cues and make plausible sense retrospectively, while enacting more or less order into those ongoing circumstances.
> (Weick, Sutcliffe, and Obstfeld 2005, 409)

An identity anchor point is comprised of intersecting identity categories that are discursively created and recreated. Anchor points are not just identity categories; they encompass the act of their creation via discursive processes, the power relations among individuals and the sensemaking processes. Anchor points assist us in securing meaning, for a brief period of time, so that we may consider the order that is (re)created through this meaning. An individual's self- and social identities and their anchor points are used together in this study to reveal the lived, ordered experience of HQP women within the Canadian space industry.

This chapter begins by presenting the Canadian industry's demographic order to highlight this underrepresentation of women. I then present the theoretical framework and the research design for this study. The results of the analysis, focused on two participants, are then discussed.

Canadian Space Industry Demographics

The space industry was born after World War II. Engineering and scientific practice morphed from a war effort to one of government-academic-private space industry alliances, where science and mathematics were stressed for achieving technological advancement and commercial enterprise (Lang, Cruse, McVey and McMasters 1999). The race to the moon, in particular, was primarily run by two global entities, the US and the USSR, but included the launch of the Canadian-designed and built Alouette satellite in 1962 (CSA 2012b). This satellite was constructed and operated via a military government department and a mix of private companies. The Canadian space industry has grown since this time, and has generated $3.32 billion in 2012 (CSA 2013a). It is recognised today for its strengths in such areas as satellite-based communications, earth observation and space robotics (AIAC 2015).

The Canadian space industry is a subset of the larger Canadian aerospace industry, which employed almost 80,000 people in 2011, 20 per cent females, of whom approximately half (55 per cent) were in administrative and clerical roles (Prism Economics and Analysis 2012). The space industry itself employed almost 8,000 people across more than 200 for-profit companies, universities and government departments (CSA 2013b). The Canadian Space Agency (CSA), in particular, employed a total of 652 women and men in 2013, where 279 women held positions in Executive, Scientific and Professional, Technical, Administrative and Foreign Services, and Administrative Support (CSA 2014). Five of the 24 CSA executive positions in 2013 were held by women, only one of whom had a scientific background (CSA 2014). There were 175 supervisors, functional managers and directors at the CSA, key population groups that can prepare for senior management and leadership positions.[2] Close to one-third (31 per cent) of this group were women, with the majority in corporate (administrative) positions. Women were underrepresented across the engineering profession and, notably, there were no women at the senior Engineering 6 level (CSA 2014). In the scientific and professional category, 66 women held positions out of a possible 302 positions. The vast majority of women (200) were in the Administrative and Foreign Services, and Administrative Support positions (CSA 2014). The situation is similar in MacDonald Dettwiler Associates (MDA), the largest private space industry company in Canada, where men held all eight senior management positions in 2012 (Catalyst 2013).

Theoretical Framework: Discourses, Social Identity and Anchor Points

The concepts of discourses, social-identity and anchor points underpin the theoretical framework for this study. Foucault's concept of discourse does not refer to language or how individuals use language with a goal of establishing a theory of language (Foucault 1978, 1980; Perrot 1980). Foucauldian discourses and their production go beyond language, texts and semiotics. Discourse and its practice encompass "everyday attitudes and behaviour, along with our perceptions of what we believe to be reality" (Grant, Keenoy, and Oswick 1998, 2). Foucauldian discourse is related to mundane social life and to social processes,[3] bringing an object or a set of objects to life. Phillips and Hardy (2002) found that social reality cannot be understood without investigating discourses. Discourse, then, is more a matter "of the social, historical and political conditions under which, for example, statements come to count as true or false" (McHoul and Grace 2007, 29).

Identity is represented in this study by two main sociological branches, self-identity and social identity. Social identity, in particular, can be influenced by a multitude of mechanisms including discursive acts such as stories, ideologies, experience, history, position in society and attachments such as emotional involvement (Ashmore, Deaux, and McLaughlin-Volpe 2004). The concept of social identity can be used to focus on the outside impact on 'who I am', and how we make sense of this outside influence. If, in contrast, focus was put only on the projection of self-identity—or the tales that an individual tells about their own projected self-identity—the study of how an individual shapes and is shaping who they are would be limited to only one specific sphere of being, that is, self-perception.

Intersectionality, or the study of intersecting identity categories and the resultant order that is created, adds an important facet to the study of the complexity of individuals. Intersectionality scholarship specifically takes into account the positioning—discrimination/ marginalisation/ oppression/ exclusion—of an individual based on interdependent and constituting identity categories (Crenshaw 1989; 1991). I believe that investigations into the complex representation(s) of an individual cannot be an exercise in determining how many demographic identities—or standpoints—a person has. Revealing a complex individual is an exercise in investigating the (gendered) discursive experiences of individuals interacting together and the impact of those discourses.

To reveal such a complex individual, the anchor point concept (Ruel, Mills, and Thomas 2015) is used. Anchor points, originally coined by Glenn (2004) and reconstructed by Ruel et al. (2015), are intersecting identity categories that are discursively created and recreated. They encompass the act of their creation via interactions among individuals, and their own, individual sensemaking processes. The discursive deployment of these anchor points within an organisational context can produce and impose limits that (re)create that order. I present my act of reflexivity to demonstrate a possible range of these ephemeral anchor points.

First 'I' in Intersectionality: My Range of Anchor Points

To better understand this theoretical framework and anchor points in particular, I present 'who I am'. I am a highly educated HQP, French-Canadian, White, mother, woman. I am also a public servant working within the

Canadian space industrial context. I freely acknowledge (now) that I adopt discursive practices and processes that reflect norms and values of this industry sometimes without realising I have done so. I am someone who is enclosed, partitioned and ranked (Marsden 1997) within the Canadian space industry as a Life Sciences Mission Manager. I am the only Canadian woman in this occupational position who leads and manages scientific, operational life sciences missions into space. When needed, I am someone who is able to discursively and behaviourally play the 'I am different than you—I am the same as you' web of games.

This social identity—Life Sciences Mission Manager—highlights not only the gendered nature of my work as a Life Scientist but also underscores the sacrifices I have had to make with respect to 'who I am', or my self-identity. In addition, the experiences I have been party to and subject to contribute to my gaining a sense of 'fit' into/with the dominant group of White men. For example, when challenged by a colleague in a meeting to an arm wrestle to resolve a contentious work-related disagreement, I obliged; or, when asked to get coffee by a visiting European male dignitary, I let another White man identify my work 'enclosure'; or, when told that it was great to have a woman at the table to act as the nurturing and caring voice, I did my best to assume this temporary (gendered) anchor point. Summarising these discursive stories, I present in Figure 10.1 my self- and social identities along with my range of anchor points.

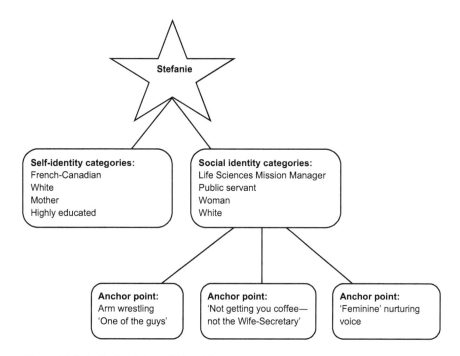

Figure 10.1 Stefanie's Map of Identities

We could spend some time analysing my unique/token status and the attempts to assimilate me within the dominant group of men. However, the focus of this study is not to rationalise the gender ideologies (Pavlenko 2001) that are at play in my particular case. This study is about bringing forth STEM-professional women's (re)created, fleeting anchor points to reveal their ordered experience.

Research Design

My research objective is to examine the dominant and the mundane in the daily discursive processes utilised by STEM-professional women, men and transgendered women/men in the Canadian space industry in such a way to reveal the complex individual and her lived experience. Helms Mills, Thurlow and Mills's (2010) critical sensemaking (CSM) framework provided me with an avenue to achieve this. CSM is four heuristics interacting together. The framework is shaped from Weick's (1995) sensemaking, Foucault's (1978; 1980) discourses, Mills and Murgatroyd's (1991) organisational rules and Unger's (1987a; 1987b) formative contexts. Interaction is the key idea here; there is no structural or procedural step-function among these heuristics.

Fundamentally, social realities cannot be understood without investigating those discourses that are practiced in that reality (Phillips and Hardy 2002). Discursive acts centred on identity—anchor points in this case—are made available to analysis since they are social constructions that reflect power relations. These discursive acts ultimately constrain the sensemaker within a social reality "to seek out familiar solutions that have worked in the past . . . and [that] maintain the social status quo" (Helms Mills and Mills 2009, 175).

These 'familiar' solutions are influenced by institutional rules and meta-rules, and formative contexts. Mills and Murgatroyd's (1991) treatment of institutional rules and meta-rules works in concert with Unger's (1987a; 1987b) formative contexts. Rules and meta-rules function as a pre-existing framework determining how 'things get done' (Mills and Murgatroyd 1991). Formative contexts, on the other hand, capture and reflect dominant social assumptions (Unger 1987b) often referred to as social values. Individuals within an organisation can express institutionally dominant social values, rules and meta-rules through narratives and stories. These organisational narratives capture the said and the unsaid.

CSM provides a framework to study discourses, weaving in an individual's sensemaking, institutional rules and meta-rules, and formative contexts all together. CSM ultimately assists in revealing "the consequences of those power effects for individuals" (Helms Mills, Thurlow, and Mills 2010, 189).

Second 'I' in Intersectionality: Participants and Data Collection

The Canadian space context is made up of a wide range of individuals. This social reality has the potential for a large web of discourses. Recalling that the research question is focused on identifying the range of anchor points, a primary form of identity category such as woman had to be chosen followed by the intersection(s) with other possible identity categories (McCall 2005). Therefore, potential participants were limited to women and transgendered individuals who identified as women with varied identity categories including race, ethnicity, sexual orientation, STEM-trained and who occupied employee or manager positions across the Canadian space industry. To be able to study women's anchor points, I necessarily had to have the participation of (gendered) men as an input to the identities of women. The goal was not, however, to investigate the range of anchor points of men.

The larger study has 10 participants, six women and four men, recruited via a snowball referral technique to avoid the introduction of my own inherent biases given my extensive network of personal contacts and position of privilege. To ensure anonymity of participants, I used pseudonyms and hid certain details such as ethnic identity and specific STEM degrees earned. Participant recruitment ceased once no new substantial themes and insights emerged. The overall sample was diverse from the perspective of STEM education level (bachelor's, master's, PhD degrees), professional and occupational roles (executives, managers, engineers, scientists), career stage (early career, mid-career and late career) and public and private Canadian space organisations. Due to the snowball sampling technique used the sample was not as diverse as I had initially planned. Notably, no transgendered individuals were recruited.

Data collected included narratives and stories and a variety of documents including participant emails and corporate reports. Unstructured interviews were specifically chosen given that identity categories are best left to the participants to identify in their own voice (Ashmore, Deaux, and McLaughlin-Volpe 2004). The tape-recorded interviews were either transcribed by one professional transcriber when participants chose to speak in English, or were translated and transcribed from French to English by another professional translator/transcriber. This option to conduct the interviews in French or English reflects the linguistic reality of the Canadian space industry.

Third 'I' in Intersectionality: Recreating the Participants' Range of Anchor Points

The interaction of Weick's (1995) sensemaking, Foucault's (1978; 1980) discourses, Mills and Murgatroyd's (1991) context of organisational rules and Unger's (1987a; 1987b) formative contexts was used to extract the range of anchor points for each participant. By focusing on the narratives and stories that people use in daily interactions, I was able to reconstruct their views of the industry, their occupation, their job and their self (Boje 1991; 2001; 2008). The result of these unstructured interviews, surprisingly needing sometimes only three questions on my part to generate stories, were analysed with a view to revealing how gendering discourses shape the interaction of HQP women and men in the space industry.

The analysis of discourses involved primarily the extraction of anchor points, with a 'making of sense' layer captured as a way to put into evidence the (re)creation of these anchor points. With respect to the range of anchor points, I first searched through the transcripts for statements such as "I am . . . ", highlighting those until I had exhausted the transcript. I then passed a second time through the transcript, searching for and highlighting statements regarding the STEM training and education achieved, as one example of social identity discourses, and other social identities that I considered inputs into her self-identity. I then passed through the transcript a third time, searching for stories specifically attributing anchor points. These stories would sometimes start with "I was at a meeting . . . " or "I was told that . . . " or "Did you hear about . . . ". For example, the 'Only girl here' anchor point was (easily) found in all the women's discourses when they would recount meetings, education, etc. experiences. I passed through the transcript one final time, looking at the highlighted identities. At times, via the application of the CSM framework, I realised that I had attributed, say, a self-identity to an anchor point, and I would correct my analysis.

With respect to the making of sense, these included influences from rules and meta-rules and social values as stated by the participant. I would highlight in the transcripts a particular story passage—that would move me, captivate me, frustrate me or make me question what the participant was trying to say—and then I would move to the STEM men's interview transcript to see if there were any parallels in their storytelling, i.e. was that meeting contentious, did that person retell the story with a completely different lens. Then I would bring these ideas together with what I 'knew' of the individual to retrace the anchor point discourses coming into being. I then graphically represented each participant, with accompanying stories and narratives captured with the sensemaking layer below the various anchor points.

Discussion

Social identities and their existence could be easily traced in the participant's discourses to influences and ideologies in society, a participant's experiences in life, history and emotional attachments (see Ashmore, Deaux, and McLaughlin-Volpe 2004). Anchor points, on the other hand, were found to be a separate and distinct manifestation of social identity. Anchor points had important influences from the space industry's rules and social values context. These anchor points were also ephemeral, varying in time and in space, depending on an individual's interactions with others and with the participant's occupational role and title. I found, therefore, a marked discursive difference between the presentation and extraction of social identities and anchor points.

Another theme across all participants was the lack of distinction among the following terms: 'female', 'girl' and 'woman'. Typically, gender and diversity scholars go to great lengths to identify that a woman is a cultural representation of an individual. However, 'female' and 'girl' were used interchangeably and easily while 'woman' almost never appeared in the discursive practices of either HQP women or men. In a similar vein, when I hazarded to ask a direct question about gender and discrimination or asked my clearing question ('is there anything you would like to add to our conversation that I have not asked you?'), all women participants stated emphatically that they had had no experiences with discrimination because of their gender or, similarly, the men stated that the industry was not discriminatory. Some participants went so far as to be completely perplexed about how our conversation tied in with my research about women in the space industry and the 'sexism' (participants' discourses) that I was 'trying to find'.

Finally, I must take a moment to reveal the emotional toll these interviews took on me. As an insider within this industry, participants talked freely and openly about both their happy and painful experiences. They often tried to include me in their experiences, saying 'you know' to me in many of our discursive exchanges. After two consecutive particularly difficult interviews— one that lasted over three hours where the participant revealed her emotional destruction within this industry, and the other that saw references made to pornographic movie nights that occurred on site in one organisation—I had to stop the interview process for a few weeks. I returned to the interview process with a realisation that I would continue to hide my own suite of identities and my emotions from participants to ensure that I could complete the data collection phase of my research. I felt that if I separated out the interviews over time, and shared my emotions with those close to me, I could continue to collect the data to complete my research.

Geirit

Geirit works in a private Canadian space organisation and has an international educational and occupational STEM background, and is at an early career stage. Her discourses revealed much of 'who I am' and 'who I am becoming'. They also revealed an extensive range of anchor points. These identities are presented in Figure 10.2.

Geirit's sense of 'who I am' was clearly stated and repeated in a number of stories she told, including that she never wants children and that she 'needs change'. One discursive example of this need for change is shown in the self-identity box in Figure 10.2. She also stated emphatically and often that she

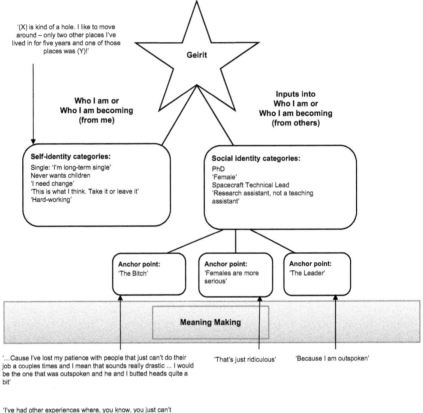

'(X) is kind of a hole. I like to move around – only two other places I've lived in for five years and one of those places was (Y)!'

Geirit

Who I am or
Who I am becoming
(from me)

Inputs into
Who I am or
Who I am becoming
(from others)

Self-identity categories:
Single: 'I'm long-term single'
Never wants children
'I need change'
'This is what I think. Take it or leave it'
'Hard-working'

Social identity categories:
PhD
'Female'
Spacecraft Technical Lead
'Research assistant, not a teaching assistant'

Anchor point:
'The Bitch'

Anchor point:
'Females are more serious'

Anchor point:
'The Leader'

Meaning Making

'…Cause I've lost my patience with people that just can't do their job a couples times and I mean that sounds really drastic … I would be the one that was outspoken and he and I butted heads quite a bit'

'That's just ridiculous'

'Because I am outspoken'

'I've had other experiences where, you know, you just can't communicate with somebody and I lose my patience'

'That's really not your decision to make' and 'I'm leading the program' versus 'Did I overstep the bounds?'

Figure 10.2 Geirit's Map of Identities

is very hard-working, and others can 'take it or leave it' when it comes to what she thinks. Geirit's social identities, by definition influenced by ideologies such as academic credentials (Ashmore et al. 2004), included the social constructions of being 'a PhD'. She also staunchly defended her job title as a 'Research Assistant, not a Teaching Assistant'. Geirit's STEM social identities—PhD, Satellite Technical Lead, Research Assistant—interacted and were interdependent. This type of interaction was found throughout her technically based stories, highlighting her extensive technical knowledge while embracing an ideology of merit and skills that she believed were independent from her gender. I must add that this interaction and interdependence of social identities was in line with Crenshaw's (1989, 1991) findings on intersectional identities, where one social identity (say, PhD) could not be separated out from another (Lead), for example.

Geirit's anchor points—'The Bitch', 'Females are more serious' and 'The Leader'—distinctly stood out in her discourses from her self- and social identities. Starting with 'The Bitch' anchor point, she recounted how she had been named as such in meeting settings. Some examples of her discourses (and sensemaking) surrounding this anchor point are presented in the meaning-making layer in Figure 10.2. Geirit tried to assume (discursively) this gendered 'Bitch' anchor point—stating emphatically in a meeting that 'I am leading this program' and losing patience when she could not communicate this message clearly with someone—while sharing through another story that she struggled with the implications of being characterised as this 'Bitch'. Notably, in one story she found herself telling others that 'this is not your decision' then trying to find her immediate supervisor after the meeting to ask him if she had overstepped her bounds by making such a statement.

Geirit was also ascribed the anchor point of 'Females are more serious'. When digging into her discourses, I found that Geirit believed this anchor point to be "just ridiculous". From Morgan (2000), women believe engineering is gender-neutral where merit and skills are held in high esteem; Geirit's discourses surrounding this anchor point reflected this notion of gender neutrality. Her skills were of merit to her, which she believed made her serious and not that her 'female-ness' would make her so. This resistance discourse was important because it highlights that not all anchor points had to be interpreted as 'simply' oppressive by the STEM-professional woman; there is room for resistance. Similarly, the attributed 'Leader' anchor point was, according to Geirit, a reflection of her technical knowledge and skills. Being the 'Leader' to her also meant that it reflected her outspokenness. This limited characterisation of leadership—outspokenness because you have the 'right' to be due to your merit and skills—is reflective of the NASA masculine discourses such as being "kings of the mountain" (Maier 1997, 954) and a "sober concern for facts" and of "making infallible decisions"(Schwartz 1989, 59, 63). Note that I did not consider this anchor point a social identity because of Geirit's oscillation between this extreme 'outspokenness' and her expressed doubts regarding whether her supervisor would agree with this 'outspokenness'.

This map of Geirit's identities reveals her intersecting identities. In her own discourses, she was a 'female' who was a PhD who embraced the 'take it or leave it' self-identity and who was unsure of assuming the social constructions of 'The Bitch' but wanted to be recognised as the 'Leader', assigning value to her merit and skills while specifically setting aside her 'female' gender in her sensemaking. It is noteworthy to underline that Geirit's focus on her merit and skills were in alignment with one of the HQP men who worked with her. The stories generated by Bramun, in particular, stated that to his mind, there was a job to get done and he didn't care who got it done.

Inenya

Inenya works within a public Canadian space organisation and is in the later career stage. Her discourses also revealed much of 'who I am' and 'who I am becoming', as did Geirit's discourses. Inenya's map of identities is shown in Figure 10.3.

Inenya's sense of 'who I am' was clearly stated and repeated in a number of stories she shared with me. She embraced her sense of humour as a self-identity, where no other participant in this study had done so. She also self-identified as being 'fierce', an identity that I found within this industry when others referred to HQP women exclusively. Being 'fierce'—often ascribed to these women via a number of discursive artefacts (e.g. emails announcing

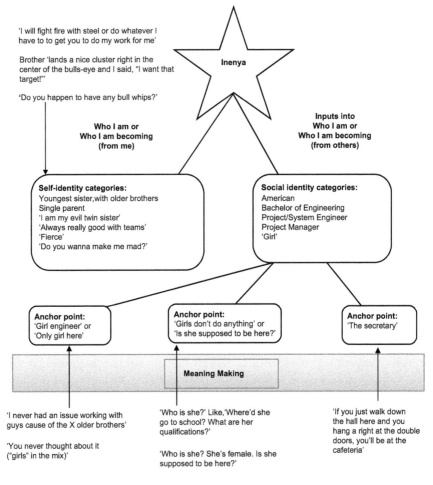

Figure 10.3 Inenya's Map of Identities

departures of HQP women, emails referring to HQP women who were closing acting appointments, etc.)—appeared to be an institutional meta-rule.
Inenya had clearly moved beyond the attribution of this possible anchor
point to embracing it in her discourses as 'who I am'. Examples of Inenya's
'fierceness' and her 'sense of humour' discourses are presented above her
self-identity box in Figure 10.3.

Inenya's social identities mostly encompassed her STEM-educational
background and her various HQP occupational roles. These STEM social
identities interacted and were interdependent with her 'girl'-ness, put into
evidence by her insistence that "they [men] all get together. I'd bring in muf-
fins and stuff" and her numerous references to "girl engineers":

> When I started working there were girl engineers in the 80s. I always
> had a team that when I first started, I was on a test team. And it was a
> mix. There were a couple girls, not a lot, but a couple (of) girls. But you
> never thought about it. It just wasn't . . . it wasn't an issue. It wasn't
> even a comment.

I found three anchor points in Inenya's discourse: the 'Only girl here', the
'Girls don't do anything' or 'Is she supposed to be here?'; and the 'Secretary'. Inenya's 'Secretary' anchor point, if you recall, was similar to my own
anchor point presented in my act of reflexivity in Figure 10.1. The other
two anchor points revealed a different discursive lived experience than
mine, however. For the 'Only girl here' anchor point, Inenya recounted
that at the beginning of her career, she never really noticed if she was the
'Only girl here', as highlighted in the story above. As far as Inenya was
concerned, this was a time when NASA astronauts Sally Wright and Judy
Resnick were important symbols to her and that overshadowed her 'Only
girl here' awareness. When she did (eventually) look around and reflect on
what she saw, she would ". . . sit there and you look up there . . . and it's all
white men". The (White) STEM-professional men around Inenya did make
attempts to include her:

> (One of the guy's said) "Let's not get into a pissing contest" and it just
> hit me one time when we were talking when he was saying that and
> I said, "Umm, unless you're talking duration, then I can't participate."
> So, every time after that, (male colleague) would say, "Let's not get into
> a contest that (Inenya) can't participate in". I just remember him saying
> that. And it would just like (be) silence around the table and every-
> body's like, "She's right. She can't participate in that one!"

This masculine 'pissing contest' discourse was a rather graphic visual representation of Inenya's 'Only girl here' anchor point. Her male colleagues
wanted to ensure her inclusion and would strive to find other 'contests' that
wouldn't need specific 'hardware'.

164 Stefanie Ruel

The middle of Inenya's career saw the appearance of another anchor point in her stories: 'Girls don't do anything' or 'Is she supposed to be here?' This anchor point, attributed by several men, can best be described as a call to her credentials in doing space and the fact that she was a 'female':

> "Who's this person?" "This is (Inenya). (Inenya's) going to be taking over. (Inenya's) got a lot of experience blah, blah, blah." He was like, "Who is she?" like, "Where'd she go to school? What are her qualifications? What's . . ." and I had walked in like a minute or so late . . . So he's going on and on and just like ripping me to shreds without even knowing me. And then finally my supervisor at the time said, "Um, she just entered the room". And so he shut up. And it was like, "Ahhhh . . . " really criticising me.

As the story around this anchor point continued, this was the point where Inenya constructed her alter ego, her 'evil twin'. She devised a curriculum vitae (CV) based on her evil twin and passed it around at a meeting. This one man who had attributed her 'Is she supposed to be here?' anchor point would, in her sensemaking, have tangible evidence that she 'belonged' and had the 'right' credentials.

The map of Inenya's identities demonstrate again the existence of interdependent and constituting identities. Specifically, per Inenya's discourse, she was a 'girl engineer' who embraced masculinist discourses—symbolically via a bullwhip and a perfect target which she displayed in her office—and who developed an alter ego as a (humorous) way to resist questions of her legitimacy around the table, pushing aside the anchor point of 'Is she supposed to be here?' and the 'Secretary'.

Conclusion

This study revealed one important aspect of 'doing space', namely the gendered discursive interactions of STEM-professional women and men. The impact of these gendering relations is reflected in two women's discursive processes and in their resultant identity maps. The revelation of these two individuals, via their self- and social-identities and range of anchor points, demonstrate the complexity of individuals and how they can be (re)created in such a way as to reveal the gendered discourses of the everyday.

What does the future hold for the Canadian space industry and these gendering relations? The industry will continue to attract individuals who subscribe to being innovators and pioneers. There will also continue to be an unequal and inequitable representation of women in the industry. This unequal and inequitable representation problem is due not only to the stagnant university graduation rates in STEM disciplines, or to the adherence to human resource critical mass ideologies. It is also due to the lack of recognition of the role of, and the impact of, gendering discourses within this industry. This study reveals the gendering nature of working in the space industry; however, there is much more work to be done both internally and externally to recognise the power-effects on who an individual is and who that individual is becoming.

Notes

1. In line with Nkomo and Cox (1999), I use diversity within the context of identities and the resultant (re)creation of many intersecting identities. The terms 'women', 'men' and 'transgendered' are used here as a form of classification that encompasses not only biological make-up (i.e. sex-based body and chromosomal classifications) but also the cultural, gendered experience that is attributable to these social positions. Given this construction, the body may play an integral part in the cultural meaning making surrounding 'women', 'men' and 'transgendered' but it is not explicitly addressed as a separate identity. There is an "essential incompleteness" (Butler 1990, 21) to these terms.
2. Personal communication with P. Tanguay, HR Advisor, 26 November 2013.
3. Social life refers to the "interconnected networks of social practices of diverse sorts (economic, political, cultural, family and so on)" (Fairclough 2001, 27). Social processes can have the following interrelated elements: productive activity, means of production, social relations, social identities, cultural values, consciousness and semiosis (Fairclough 2001).

References

AIAC (Aerospace Industries Accociation of Canada). 2015. *AIAC 2015–2016 Guide to Canada's Aerospace Industry*. AIAC. http://aiac.ca/guide/.
Ashmore, R., Deaux, K. and McLaughlin-Volpe, T. 2004. "An Organizing Framework for Collective Identity: Articulation and Significance of Multidimensionality." *Psychological Bulletin* 130(1): 80–114.
Boje, D. 1991. "The Storytelling Organization: A Study of Story Performance in an Office-Supply Firm." *Administrative Science Quarterly* 36(1): 106–126.
Boje, D. 2001. *Narrative Methods for Organizational and Communication Research*. Thousand Oaks, CA: Sage.
Boje, D. 2008. *Storytelling Organizations*. Thousand Oaks, CA: Sage.
Butler, J. 1990. *Gender Trouble*. New York, NY: Routledge.
Canadian Space Agency (CSA). 2012a. *CSA Demographic Profile and Organizational Review (2011–2012)*. Saint-Hubert: Author.
Canadian Space Agency (CSA). 2012b. *Alouette I and II*. Saint-Hubert: Author. www.asc-csa.gc.ca/eng/satellites/alouette.asp.
Canadian Space Agency (CSA). 2013a. *State of the Canadian Space Sector 2012*. Saint-Hubert: Author. www.asc-csa.gc.ca/pdf/eng/industry/state-2012.pdf.
Canadian Space Agency (CSA). 2013b. "Canada's Space Sector." *Canadian Space Agency Website*, July 22. www.asc-csa.gc.ca/eng/publications/spacesector.asp.
Canadian Space Agency (CSA). 2014. *CSA Demographic Profile 2012–2013, Version 2*. St-Hubert: Author.
Catalyst. 2013. "2012 Catalyst Census: Financial Post 500 Women Senior Officers and Top Earners." *Catalyst*. www.catalyst.org/knowledge/2012-catalyst-census-financial-post-500-women-senior-officers-and-top-earners-0.

Chu, H. 2006. "Being a Female Engineer: Identity Construction and Resistance of Women in Engineering Schools." PhD thesis, Texas A&M University. http://oaktrust.library.tamu.edu/bitstream/handle/1969.1/4364/etd-tamu-2006B-SOCI-Chu.pdf?sequence=1.

Corlett, S. and Mavin, S. 2014. "Intersectionality, Identity and Identity Work: Shared Tenets and Future Research Agendas for Gender and Identity Studies." *Gender in Management: An International Journal* 29(5): 258–276.

Crenshaw, K. 1989. "Demarginalizing the Intersection of Race and Sex: A Black Feminist Critique of Antidiscrimination Doctrine, Feminist Theory and Antiracist Politics." *University of Chicago Legal Forum* 1989: 139–167.

Crenshaw, K. 1991. "Mapping the Margins: Intersectionality, Identity Politics, and Violence Against Women of Color." *Stanford Law Review* 43(6): 1241–1299.

Fairclough, N. 2001. "Critical Discourse Analysis." In *How to Analyze Talk in Institutional Settings: A Casebook of Methods*, edited by A. McHoul and M. Rapley, 25–38. London: Continuum.

Faulkner, W. 2007. "'Nuts and Bolts and People': Gender-Troubled Engineering Identities." *Social Studies of Science* 37(3): 331–356.

Foucault, M. 1978. "Politics and the Study of Discourse." *Ideology & Consciousness*, Spring 1978(No. 3): 7–26.

Foucault, M. 1980. *Power/Knowledge: Selected Interviews and Other Writings 1972–1977*. Edited by C. Gordon. Translated by C. Gordon, L. Marshall, J. Mepham, and K. Soper. New York: Pantheon Books.

Fraser, N. 1989. *Unruly Practices: Power, Discourse, and Gender in Contemporary Social Theory*. Minneapolis: University of Minnesota Press.

Glenn, E. N. 2004. *Unequal Freedom: How Race and Gender Shaped American Citizenship and Labor [Kindle DX Version]*. Cambridge, MA: Harvard University Press.

Grant, D., Keenoy, T. and Oswick, C. 1998. "Introduction: Organizational Discourse: Of Diversity, Dichotomy and Multi-Disciplinarity." In *Discourse and Organization*, edited by D. Grant, T. Keenoy and C. Oswick, 1–13. Thousand Oaks, CA: Sage.

Hanappi-Egger, E. 2013. "Backstage: The Organizational Gendered Agenda in Science, Engineering and Technology Professions." *European Journal of Women's Studies* 20(3): 279–294.

Helms Mills, J. and Mills, A. 2009. "Critical Sensemaking and Workplace Inequities." In *Equality, Diversity and Inclusion at Work: A Research Companion*, edited by M. Özbilgin, 171–178. Cheltenham, UK: Edward Elgar.

Helms Mills, J., Thurlow, A. and Mills, A. 2010. "Making Sense of Sensemaking: The Critical Sensemaking Approach." *Qualitative Research in Organizations and Management: An International Journal* 5(2): 182–195.

Hill Collins, P. 2000. "Moving Beyond Gender: Intersectionality and Scientific Knowledge." In *Revisioning Gender*, edited by M. Marx Ferree, J. Lorber and B. Hess, 261–284. Walnut Creek, CA: AltaMira Press.

Jorgenson, J. 2002. "Engineering Selves Negotiating Gender and Identity in Technical Work." *Management Communication Quarterly* 15(3): 350–380.

Lang, J., Cruse, S., McVey, D. and McMasters, J. 1999. "Industry Expectations of New Engineers: A Survey to Assist Curriculum Designers." *Journal of Engineering Education* 88(1): 43–51.

Maier, M. 1997. "Gender Equity, Organizational Transformation and Challenger." *Journal of Business Ethics* 16(9): 943–962.

Marsden, R. 1997. "Class Discipline: IR/HR and the Normalization of the Work-force." In *Managing the Organizational Melting Pot: Dilemmas of Workplace Diversity*, edited by P. Prasad, A. Mills, M. Elmes, and A. Prasad, 107–128. Thousand Oaks, CA: Sage.

McCall, L. 2005. "The Complexity of Intersectionality." *Signs* 30(3): 1771–1800.

McHoul, A. and Grace, W. 2007. *A Foucault Primer: Discourse, Power and the Subject*. New York: New York University Press.

Mills, A. and Murgatroyd, S. 1991. *Organizational Rules: A Framework for Understanding Organizations*. Milton Keynes, UK: Open University Press.

Morgan, L. 2000. "Is Engineering Hostile to Women? An Analysis of Data from the 1993 National Survey of College Graduates." *American Sociological Review* 64(2): 316–321.

Nkomo, S. and Cox, T. 1999. "Diverse Identities in Organizations." In *Managing Organizations: Current Issues*, edited by S. Clegg, C. Hardy and W. Nord, 88–106. London: Sage.

Parker, I. 1992. *Discourse Dynamics*. London: Routledge.

Pavlenko, A. 2001. "Bilingualism, Gender, and Ideology." *International Journal of Bilingualism* 5(2): 117–151.

Perrot, M. 1980. "Table ronde du 20 mai 1978. L'Impossible prison: Recherches sur le système pénitentiaire au XIXe siècle. Dits Ecrits Tome IV texted n 278Web." http://1libertaire.free.fr/MFoucault300.html.

Phillips, N. and Hardy, C. 2002. *Discourse Analysis: Investigating Processes of Social Construction*. Thousand Oaks, CA: Sage.

Prism Economics and Analysis. 2012. "Current and Future Human Capital Needs in the Aerospace Industry and Strategies for Harnessing the Potential Workforce: A Report Prepared for The Aerospace Review." http://aerospacereview.ca/eic/site/060.nsf/vwapj/Aerospace_Human_Captial_Needs_-_Final_Report_draft_July_16.pdf/$FILE/Aerospace_Human_Captial_Needs_-_Final_Report_draft_July_16.pdf.

Ruel, S., Mills, A. and Thomas, J. 2015. *Intersectionality at Work: The Case of Ruth Bates Harris and NASA*. Administrative Sciences Association of Canada (ASAC) 2015 Conference, Gender and Diversity Division, Halifax, Nova Scotia. Accessed June 26, 2015. www.asac.ca/asac2015confrpp.

Schwartz, H. S. 1989. "Organizational Disaster and Organizational Decay: The Case of the National Aeronautics and Space Administration." *Organization & Environment* 3(4): 319–334.

Unger, R. 1987a. *Plasticity into Power*. Cambridge: Cambridge University Press.

Unger, R. 1987b. *Social Theory: Its Situation and Its Task*. Cambridge: Cambridge University Press.

Watson, T. 2008. "Managing Identity: Identity Work, Personal Predicaments and Structural Circumstances." *Organization* 15(1): 121–143.

Weick, K. 1995. *Sensemaking in Organizations*. Thousand Oaks, CA: Sage.

Weick, K., Sutcliffe, K. and Obstfeld, D. 2005. "Organizing and the Process of Sensemaking." *Organization Science* 16(4): 409–421.

11 Will the Head of Engineering Please Stand Up? The Underrepresentation of Women in Engineering

Susan Durbin and Ana Lopes

Introduction

Gender segregation in the UK labour market is persistent and partly the consequence of little change in the numbers of women employed in male-dominated industries. A number of these industries, some of which are economically critical, are facing skills shortages, which could be addressed through the recruitment and retention of more women (Munn 2014). There are currently 14.7 million women in employment in the UK (Deloitte 2016) out of a total workforce of just over 30 million. While women have entered some previously male-dominated professions in greater numbers such as human resources and law, they comprise just 13 per cent of the STEM (science, engineering, technology and mathematics) workforce, 11.5 per cent of STEM managers and just 5.7 per cent of engineers (WISE 2015).

This chapter examines a highly gender segregated area of employment—engineering—a profession where gender segregation begins at school, continues through to the workplace and is underpinned by gender stereotypical views of what constitutes 'men's work' and 'women's work' (Bradley 1989). The chapter offers an insight into what life is like for a sample of female engineers, specifically in relation to their numerical underrepresentation, how they think women engineers are perceived and the challenges they face as female professional engineers in male-dominated workplaces.

The chapter begins by presenting a general picture of the engineering sector, focusing on the aviation and aerospace industry. We then briefly review extant literature on women in male-dominated industries and engineering in particular. After a brief explanation of the methods used, we then present and discuss empirical material collected through 16 semi-structured interviews with female engineers who work in the UK aviation and aerospace industry, in an attempt to understand their work experiences, challenges and perceptions of how women are viewed in the industry.

Engineering and the Aviation and Aerospace Industry

The engineering sector is important to the UK economy, contributing 27.1 per cent of the total UK Gross Domestic Product (GDP) and employing over

5.5 million people, with approximately two-thirds employed as practising engineers and technicians (Kumar, Moss and Johnson 2016). Employers report a skills shortage in the sector, especially at technician and graduate levels, which is exacerbated by the majority of young women not choosing a career in engineering and half of those who graduate with engineering degrees opting not to follow an engineering career. This leads to a lack of gender diversity and the underutilisation of the female workforce. The UK compares poorly to other EU countries, such as Latvia and Sweden, where women make up 30 per cent and 26 per cent of engineers respectively (Kiwana, Kumar and Randerson 2011). It is claimed that increasing the numbers of women in STEM employment could contribute an additional £2 billion to the UK economy (Kumar et al. 2016). This skills shortage could be addressed by encouraging more women to join the profession and thereby enable employers to improve their 'bottom line'. But is this an attractive proposition for the women themselves, who may be deterred by the masculine image of engineering? Do the gendered power relations and the masculine culture in engineering need to be challenged before more women will set foot in engineering (Sharp, Franzway, Mills and Gill 2012)?

The shortage of women engineers and the segregation of women within it, begins in education and is reflected in employment figures. 'Leaks' in the pipeline of potential engineers begin at 'A' level[1] stage for women as just 20 per cent of physics 'A' level students are girls (Institute of Physics 2012). Girls tend to become attracted to engineering at the age of 11 but lose that interest by the age of 14, believing it to be 'unglamorous and anti-social' (Kumar et al. 2016). Poor careers advice and unacceptable stereotypes about STEM jobs, amongst other factors, means that many girls are not choosing engineering. Despite first degree achievements in engineering and technology being at an all-time high, just 15 per cent of those degrees were awarded to women and just over half of all female engineering and technology graduates entered engineering jobs. This is compounded by engineering attracting the lowest proportion of female applicants in the first place (Kumar et al. 2016).

The aviation and aerospace industry, where we conducted our research with female engineers, is particularly significant to the UK, contributing around 1.2 per cent of the total GDP and employing 300,000 directly and 700,000 indirectly. The industry has a persistent, ongoing skills shortage which could be addressed through recruiting and retaining more women (RAeS 2009; Munn 2014). However, in this industry, women tend to be segregated into occupations that are gender-typical, such as clerical, administrative, sales, human resources and marketing and remain very poorly represented in the industry-critical jobs such as pilots, senior managers, directors and, crucially, engineers. Interestingly, the Royal Aeronautical Society (RAeS), the professional body representing the aviation and aerospace industry, welcomed its first female president, Jenny Body, in 2013 and has a Women in Aviation and Aerospace Committee. The industry, however, remains one of the most underrepresented for female engineers and the second least likely destination for a female engineering graduate.

Women in Male-Dominated Industries: Challenges, Barriers and Stereotypes

This begs the question, why are women being deterred from following a career in engineering? Women who work in male-dominated industries face challenges that differ from those who work in female-dominated or gender balanced industries and sectors. Martin and Barnard (2013) argue that these challenges either emanate from organisational practices that, overtly or covertly, perpetuate discrimination, or from women having unique, physical work-identity and work-life balance needs that are not recognised in male-dominated environments. Many of these challenges and barriers to progression emanate from what Bradley (1989, 69) calls "gender work environments" or "work cultures", which both reflect and enhance segregation. Women in male-dominated industries may also feel that they are not accepted into certain roles, especially those that have been historically maintained as 'masculine' through masculine organisational practices (Mills 1998; Neal-Smith and Cockburn 2008; McCarthy, Budd and Isan 2015). Women end up being stereotyped as emotional and less committed to their work than their male colleagues (Von Hippel 2015). There is also a lack of role models, mentors and networks that could act as a means of support for women (Germain, Herzog, Hamilton and Hamilton 2012). Women thus find themselves having to prove their suitability for the job and to challenge the masculine norms in their industries and workplaces (Woodfield 2016).

The culture of presenteeism, long working hours and the expectation of infinite availability have also been identified as barriers to the retention of women and their progression in male-dominated industries. In a study of women working as civil engineers in the construction industry, Watts (2009) found that success was linked to being able to fit into these features of the dominant masculine culture and that the issue is experienced as particularly stressful by women with family commitments. Moreover, despite the introduction and development of family-friendly policies and legislation in the UK, combining work and caring/domestic responsibilities remains a persistent problem for the majority of working women, who still perform the majority of domestic and child-rearing responsibilities in the home, regardless of class or occupation (Sullivan 2000). Almost half of women in employment work part-time, which has been linked to low-quality work and with fewer possibilities for promotion (Durbin 2015; Durbin and Tomlinson 2010; 2014). Working part-time still carries a stigma, with part-time workers being considered uncommitted or peripheral (Alvesson and Billing 2009) and impacting negatively on one's professional identity (Watts 2009).

All of these factors lead to a 'leaky pipeline', with the continuous loss of women as they progress in STEM careers, underpinned by the prevalence of gender stereotyping (Damaske 2011). Although connected to the experiences of women in employment, stereotyping predates a person's entry to the labour market, starting early on, in the way boys and girls are socialised in the family and schools (Jenkins 2004; Powell 2011). While stereotypes also affect men, they are more detrimental for women because they can limit women's aspirations and occupations (Heilman 2012). The gender stereotypes are particularly harmful for women's occupations that seem to 'fit' with descriptive stereotypes about men and 'not to fit' with descriptive stereotypes about women (Caleo and Heilman 2014). This may lead to some women adopting masculine attributes, although they may find themselves in a new predicament, as they risk being seen as violating gender-normative expectations. Women in male-dominated industries may feel a disproportionate need to prove themselves when compared to their male counterparts (Smith 2013).

Women in Engineering: An Overview

Entry into the engineering profession follows several years of post-compulsory education and on-the-job professional workplace training. The low numbers of women in STEM occupations have been well-documented (Evetts 1998; Fox and Stephan 2001; Herman, Lewis and Humbert 2012). So why do women stay in engineering? Buse, Bilimoria and Perelli (2013) claim this is because female engineers are adaptable and have high levels of efficacy, identify as engineers and are motivated by the challenges of being an engineer but they also found that these women are less likely to be married and to have fewer children. In a study of female engineering students, Powell and Bagilhole (2006) found that their interviewees accepted gender discrimination, viewed the industry positively, valued their novelty status, were critical of other women and acted like 'one of the boys'. They argue that this indicates women may be assimilating to the dominant male culture and/or share the attitudes and values of their male colleagues or are 'fronting it out' (Evetts 1998) to become accepted by their male colleagues.

Engineering has been described as a 'masculine' profession that is unsuitable for women, as it is perceived as being 'tough, heavy and dirty' (Powell and Bagilhole 2006). Gender stereotypes of this nature have long functioned as exclusionary mechanisms. Holth's (2014) study of IT engineers demonstrates that while stereotypes can be challenged, entering an engineering career can be seen as a 'straight road' for men, following a natural connection to technology, and as a 'winding road' for women as it is seen as 'gender inauthentic', with women often asked to justify their career choices. Conversely, Cech, Rubineau, Silbey and Seron (2011) argue that the problem is that when compared to men, women tend to lack professional role confidence and this contributes to more women leaving the profession. Cech (2015) points out that men and women develop somewhat different professional identities and this has an impact on men's and women's intentions to remain or leave engineering.

Various strategies to try to increase the numbers of women entering engineering education and employment have enjoyed limited success (Durbin 2010; Powell et al. 2008). Government initiatives include the setting up and funding of Women in Science and Engineering (WISE) to tackle women's underrepresentation in science and engineering with a target to increase the numbers of women to 30% by 2020. On current figures, this looks challenging, particularly as funding to bodies such as WISE has been progressively cut and little has been done to address the lack of flexible working in some of these industries. Despite all of the above, there has been no significant advance in the gender diversity of the sector. As one of the authors of the UK Engineering (2016) report argues, the participation of women in engineering must change (Kumar et al. 2016).

Methods

This chapter is based upon 16 semi-structured interviews with female engineers (pseudonyms are used to protect their identities) in six large engineering companies in the aviation and aerospace industry. Interviewees are employed in a variety of engineering roles and at different levels such as professional or manager, spread across the UK public and private sectors (see Table 11.1 below). Interviews were conducted between February and May 2015, as part of a broader study on mentoring. Interviews were predominantly face-to-face in the interviewees' workplace with a small number by telephone. Interviews lasted approximately one hour and explored the interviewee's career history, the availability of mentoring support and experiences and challenges associated with working in a male-dominated industry (the latter being the focus of this chapter). Interview data was analysed by a team of three researchers, using thematic analysis, an approach chosen due to its embedded flexibility as it allowed us to follow pre-chosen themes that guided the interview questions as well as enabling us to spot emerging themes. The following section explores these themes in more detail.

Findings

Women Engineers as 'Tokens'

To set the context, we asked interviewees to identify the approximate percentage of female engineers in their organisations, estimates ranging from 5 to 10 per cent, which were in some cases higher than the industry average (WISE 2015). We then asked interviewees whether they felt that this lack of women's presence had any impact for women in the profession and several felt that it did. As an example, Nancy explained how she found it difficult to encourage more girls to become interested in engineering as part of her outreach work with schools. She also identified further challenges associated with returning from maternity leave and working part-time. She felt

Table 11.1 Participants' Profiles

Pseudonym	Sector	Contract	Length of Service (years)	Age	Ethnic Group	Marital Status	Children
Maria	Private	FT	5	26–35	White (Other)	Single	No
Linda	Private	FT	16.5	36–45	White (British)	Divorced/separated	No
Cristina	Private	FT	3	26–35	White (Other)	Living with partner	No
Jennifer	Private	FT	16	36–45	Mixed	Single	No
Margaret	Private	FT	6	26–35	White (Other)	Married	Yes
Dorothy	Private	PT	15	36–45	White (British)	Married	Yes
Nancy	Private	FT	24	Unknown	Unknown	Married	Yes
Helena	Private	FT	3	26–35	White (Other)	Unknown	No
Sandra	Private	PT	14	41–45	White (British)	Married	Yes
Donna	Private	FT	9.5	26–35	White (British)	Living with partner	No
Cynthia	Public	Unknown	2.5	Unknown	Unknown	Unknown	No
Ruth	Private	FT	5	Unknown	Unknown	Unknown	Unknown
Paula	Private	FT	2	26–35	White (Other)	Unknown	No
Angela	Private	FT	30	Unknown	Unknown	Unknown	Yes
Brenda	Public	FT	11	26–35	White (British)	Married	No
Pamela	Public	FT	10	Unknown	Unknown	Unknown	Unknown

this would perhaps not be an issue in a more gender-balanced industry. A lack of female role models was an issue for Paula, who felt that there was a 'prototype' of personality which normally made it to the higher grades. Interviewees were clearly aware of their token status and were able to cite several examples of how this manifests itself when trying to attract and retain women in engineering. Interviewees then told us their views on why they believed that women were so poorly represented in their industry.

The Underrepresentation of Women in the Industry

The poor perception of engineering as a profession in the UK, a lack of focus on engineering in schools/poor careers advice, the physical demands of the job and speculation about women planning families, which often did not fit in with a masculine work environment, were amongst the reasons cited by interviewees for women's underrepresentation.

Comparisons with other countries revealed an awareness of a much poorer representation of women in engineering in the UK. Maria, Cristina and Paula, all of whom had studied or worked abroad, pointed out that it was more acceptable for women to become engineers in other European countries. This, they reflected, could be 'a cultural issue', especially at university where numbers of women studying engineering are higher and engineering as a profession is more highly regarded than in the UK. One reflected that this may be due to a combination of the education system and social perceptions of what is an acceptable occupation for women.

Poor schooling, a lack of careers advice and the consequent misunderstanding of the role of an engineer were offered as some of the main reasons for women's poor representation (Institute of Physics 2012; Kumar et al. 2016). Jennifer articulated that this was possibly connected with both the 'preconditioning' of girls to consider certain roles and the belief that they should emulate their mothers and sisters to 'do things such as caring' (see Jenkins 2004; Powell 2011). She felt that women had to be a little nonconformist to follow an engineering career. For Helena, the main issue for women was that as children, they were led to believe that engineering was related to being male, which she felt pushed women back from choosing an engineering career. Donna's awareness of engineering was sparked by a close male relative, which she notes was quite common for other female engineers she had spoken to. Her belief was that women had to be 'quite thick-skinned' to survive in engineering. Ruth and Pamela also thought that the problem stemmed from engineering being perceived as a traditionally male environment with the perceptions of what women can and cannot do starting at school age.

Military engineers identified slightly different reasons: the physical aspects of the job and being posted to other countries, irrespective of whether the woman had children. Brenda and Pamela had recently had to make a choice between their next posting and a promotion (respectively) or starting a family. They both chose future career progression, their intention being to start a family once they had gained promotion.

How Women Engineers Are Perceived by Others

Women's underrepresentation in engineering was also linked to how the interviewees felt women engineers were generally perceived by others. This included the perception that engineering was a 'masculine' occupation with 'masculine characteristics' being required to do the job (Neal-Smith and Cockburn 2008; McCarthy et al. 2015), that women entering this male-dominated profession were 'unusual' and 'different' and that being on the receiving end of men's derogatory comments was part and parcel of being a female engineer.

Linda felt that the perception that engineering was 'masculine' and an unusual choice for women was linked to a widespread lack of understanding of engineering in the UK:

> If I say I work in engineering they [other people] imagine I wear a boiler suit and get greasy . . . so I think there is a combination of sides, let's say, in terms of an overall misunderstanding of what the role is about and therefore with that a surprise that it's a topic that, why would I would work in engineering, which doesn't have the same status as other professions in the UK?

For Angela, engineering was perceived as 'a mechanic type, dirty role' and maybe limited in scope, when in reality there is a broad range of roles that are not fully understood. During her time as an engineer, she had observed women entering engineering but then moving into areas such as HR or finance, which she felt was partly due to these areas being more acceptable for women and where they were more readily able to progress.

Dorothy felt that women were perhaps perceived as being less intelligent or technical than men. She saw this stereotype played out in the workplace, where she observed that while women tended to carry out most of the administrative tasks, men tended to deal with the ordering of parts and liaising with suppliers. She also felt that there was a perception that women under the age of 30 would go off and have children at some point, which meant they were not taken seriously by their managers. She explained the flexible working policy that was being rolled out in her organisation but pointed out that in all her time at the organisation, she had not seen a job advertised on a part-time basis. She believed part-time working was discouraged, which has implications for women returning to work after having children (Alvesson and Billing 2009). Nancy described the perception of women in the industry in two categories: the first category being women who are perceived as being very feminine, who cry or become upset quite easily and are quite fragile; the second category being women who are a little bit desensitised and probably act more like men.

Sandra began on a positive note, explaining that, provided women perform in their jobs, they can progress and that an ultimate increase in numbers would help to change perceptions and increase the flow of women to the top. But she also acknowledged that there was a perception that perhaps women needed to have certain masculine characteristics. In her own organisation, there was an expectation that women should not show their emotions at work. Ruth did not believe there was a stereotype of women in the industry, dispelling what she described as, the 'blokey' versus 'girly girls' perceptions, although she did acknowledge that people's perceptions were perhaps that to be an engineer, you had to be interested in cars or things perceived as being 'typically blokey'. As an engineer herself she simply wanted to be perceived as being good at her job and to take the 'woman factor' out of the equation.

Linda acknowledged that there were aspects to being in the industry that were unpleasant for women, citing wolf whistling on site and occasional aggressive behaviour by men. This made her feel uncomfortable as a female. While she felt she could live with most of this, she found aggressive behaviour a challenge and difficult to deal with. Cristina felt her organisation was doing quite well in trying to dispel negative perceptions of women in the industry but that there was still a long way to go. This view had been confirmed when she was on secondment with an airline where she had experienced male behaviours similar to those cited by Linda. Angela described how some men had found it difficult to adapt their style to working with women and thus ended up feeling uncomfortable and trying to avoid working with them. While Donna had initially felt there were no negative perceptions about women, over time she started to change her mind. She felt that the negative perception lay with the older male workers, near retirement age, who had grown up in a very different environment where there were no technical women.

Personal Challenges

Finally, we asked interviewees about any personal challenges they had experienced. Unsurprisingly, the majority identified a number of these, including, being the only woman in the room; challenges around childcare, maternity leave and part-time working; having to 'prove yourself' as a woman; resistance from men to being managed by a woman; and general sexism.

Dorothy discussed the challenges and stigma attached to part-time working and how its acceptability depended upon the attitudes of line managers. She believed that her organisation would abolish part-time working given the opportunity. She also raised the 'only woman' challenge in a technical team of men—all white and in their mid-fifties. She reflected on situations when her opinion was not taken into consideration as much as the more experienced males in the team and how this was exacerbated when she became the leader of the team itself.

Having to prove herself to gain acceptance because she was a woman in engineering had been an ongoing challenge for Cristina. She described 'older people' as having an 'old-fashioned mentality' and being 'a bit sexist sometimes'. Not being able to join in the male conversations centring around cars and sport also made her feel excluded: "so I think because I was not interested in all the same topics as these guys were, so I think I had to prove myself as a good engineer even though I don't talk about cars all the time."

Nancy had experienced sexism and offered the example of male colleagues not wanting to go away with her on business trips as they were nervous about going away with a woman. She felt she had 'proved herself' and had steadily progressed, finding it easier to work with her male colleagues. For Paula, having to prove herself meant demonstrating she had performed as well as or better than her male colleagues. In addition to undergoing the usual performance management reviews, based on objective criteria, she also felt that she was being assessed as a woman, believing the question 'when is she going to have children?' was at the back of the assessor's mind.

Cynthia's challenge was not being taken seriously because of her gender. A female colleague who had been promoted the year before had gone on maternity leave and she had heard a number of negative comments about this from her male colleagues. She felt that these male colleagues expected that she would also be going off on maternity leave soon and for that reason, were not regarding her as a serious candidate for promotion. More recently, upon attending a meeting in her role as head of engineering:

> I walked in and they said, 'could the head of engineering not make it then'! I said, 'I am the head of engineering' . . . because clearly you need to be engineering qualified to understand the details and they just assumed I was a business function leader with no practical experience.

She believed this would not have happened had she been a man.

The main challenge for Linda was being 'treated in a derogatory way', as some comments she had experienced had been inappropriate and sexist. A previous manager, whom she described as having a problem working with women, had been a particular challenge. Despite trying to build a relationship with him over a number of years, she finally gave up, which she felt negatively impacted on her career as he would not consider her for development or progression. Her replacement was a male 'hotshot' who was one of the boys and was evidently viewed as more credible to do the job. Jennifer revealed how she had to put up with inappropriate comments from male colleagues. Having studied and then worked in a male-dominated environment, she had been exposed to what she described as 'certain inappropriate comments and attitudes' to which she learned to either respond, react, ignore or defend herself. While she did not feel she had been discriminated against, there had been moments when certain colleagues had behaved inappropriately.

Pamela had encountered men who did not like working for women, which she attributed to being younger, less experienced and female. She believed there were definitely some people who still felt awkward answering to a female, particularly amongst the chief technical ranks with those who had been in the job a long time. She described it as 'very subtle' and something she could not always put her finger on, as it was more of a gut feeling. She had not experienced too much sexism until her second pregnancy, where-upon her male line manager's attitude towards her changed.

Discussion

Our analysis reveals a number of key themes that cut across the public and private sector divide, age groups and length of service/experience in the industry. There was a general awareness of the token status of women in the profession and its repercussions (Kanter 1977) and while increased pressure over performance, social isolation and role encapsulation have been widely discussed, in our study female engineers highlighted the relationship between this token status in the profession and the difficulties around attracting more young women. There was a feeling that if women were not merely 'tokens' and if there were more female role models, the profession would become much more attractive to young women. Tokenism was also linked to the part-time issue, with female engineers reflecting on the relation between part-time work and motherhood, either having seen other women with children who work part time being treated differently by their line managers (or colleagues) and having had responsibilities taken away from them, or experiencing this first-hand. This is also linked to some feeling that they have to make a choice between family and career, pointing out how part-time work has negative implications for women's careers (Durbin and Tomlinson 2010; 2014). This links to the issue of organisations failing to encourage and genuinely value part-time and flexible working, despite previous research which has shown that part-time workers can be as committed as their full-time counterparts (Warren and Walters 2002). Critically, unless social attitudes toward men's role in childcare, domestic chores and family life change, women who work part-time will continue to be at a disadvantage.

Our interviewees cited many reasons why women are underrepresented in their industry, ranging from the status of the engineering profession in the UK, early socialisation of boys and girls (Bradley 2012), through to the 'masculine' image of the profession (Powell and Bagilhole 2006; Evetts 1998). To this can be added having to 'prove yourself' as a woman, resistance from men to being managed by a woman and overt sexism. Poor schooling and a lack of careers guidance was another issue highlighted by many interviewees, as was the male culture within engineering, making women feel like they are the 'other'. The physical aspects of the job do not appear to be a particular deterrent for women, apart from women in the military. Being accepted as a woman and having to prove yourself were recurrent themes.

Conclusions

Breaking down the barriers and in particular, making it easier for women to enter skilled occupations in higher-paying male-dominated industries/occupations is widely considered to be one of the ways forward for improving gender equality. It is recognised that we urgently need to increase the numbers of women in engineering/STEM based on the business case argument, linked to the idea that this will help to address the skills gap and improve productivity in the sector. But until the gender power relations in engineering organisations (Sharp et al. 2012) are tackled, women will remain the outsiders in this male world. Women are deterred from engineering due to its 'masculine' and 'dirty' image (Powell and Bagilhole 2006; Evetts 1998) from a young age and many of those who do enter the sector change career or leave. This is worrying, but perhaps these women can see the writing on the wall.

This begs the question, why do some women choose a career in a profession that has both a negative image and is one of the most male-dominated professions in the UK? Our sample of women engineers has given us an insight into this. They decided they were going to follow this career early on, enjoyed the challenges of the job and most were intending to stay. While they were not deterred by the negative masculine image of engineering, they were, however, experiencing challenges related to their gender and satisfaction with career progression was mixed. It is therefore unsurprising that women are being deterred from pursuing a career in engineering at several points of the 'leaky pipeline' (at school, upon graduating and upon becoming mothers). Could this change if the numbers of women increased? So far, efforts in this area have enjoyed limited success. We are not arguing that increasing the numbers would automatically lead to gender equality, however, we do believe it would be a step in the right direction.

Perhaps the presence of more women professionals in a better 'gender-balanced' environment could lead to a more supportive culture, where women are assessed on their performance as engineers and not on their gender. This requires a greater change effort and flexibility from employing organisations, an increased self-reflection from men and greater help from those experienced women in engineering to support the young women contemplating or just starting out in engineering (Durbin 2015).

Understanding the educational backgrounds and employment experiences of those who choose a career in engineering offers some insights into why women do or do not choose this career path. It also helps to explain

why there are so few women in engineering, where cultural and gender stereotypes are played out from the critical formative years, when very little
help and support from teachers and careers advisers is available, through to
the workplace where there are a myriad of challenges for female engineers.
Change has to come and soon!

Note

1. 'A' level is a school-leaving qualification used in the UK.

References

Alvesson, M. and Due Billing, Y. 2009. *Understanding Gender and Organizations.*
London: Sage.
Bradley, H. 1989. *Men's Work, Women's Work.* Cambridge: Polity.
Bradley, H. 2012. *Gender*, 2nd ed. Cambridge: Polity.
Buse, K., Bilimoria, D. and Perelli, S. 2013. "Why They Stay: Women Persisting in
the Engineering Profession." *International Journal of Career Development* 10(3):
139–154.
Caleo, S. and Heilman, M. E. 2014. "Is this a Man's World? Obstacles to Women's
Success in Male-Typed Domains." In *Gender in Organizations: Are Men Allies
Or Adversaries to Women's Career Advancement?* edited by R. J. Burke and D. A.
Major. Cheltenham: Edward Elgar Publishing.
Cech, E. 2015. "Engineers and Engineeresses? Self-Conceptions and the Develop-
ment of Gendered Professional Identities." *Sociological Perspectives* 8(1): 56–77.
Cech, E., Rubineau, B., Silbey, S. and Seron, C. 2011. "Professional Role Confidence
and Gendered Persistence in Engineering." *American Sociological Review* 76(5):
641–666.
Damaske, S. 2011. "A 'Major Career Woman?' How Women Develop Early Expectations About Work." *Gender and Society* 25(4): 409–430.
Deloitte. 2016. "Trailblazing Transparency: Mending the Gap." www.gov.uk/govern
ment/publications/trailblazing-transparency-report-on-closing-the-gender-pay-
gap.
Durbin, S. 2010. "SET Women and Careers: A Case Study of Senior Female Scientists in the UK." In *Women in Engineering, Science and Technology: Education
and Career Challenges*, edited by A. Cater-Steel and E. Cater. IGI Global.
Durbin, S. 2015. *Women Who Succeed: Strangers in Paradise?* Basingstoke: Palgrave
Macmillan.
Durbin, S. and Tomlinson, J. 2010. "Female Part-Time Managers: Networks and
Career Mobility." *Gender, Work and Organization* 24(4): 621–640.
Durbin, S. and Tomlinson, J. 2014. "Female Part-Time Managers: Careers, Mentors
and Role Models." *Gender, Work and Organization* 21(4): 308–320.
Evetts, J. 1998. "Managing the Technology But Not the Organisation: Women and
Career in Engineering." *Women in Management Review* 13(8): 283–290.
Fox, M. F. and Stephan, P. E. 2001. "Careers of Young Scientists: Preferences, Pros-
pects and Realities by Gender and Field." *Social Studies of Science* 3(11): 109–122.
Germain, M., Herzog, M., Hamilton, J. R. and Hamilton, P. R. 2012. "Women
Employed in Male Dominated Industries: Lessons Learned from Female Aircraft

Pilots, Pilots in Training and Mixed Gender Flight Instructors." *Human Resource Development International* 14(4): 435–453.

Heilman, M. E. 2012. "Gender Stereotypes and Workplace Bias." *Research in Organizational Behavior* 32: 113–135.

Herman, C., Lewis, S. and Humbert, A. L. 2012. "Women Scientists and Engineers in European Companies: Putting Motherhood Under the Microscope." *Gender, Work and Organization* 20(5): 467–478.

Holth, L. 2014. "Passionate Men and Rational Women: Gender Contradictions in Engineering." *NORMA* 9(2): 97–110.

Institute of Physics. 2012. *It's Different for Girls: The Influence of Schools*. London: Author.

Jenkins, R. 2004. *Social Identity*, 2nd ed. London: Routledge.

Kanter, R. M. 1977. *Men and Women of the Corporation*. New York: Basic Books.

Kiwana, L., Kumar, A. and Randerson, A. 2011. *An Investigation into Why the UK Has the Lowest Proportion of Female Engineers in the EU*. London: EngineeringUK.

Kumar, A., Moss, A. and Johnson, E. 2016. *The State of Engineering*. London: EngineeringUK.

Martin, P. and Barnard, A. 2013 "The Experience of Women in Male-Dominated Occupations: A Constructivist Grounded Theory Enquiry." *South African Journal of Industrial Psychology* 39(2): Article #1099. DOI: 10.4102/sajip.v39i2.1099.

McCarthy, F., Budd, L. and Isan, S. 2015. "Gender on the Flight Deck: Experiences of Women Commercial Airline Pilots in the UK." *Journal of Air Transport Management* 47(5): 32–38.

Mills, A. J. 1998. "Cockpit Hangars, Boys and Galleys: Corporate Masculinity and the Development of British Airways." *Gender, Work and Organization* 5(3): 172–188.

Munn, M. ed. 2014. *Building the Future: Women in Construction*. London: The Smith Institute.

Neal-Smith, S. and Cockburn, T. 2008. "Cultural Sexism in the UK Airline Industry." *Gender in Management: An International Journal* 24(1): 32–45.

Powell, A. and Bagilhole, B. 2006. "The Problems of Women's Assimilation into UK Engineering Cultures: Can Critical Mass Work?" *Equal Opportunities International* 25(8): 688–699.

Powell, A., Bagilhole, B. and Dainty, A. 2008 "How Women Engineers Do and Undo Gender: Consequences for Gender Equality." *Gender, Work and Organization* 16(4): 411–428.

Powell, G. N. 2011. *Men and Women in Management*, 4th ed. London: Sage.

Royal Aeronautical Society—RaeS. 2009. *The Future of Women and Aviation: A Specialist Report by the Royal Aeronautical Society's Women in Aviation and Aerospace Committee*. London: Royal Aeronautical Society.

Sharp, R., Franzway, S., Mills, J. and Gill, J. 2012. "Flawed Policy Failed Politics? Challenging the Sexual Politics of Managing Diversity in Engineering Organisations." *Gender, Work and Organization* 19(6): 555–572.

Smith, L. 2013. "Working Hard with Gender: Gendered Labour for Women in Male Dominated Occupations of Manual Trades and Information Technology (IT)." *Equality, Diversity and Inclusion* 32(6): 592–603.

Sullivan, O. 2000. "The Division of Domestic Labour: Twenty Years of Change?" *Sociology* 34(3): 437–456.

Von Hippel, C. 2015. "Negative Stereotypes Stifle Women's Banking Careers." *American Banker*, 29 September, 180, 151.

Warren, T. and Walters, P. 2002. "Appraising a Dichotomy: A Review of 'Part-Time/ Full-Time' in the Study of Women's Employment in Britain." *Gender, Work and Organization* 5(2): 102–118.

Watts, J. H. 2009. "Allowed into a Man's World' Meanings of Work-Life Balance: Perspectives of Women Civil Engineers as 'Minority' Workers in Construction." *Gender, Work and Organisation* 16(1): 37–57.

WISE. 2015. "Women in the UK STEM workforce. Women in Science and Engineering." www.wisecampaign.org.uk/resources/2015/09/women-in-the-stem-workforce.

Woodfield, R. 2016. "Gender and the Achievement of Skilled Status in the Work-place: The Case of Women Leaders in the UK Fire and Rescue Service." *Work, Employment and Society* 30(2): 237–255.

12 Gender Experiences in a Female-Dominated Industry

The Case of Nurses in Thailand

Uraiporn Kattiyapornpong and Anne Cox

Introduction

Thailand, an upper middle income economy (World Bank 2016), is similar to any developing country in Southeast Asia where politics, laws and regulations are in the process of developing to meet the world standard of human rights. The issue of gender equality in Thailand has been evolving gradually. Thailand presents a 'gender paradox' (Vichit-Vadakan 2008; Bjarnegård 2009), where women's newly gained success in educational and economic spheres does not translate into gender equality in other spheres. Compared to neighbouring countries, the Thai government acknowledged gender equality relatively late when it was included in the Constitution in 1997. Women's role in Thai society continues to be influenced by Buddhist beliefs and cultural norms that emphasise the superiority of men. Yukongdi and Rowley (2009) argue that social attitudes towards women in Thailand have not kept pace with the changes in legislation.

This chapter looks at gender issues around nursing in Thailand, a female-dominated profession in a transforming but still largely traditional society. Issues of gender have been identified as being of considerable importance in explaining the position of nurses in developed countries (for example, Mackay 1990), however "the conceptualisation of gender varies from one country to another, depending on cultures, traditions and values" (Cubillo and Brown 2003, 285). This research contributes to the understanding of gender and how it affects working and power relationships in a non-Western context. The empirical study investigates how gender influences career choices and defines working and power relations between doctors of both genders and nurses of both genders, and how female nurses interpret issues of gender differences.

Focusing on nursing, this chapter asks whether and how gender shapes the choice of careers and influences the interactions of nurses with doctors and patients. It argues that gender segregation exists between the professions of medicine and nursing, founded on Thai traditional values and the social construction of a skills/caring dichotomy. The study also shows how the gender of nurses and doctors affects their interactions with co-workers and patients. It presents strong evidence of negative discrimination towards male nurses. Examination of nurses' attitudes to gender demonstrates that they are aware of the problem, however, they accept credential justifications of inequality between doctors and nurses and display a submissive attitude to gender issues at work.

Background

Traditional Values and the Status of Women

Gender inequality in Thailand is rooted in the nation's culture where inequality is seen as a societal practice (Chompookum and Derr 2004). A traditional Thai allegory describes Thai people as the legs of an elephant (an animal revered in Thai culture), the men being equated with the elephant's front legs and the women with the hind legs. Thus the role of men is, like the elephant's forelegs, to lead, while the role of women is to follow. This cultural perception of women's value has long played a significant role in determining their status in Thai society.

Confucian values have pervaded local cultures and resulted in patriarchal family relations among Thai people (Bao 2005). In addition, the principles of Buddhism have underpinned Thai culture and guided the lives of the vast majority of Thai people (Elliott and Gray 2000). From the Buddhist perspective, women are seen in a subordinate position compared to men (Kirsch 1975; 1982; Hantrakul 1988; Mills 1995; Tantiwiramanond 1998; Harrison 1997). Buddhist law does not allow women to enter the priesthood and their roles are restricted to more material, bodily-oriented activities, such as providing the monks with sustenance. Within the family, daughters are taught to serve their brothers (Vichit-Vadakan 1997). In this manner, Buddhist law has promoted male dominance, endorsing the notion of men holding supreme power while women are never accepted as leaders and must support men unquestioningly.

Historically, men were expected to be the breadwinners, while women were expected to stay at home and be responsible for domestic roles such as rearing children, housework and satisfying men's sexual desires (Patana 2004). The 1974 Constitution explicitly addressed gender issues and the civil-commercial code of 1976 freed women from requiring their husbands' consent for disposing of their property or travelling abroad (Pongsapich 1997). Although many national policies target women for further development, they are criticised for ineffective outcomes. For instance, Tantiwiramanond and Pandey (1997) observed that cooperation among women's institutions is not strong enough to upgrade the status of Thai women. Such organisations were constrained by problems such as a lack of staff, budget and other resources. Non-governmental organisations are also vulnerable in terms of funding and long-term sustainability. Pongsapich (1997) pointed out that national gender policies promote equal access to opportunity between men and women but failed to introduce a change in social values.

Women at the Workplace

In recent years the gender gap in educational attainment has been narrowing. From 1992, Thailand, like other middle- and high-income countries, experienced a reversal in the education gender gap as more female than male students enrolled in higher education (World Bank 2010). By 2000, girls were twice as likely to continue in schooling than boys in all regions (Archavanitkul, Lyson, Pattaravanich and Williams 2005) and they outperformed boys in secondary school participation and completion at the tertiary level. However, gender stereotyping is still apparent in Thai education. Women tend to choose to study the humanities and social sciences, while men prefer engineering, information systems and sciences, which tend to receive higher remuneration. Recently, the awareness of gender stereotyping within the national education system has increased and the curriculum has been revised to eliminate gender stereotyping and encourage girls to enter male-dominated fields, including politics.

Rapid economic growth has enhanced women's opportunities and challenged the pattern of gender segregation. During the last few decades, the Thai economy has undergone a structural transformation, with the reallocation of labour and capital away from agriculture to manufacturing and services. Most of the changes in the composition of the female paid labour occurred in the service sectors while men have shifted to new sectors such as electricity, gas, water supply or public administration, transportation and construction. Women are still employed in traditionally female occupations in health and social work, hotels and restaurants and education, while men are more likely to work in male-dominated occupations in construction, mining and public utilities (Bui and Permpoonwiwat 2015). Contemporary Thai women bear double obligations, one that conforms to the traditional social values and confines them to household duties, and the other of earning income for the family (Siengthai and Leelakulthanit 1994). As in other countries, women spend more time on household work than men, while working/studying a similar number of hours per day (National Statistical Office and Office of Women's Affairs and Family Development 2008).

Pay discrimination was made illegal in the 1997 Thai National Constitution (Section 26), which states that whenever the job is of the same type, quality and quantity, the basis of pay including working hours, overtime and holidays, must be equal regardless of the gender (Liamvarangkoon 2002). However, in spite of the increased labour market participation of women, there is a gender wage gap in most industries (Monk-Turner and Turner 2001; Son 2007; Elder 2010; Nakavachara 2010). For example, the wages for formal workers in the service sector were relatively equal at 54 Bahts per hour, but men in the agricultural sector earned 32 Bahts per hour, while women earned 30 Bahts per hour (94 per cent). In the industrial sector, on average women earned 82 per cent of the male rate. The average earnings of informal workers are less, with men in the agricultural sector earning 17 Bahts per hour and women 15 Bahts per hour (88 per cent) and in the industrial sector men earned 23 Bahts per hour, compared to women's wages of 18 Bahts per hour (78 per cent). In the service sector, the income gap was the smallest, with men earning 25 Bahts per hour and females earning 24 Bahts per hour (96 per cent) (Pooittiwong 2016, 36–37). Some researchers argue that the gender wage gap is narrowing due to an improvement in women's education achievements, especially in higher education (Adireksombat, Fang, and Sakellariou 2010; Nakavachara 2010; van der Meulen Rodgers and Zveglich 2012).

Nursing—A Female-Dominated Profession

This study argues that the dominant coalition (men) works to reproduce itself in a systematic manner and strives to 'carefully guard power and privilege' (Kanter 1977, 48) and thus the status quo of male domination in managerial structures is maintained. This systematic reproduction is accomplished by the hiring and promoting of other men and poses a structural barrier that prevents the advancement of women in many occupations and "reproduces male hegemony" (Stangl and Kane 1991, 59), when men are overrepresented in an organisation or occupation.

The situation in the health care industry is different as more than 90 per cent of nurses are women and therefore men are a numerical minority (Kouta and Kaite 2011; Perkins 2016). Despite the numerical superiority of women, gender discrimination exists in nursing careers (Kouta and Kaite 2011). Porter (1992) concludes that gender affects nursing in three interconnected ways: it is devalued as it is women's work; gender over-determines inter-occupational inequalities in the male-predominant profession of medicine; and the development of a predominantly male managerial elite is an increasing issue of gender inequality. Moreover, barriers influencing gender inequality in nursing still exist, namely the image of nursing as a nurturing role, cultural/social expectations on gender roles, gender-role stereotypes, opportunities for nursing education, stable economic rewards condition and career development opportunities (Kouta and Kaite 2011; Porter 1992).

Theoretical Framework

At the macro level, traditionally institutions were defined as formal political structures and organisations (Mackay and Meier 2003), but new institutionalism defines institutions as comprising "rules, informal structures, norms, beliefs and values, routines and conventions and ideas about institutions" (Mackay and Meier 2003, 6). Lane (1992) emphasised the values and interests of powerful social actors, arguing that "if institutions are conceived of as concrete manifestations of societal values and norms, then it appears logical to specify that values and norms are seen to be congruent with given institutional structures" (37). Gender "is a crucial dimension in the study of institutions" (Mackay and Meier 2003, 2) and major social divisions such as gender, class and race are key elements in understanding institutional resistance to change. This also indicates that the social position of individuals is not only laid down by their capital, but also modelled on the gendered value given by society (Skeggs 2004).

At the organisational level, Acker (2006, 443) argued that "all organizations have inequality regimes, defined as loosely interrelated practices, processes, actions, and meanings that result in and maintain class, gender, and racial inequalities within particular organizations". She pointed out that these regimes are linked to inequality in the surrounding society, its politics, history and culture. Gendered and sexualised assumptions result in continuing inequalities in all organisations (Acker 2009). The gendered substructure is persistent as it is created and maintained in the organising processes in which inequalities are built into job design, wage determination, distribution of decision-making and supervisory power, the physical design of the work place, and rules, both explicit and implicit, for behaviour at work (Acker 2012).

Research specifically relating to women in the workplace and the unequal power relations includes Kanter's (1977) investigation of the lives of female managers in an American corporation, which was reaffirmed in her 1987 study which concluded that career success, motivation and productivity are largely determined by organisational structure and social circumstance rather than by an individual's ability and/or competence (Kanter 1987).

More recent research produced many "rich descriptions" of how power is produced and reproduced through gender (Kenny and Mackay 2009, 275).

Methodology

The largely exploratory nature of the research, the need to examine in detail the gendered experience in the female-dominant career of nursing in Thailand perceived by female nurses and the importance of contextualising their experience meant that qualitative methods were the most appropriate strategy (Yin 1994; Kelly 1999). A qualitative method also provided a sophisticated instrument to capture the often subtle, complex and changing ways in which nurses operated. It allowed unpacking nurse behaviour and experience at work under intertwined interactions with different actors (other nurses, doctors and patients).

Twelve female nurses who worked in public and private hospitals in Bangkok were selected using convenience and snowball methods. Respondents were registered nurses with bachelor's degrees and were aged from 24 to 48 years. Most (eight nurses) had between two and six years professional work experience, and two had more than 20 years of experience (see Table 12.1). Interviews of 30 to 45 minutes were conducted in October 2016.

Table 12.1 Participants' Profiles

Nurse	Age	Years of Experience	Work Unit/ Department	Career Level	Hospital Type
Mary	36	14	Out-patient department	Supervisor	Private
Patricia	26	4	Premium in-patient ward	Nurse level 2	Private
Susan	48	26	Management	Head of Nursing Department	Government
Nadia	28	6	Children's in-patient ward	Nurse level 2	Private
Anita	25	3	Fertility unit	Nurse level 1	Private
Valerie	38	16	Disease prevention and control	Head of Nursing Department	Government
Jennifer	46	24	Anesthesiology	Supervisor	Government
Elaine	24	2	General practice	Nurse level 1	Government
Casey	24	2	Men's health	Nurse level 1	Government
Tanya	25	3	Women's health	Nurse level 1	Government
Helen	27	5	Midwifery	Nurse level 2	Private
Tina	29	4	Dermatology	Nurse level 2	Private

The use of semi-structured interviews allowed the interviewees to dictate the character of information, at least to some extent, and allowed new issues to emerge.

The interview questions focused on two major themes: respondent's profile, including job role, type and level, nursing education and work place; and perspective/attitude on nursing career and social/cultural expectation on gender role including experiences regarding working relationships and power relationships between male/female nurses, male/female doctors and with patients. English interview questions were translated into the Thai language and reviewed by two Thai nurses. Then the revised Thai-version questions were translated back into English to ensure they were valid and correctly translated. All interviews were recorded and transcribed, then translated into English, and the back translation was applied again prior to data analysis. The Nvivo program was used to analyse data. The findings focus on two themes: tradition defines career choices; and gender defines relationships and powers at work and discrimination against male nurses.

Traditions Define Career Choices

Nursing is considered a suitable career for women because women, as an extension of their maternal functions, are seen to possess expressive, emotional and caring qualities, while men are seen as 'naturally' more instrumental, rational, scientific and decisive (Porter 1992). Hearn (1982) describes this social construction as 'patriarchal feminine'. 'Feminine' because it accords to the feminine caring stereotype and 'patriarchal' because in doing so it reinforces female subordination. This is especially the case in Thailand, where the negative traditional cultural perception of women's value is tied with domestic roles such as rearing children, caring for other family members and if they work outside the house, engaging in low-status, gender-stereotyped jobs. Interviewees perceived nursing as a suitable career for women due to these gender stereotypes. Susan noted that:

> when we think about a nursing career, nursing is the caring job that requires nurses to touch the patients in order to provide treatment; it is not just communication and conversation. The nature of the job requires nurses to be gentle and attentive to detail. It is not appropriate for male nurses to touch female patients. Thai social expectations demand that nursing is performed by females because of its physical nature. When we look at traditional Thai family roles, the duty of caring is designated to females.

Society's expectations are reinforced by family pressure. Showing gratitude and paying back the gratitude to parents are expected. Children, especially girls, are taught that it is their duty to repay their parents throughout their lives through performing household chores, giving money to their parents monthly when they work and caring for their parents. Many interviewees revealed the pressure of being a daughter, especially the eldest child. Casey observed that:

> My family strongly influenced me to choose nursing, especially my father, who thinks that this career is suitable for women. I am also the eldest and it was expected that I would look after my family, especially when my parents got old.

Families encouraged their daughters to pursue a nursing career because it is perceived as a way to raise the families' status. Anita commented: "I chose nursing as my career because my family encouraged me. In a country town, nursing is considered a very good job. It is a respectable and honoured job. It is distinguished and worthy for upcountry people".

Apart from the effect of tradition and family pressure, the findings highlight the influence of personal circumstances, especially when someone in the family became ill. Valerie selected

> nursing because I can help take care of my family when they are ill. . . . When I was in grade 10 my father had an accident and needed a brain operation. I was so worried and wanted to know about his condition and ways to help him. So if I studied nursing, I would be able to know what was going on and how to help my father, how to talk to the doctors to get more detailed information and treatment alternatives.

Due to a shortage of nurses and increasing demands in the health sector, there is a need to increase the number of male nurses. Cultural stereotypes posed a strong barrier for men to enter this profession, as Tanya's views illustrate: "it would be said that they [men] could have done something better than taking a female job. They would not be seen as important doing this job and looked down on as it is can be done by females". Interviewees saw the importance and need of having more male nurses and believed economic factors were important in the men's decisions to undertake nursing. Patricia had talked to some male nurses about this: "One of them said his parents wanted him to study nursing as it would be easy to find a job as nurses are in demand. Nurses will not be unemployed. Therefore it is about job security".

Gender Defines Relationships and Powers at Work

Doctors and nurses work together to in hospitals and the health care system, yet a power differential clearly exists between the male-dominated profession of medicine and the female-dominated profession of nursing (Manias and Street 2001; Reynolds and Timmons 2005; Reeves, Nelson and Zwarenstein 2008; Siedlecki and Hixson 2015; Vasey and Mitchell 2015). For Patricia:

> it is definitely a different status with doctors . . . some have quite high egos, some have unrealistic expectations that nurses have to know everything. . . . If we cannot answer their questions, they will not talk to us again and they will report to our Head of Nurses that we have no knowledge in doing our job . . . We do not really receive any respect from doctors.

While Anita noted that:

> There is discrimination between doctors and nurses in my workplace. They [hospitals and staff] always treat doctors better as they are seen as higher roles and status. The doctors can have very large egos and be arrogant. In private hospitals, we have to call them 'Master Doctor' or 'Professor'.

Jennifer concluded however, that "it is like India's social caste system. . . . They [doctors] are in much higher positions. They are so big in the hospital in Thailand".

In most cases nurses accepted that the superior position of doctors was due mainly to their credentials, but this did not mean that they saw doctoring as a more important facet of health care than the activities of nurses. Most nurses feel that they are closer to patients and know more about them than doctors. Nadia commented that:

> Doctors normally ask about the patients' well-being and any progress. As nurses are with the patients all the time, they will believe us . . .

Sometimes, some doctors or new doctors will ask about new medications if they do not know. So nurses provide their knowledge and experience of using such medication.

There is an acceptance apparent in female nurses concerning doctors' assumptions about their inferior gender and occupational roles. The value judgements that they attached to this fact are deeply rooted in the belief of the inferiority of females' ability compared to that of males. Mary remarked that "I did not choose to be a doctor because I thought it would be too difficult for me; I had no possibility to pursue that course". This view was echoed by Valerie: "I thought I might not be smart enough or good enough to be a doctor, so I did not think I could study to be a doctor". Bhanthumnavin (2003) observed that Thai women are more vulnerable to social influence in the workplace than men, and are more sensitive to work conflicts than men. It is worth noting that some female nurses chose to avoid conflicts by lowering their self-value and push themselves to work harder to compensate for their 'shortcomings'. As Patricia observed:

> We have to be humble and accept the fault that we did not know every new medicine and their side effects. And we will do further study in order to keep up to date and be able to answer the questions next time.

Interviewees believed that most male doctors preferred to work with female nurses if they could. Jennifer said that "I notice that male doctors prefer or like to work with female nurses . . . I feel that female nurses have more advantages than male nurses, especially when working with male doctors". Thai female nurses try to avoid conflicts by working hard and maintaining harmonious relationships with male doctors as part of their working style and rely on their femininity to negotiate at work. As Helen observed, "Female nurses can plead or use their femininity to ask for compassion and gentler treatment. Male nurses cannot do such things". This can be related to the work of other researchers who view the nurse-doctor relationship as patriarchal and draw parallels between the husband-wife relationship in the family (Dingwal and McIntosh 1978; Porter 1992; Sweet and Norman 1995).

In contrast, the relationship between male doctors and male nurses does not appear to function as effectively as male doctors and female nurses. In Jennifer's view:

> Male doctors and male nurses sometimes clash. In the case that the nurse does something wrong, if it is a female nurse, the male doctor typically will not complain too much or use harsh words. But if it is a male nurse, the male doctor will be very awful to the male nurse.

Interviewees believed that female doctors attempt to avoid working with male nurses if possible. This can be explained through gender role stereotypes as societal and cultural perceptions play important parts in this situation. Female doctors do not feel comfortable giving orders to male nurses due to gender role stereotype and society and cultural perceptions of the submissive role of females. Jennifer noted that:

> Female doctors are comfortable with female nurses. They prefer to work with female nurses than male nurses. It is because in the Thai cultural system it is seen as fitting for female nurses to receive order from the doctors, but it is not the case with male nurses. It is very much like the situation where a parent wants something or wants to ask for a favour, they will ask a daughter, not a son because a daughter will be more disciplined and more obedient compared to a son.

Discrimination Against Male Nurses

Male nurses face discrimination at entry level, a condition seen in Western countries (see for example, Keogh and O'Lynn 2007). In Thailand nursing schools limit the number of male students. Patricia reported that this was "no more than 20 per cent of all nursing students. The male applicants are typically less than the restriction anyway". Although many studies (for example, McCucheon 1996; Fisher 1996; Loughrey 2008) confirm no significant difference in masculinity and femininity between male and female nurses, male nurses are still seen as deviant, gays, homosexuals, low achievers and feminine-like (Porter 1992; Loughery 2008). In the Thai language, the word 'nurse' represents female nurses, while the counter-gender term is 'male nurse'. As we can observe, the use of language reflects the society's perception of this gendered industry. Casey described her views of the male nursing students:

> There were very few male nursing students. Some were female-like. I felt pity for straight men [who attended the nursing course], as no girls would date them. Most of the male nursing students were unattractive. Compared to the doctor students, even if they were so ugly, the girls still saw them as attractive because they were doctors.

Male nurses face discrimination in work allocation. The profession of nursing developed in the 20th century as a female profession, and this legacy can carry over into nurse-patient relationships. Patients also don't prefer male nurses, especially female patients who need intimate care. Mary discussed this in her interview:

> Due to Thai traditional culture and the need for privacy, male nurses may find it difficult to work in some sections of the hospital as patients are more comfortable with female nurses. There have been a few cases

where they had male nurses, but ended up calling for female nurses because the male nurses were not supposed to expose/see the private parts of female patients. . . . Heads of Nursing and supervisors will have to assign jobs to female nurses for patients that require close care. Some tasks are simply not suitable for male nurses. Patients do not feel comfortable receiving personal care from male nurses.

Responding to patient demand, Nursing Heads take Thai cultural norms and tradition into consideration when assigning tasks to nurses. Discrimination against male nurses in work allocation then becomes unavoidable, and some interviewees discussed the restricted work allocation of male nurses. Mary commented: "Male nurses are assigned to only a few departments that are suitable for male nurses, for example, emergency unit, ICU, or specific male care/treatment units". Patricia described even more restrictions:

Male nurses at my hospital only work in the emergency unit. They are not allowed to work in the ward. The night shift consists of only one staff member, so male nurses are not appropriate to look after patients at any time. All foreign patients in this premium ward require female nurses as male nurses are not allowed to touch female patients due to religious and traditional practices.

Although being male is seen as of high value in a patriarchal system, role tension in nursing still exists. Research has found that male nurses are motivated to upgrade their professional status (Dassen, Nijhuis and Philipsen1990) and achieve administrative and elite specialty positions to be distinctive from female nurses (Evans 1997; Ozdemir, Akansel and Tunk 2008). This is also the case for Thai male nurses, where it is usual for them to undertake further studies and progress their career in administrative and managerial roles. Male nurses are invariably regarded as being on their way to higher levels or managerial positions because of their gender. Thus their gender opens up greater career opportunities in the future but it does not give them any advantage over their female counterparts in their hospital work after graduation.

Conclusion

This chapter on the nursing profession in Thailand and is based on interviews with a small number of participants and the one-sided (female) perspective only. This study only collected data from female nurses in Bangkok, and there is a need for wider research within Thailand. This exploratory study reveals the impacts of tradition, society and culture on women's choice of nursing career in Thailand. Thai women are regarded as inferior to men as a result of the practice of Buddhism and traditional social values. However, nursing is seen as a suitable career for women, and family expectation is a main influence in choosing nursing career. This is consistent with research in Western contexts on the stereotype of nursing profession as a female career. Caring for others, including their intimate bodily needs, reinforces nursing as a female career, and limits the roles male nurses can play in Thai culture, where men are not allowed to touch women.

This study points out that gender plays a significant role in the interactions, working and power relationships between doctors and nurses. In many cases, it has negative impacts and corrodes working relationships in the hospitals. It is interesting to see the female nurse interviewees report that femininity can give female nurses an advantage in working with male doctors. This research also finds that most Thai female nurses try to avoid conflicts by working hard and maintaining harmonious relationships with male doctors as part of their working style. This perhaps adheres to Thai social norms and Buddhism, which focuses on harmony (Maneerat, Hale and Singhal 2005). Polite manners are favoured particularly by women (Patana 2004). On the other hand, although female doctors have accumulated education and experience in a doctor role and have gained highly respectable status over time, when it comes to gender roles between male and female, their subconscious recognition of male superiority seems to hinder the way they think and act towards male nurses.

There is a distinctive cultural barrier between male nurses and patients. Female nurses are often explicitly required by patients, especially female patients who need intimate care.

This study provides as an excellent example of reserved discrimination in a female-dominated industry. Studies in the US and other Western countries show substantial gender bias and barriers against males being nurses (Curtis, Robinson and Netten 2009; LaRocco 2007; O'Connor 2015; O'Lynn 2004; Whittock and Leonard 2003). In Thailand, the biggest career barrier for male nurses comes from the role that society expects them to play. Thai gender stereotypes socialise women to become emotional and nurturing while men are taught to be rational and aggressive (Yingchoncharoen 2007). Therefore, masculine characteristics are not welcome in Thai nursing. Gender orientation of male nurses is automatically and irrelevantly questioned when they choose to pursue a career in nursing.

This study found that although Thai women are aware of the existence of gender inequality in the hospitals and see how this affects their working life, but they largely accept such discrimination. The gender-based attitude that men are more suitable for leadership (doctor role) is widely accepted among Thai women in nursing. Such a belief originates from Thai traditional values and female nurses act in compliance with these gendered roles. According to the liberal feminist lens which focuses on the notion of rights and equality (Holmes 2007), Thai women are seen as equal to men, confirmed in the Thai Constitution and reinforced by their advancement and achievement in education, yet the actual gains for women are still limited. Although they have accumulated human capital, Thai female nurses' status at work is greatly diminished by social norms and organisational values. This finding indicates that the social position of individuals is not only laid down by their capital, but also modelled on the value given to their gender by society.

References

Acker, J. 2006. "Inequality Regimes Gender, Class, and Race in Organizations." *Gender and Society* 20(4): 441–464.

Acker, J. 2009. "From Glass Ceiling to Inequality Regimes." *Sociologie du Travail* 1(2): 199–217.

Acker, J. 2012. "Gendered Organizations and Intersectionality: Problems and Possibilities." *Equality, Diversity and Inclusion: An International Journal* 31(3): 214–224.

Adireksombat, K., Fang, Z. and Sakellariou, C. 2010. *The Evolution of Gender Wage Differentials and Discrimination in Thailand: 1991–2007—an Application of Unconditional Quantile Regression*. MPRA Paper No. 27516.

Archavanitkul, K., Lyson, T., Pattaravanich, A. and Williams, L. 2005. "Inequality and Educational Investment in Thai Children." *Rural Sociology* 70(4): 561–583.

Bao, J. 2005. *Marital Acts: Gender, Sexuality, and Identity Among the Chinese Thai Diaspora*. Honolulu: University of Hawaii Press.

Bhanthumnavin, D. 2003. "Perceived Social Support from Supervisor and Group Members' Psychological and Situational Characteristics as Predictors of Subordinate Performance in Thai Work Units." *Human Resource Development Quarterly* 14(1): 79–97.

Bjarnegård, E. 2009. "Thailand—Approaches to the Gender Paradox." In *Women and Politics Around the World*, edited by J. Gelb and M. Lief-Palley, Santa Barbara, CA: ABC-CLIO.

Bui, T. and Permpoonwiwat, C. 2015. "Gender Wage Inequality in Thailand: A Sectoral Perspective." *International Journal of Behavioral Science* 10(2): 19–36.

Chompookum, D. and Derr, C. 2004. "The Effects of Internal Career Orientations on Organizational Citizenship Behavior in Thailand." *Career Development International* 9(4): 406–423.

Cubillo, L. and Brown, M. 2003. "Women into Educational Leadership and Management: International Differences? *Journal of Educational Administration* 41(3): 278–291.

Curtis, L., Robinson, S. and Netten, A. 2009. "Changing Pattern of Male and Female Nurses' Participation in the Workforce." *Journal of Nursing Management* 17: 843–852.

Dassen, T., Nijhuis, F. and Philipsen, H. 1990. "Male and Female Nurses in Intensive-Care Wards in the Netherlands." *Journal of Advanced Nursing* 14(4): 387–393.

Dingwal, R. and McIntosh, J. 1978. *Readings in the Sociology of Nursing*. Edinburgh: Churchill Livingstone.

Elder, S. 2010. "Women in Labour Markets: Measuring Progress and Identifying Challenges." www.ilo.org/empelm/pubs/WCMS_123835/lang—de/index.htm.

Elliott, S. and Gray, A. 2000. *Family Structure: A Report for the New Zealand Immigration Service*. New Zealand: Department of Labour.

Evans, J. 1997. "Men in Nursing: Issues of Gender Segregation and Hidden Advantage." *Journal of Advanced Nursing* 26: 226–231.

Fisher, M. 1996. "Sex Role Characteristics of Males in Nursing." *Contemporary Nurse* 8(3): 65–71.

Hantrakul, S. 1988. "Prostitution in Thailand." In *Development and Displacement: Women in Southeast Asia*, edited by G. Chandler, N. Sullivan and J. Branson, 115–136. Clayton, VIC: Centre of Southeast Asian Studies, Monash University.

Harrison, R. 1997. "The 'Good', the 'Bad' and the Pregnant: Why the Thai Prostitute as Literary Heroine Can't Be Seen to Give Birth." In *Women, Gender Relations and Development in Thai Society*, edited by V. Somswasdi and S. Theobald, 323–348. Chiang Mai: Chiang Mai University Press.

Hearn, J. 1982. "Notes on Patriarchy, Professionalization and the Semi-Professions." *Sociology* 16: 184–202.

Holmes, M. 2007. *What Is Gender? Sociological Approaches*, 1st ed. London: Sage.

Kanter, R. M. 1977. *Men and Women of the Corporation*. New York: Basic Books.

Kanter, R. M. 1987. "Men and Women of the Corporation Revisited." *Management Review* 76: 14–16.

Kelly, D. 1999. "Making a Good Case: The Case Study." In *Researching Industrial Relations*, 2nd edition, edited by D. Kelly, 119–135. Sydney: Federation Press.

Kenny, M. and Mackay, F. 2009. "Already Doin' It for Ourselves? Skeptical Notes on Feminism and Institutionalism." *Politics and Gender* 5: 271–280.

Keogh, B. and O'Lynn, C. 2007. "Male Nurses Experiences on Gender Barriers: Irish and American Perspectives." *Nurse Educator* 32: 256–259.

Kirsch, A. 1975. "Economy, Polity and Religion in Thailand." In *Change and Persistence in Thai Society*, edited by G. W. Skinner and A. T. Kirsch, 172–196. Ithaca, NY: Cornell University Press.

Kirsch, A. 1982. "Buddhism, Sex-Roles and the Thai Economy." In *Women of Southeast Asia*, edited by P. Van Esterik, 13–32. Dekalb, IL: Northern Illinois University Press.

Kouta, C. and Kaite, C. 2011. "Gender Discrimination and Nursing: A Literature Review." *Journal of Professional Nursing* 27(1): 59–63.

Lane, C. 1992. "European Business Systems: Britain and Germany Compared." In *European Business Systems: Firms and Markets in Their National Contexts*, edited by R. Whitley. 65–97. London: Sage.

LaRocco, S. 2007. "A Grounded Theory Study of Socialising Men into Nursing." *Journal of Men's Studies* 15: 120–129.

Liamvarangkoon, S. 2002. *Effect of Gender Role on Career Advancement in Thai Civil Service*. Bangkok: National Institute of Development Administration.

Loughery, M. 2008. "Just How Male Are Male Nurses?" *Journal of Clinical Nursing* 17: 1327–1334.

Mackay, F. and Meier, P. 2003. "Institutions Change and Gender—Relations: Towards a Feminist New Institutionalism?" Paper presented at the European Consortium for Political Research Joint Sessions of Workshops, Edinburgh, 28 March–2 April.

Mackay, L. 1990. "Nursing: Just Another Job?" In *The Sociology of the Caring Professions*, edited by P. Abbott and C. Wallace. 54–72. London: Falmer.

Maneerat, N., Hale, C. and Singhal, A. 2005. "The Communication Glue that Binds Employees to an Organization: A Study of Organizational Identification in Two Thai Organizations. *Asian Journal of Communication* 15(2): 188–214.

Manias, E. and Street, A. 2001. "The Interplay of Knowledge and Decision Making Between Nurses and Doctors in Critical Care." *International Journal of Nursing Studies* 38(2): 129–140.

McCucheon, L. 1996. "Male Nurses: More Like John Does Than Jane Doe." *Psychological Reports* 79: 1227–1232.

Mills, M. 1995. "Attack of the Widow Ghosts: Gender, Death and Modernity in Northeast Thailand." In *Bewitching Women, Pious Men: Gender and Body Politics in Southeast Asia*, edited by A. Ong and M. Peletz, 244–273. Berkeley, CA: University of California Press.

Monk-Turner, E. and Turner, C. 2001. "Sex Differentials in Earnings in the South Korean Labor Market." *Feminist Economics* 7(1): 63–78.

Nakavachara, V. 2010. "Superior Female Education: Explaining the Gender Earnings Gap Trend in Thailand." *Journal of Asian Economics* 21(2): 198–218.

National Statistical Office and Office of Women's Affairs and Family Development. 2008. *Gender Development: Similarities and Differences*. Bangkok: United Nations Development Programme and National Statistical Office.

O'Connor, T. 2015. "Men Choosing Nursing: Negotiating a Masculine Identity in a Feminine World." *Journal of Men's Studies* 23(2): 1–18.

O'Lynn, C. 2004. "Gender-Based Barriers for Male Students in Nursing Education Programs: Prevalence and Perceived Importance." *Journal of Nursing Education* 43: 229–236.

Ozdemir, A., Akansel, N. and Tunk, G. 2008. "Gender and Career: Female and Male Nursing Students' Perceptions of Male Nursing Role in Turkey." *Health Science Journal* 2(3): 153–161.

Patana, S. T. 2004. "Gender Relations in Thai Society: A Historical Perspective." In *Women's Studies in Thailand: Power, Knowledge and Justice*, edited by S. Satha-Anand, 65–83. Seoul: Ewha Womans University Press.

Perkins, S. 2016. "Gender Equality Issues in Nursing Careers." Accessed October 2. http://work.chron.com.

Pongsapich, A. 1997. "Feminism Theories and Praxis: Women's Social Movement in Thailand." In *Women, Gender Relations and Development in Thai Society*, edited by V. Somswasdi and S. Theobald, 3–51. Chiang Mai: Ming Muang Navarnt.

Pooittiwong, A. 2016. "Three Essays on Gender Wage Gap." PhD thesis, Claremont Graduate University.

Porter, S. 1992. "Women in a Women's Job: The Gendered Experience of Nurses." *Sociology of Health & Illness* 14(4): 510–527.

Reeves, S., Nelson, S. and Zwarenstein, M. 2008. "The Doctor-Nurse Game in the Age of Interprofessional Care: A View from Canada." *Nursing Inquiry* 15(1): 1–2.

Reynolds, A. and Timmons, S. 2005. "The Doctor-Nurse Relationship in the Operating Theatre." *British Journal of Perioperative Nursing* 15(3): 110–115.

Siedlecki, S. and Hixson, E. 2015. "Relationships Between Nurses and Physicians Matter." *The Online Journal of Issues in Nursing* 20(3). DOI: 10.3912/OJIN.Vol20No03PPT03.

Siengthai, S. and Leelakulthanit, O. 1994. "Women in Management in Thailand." In *Competitive Frontiers: Women Managers in a Global Economy*, edited by N. Adler and D. Izraeli, 160–171. Cambridge: Blackwell.

Skeggs, B. 2004. "Exchange, Value and Affect: Bourdieu and 'the self'." In *Feminism After Bourdieu*, edited by L. Adkins and B. Skeggs, 75–95. Oxford: Blackwell.

Son, H. 2007. *Occupational Segregation and Gender Discrimination in Labor Markets: Thailand and Viet Nam.* ERD Working Paper No. 108. Asian Development Bank. http://hdl.handle.net/11540/1868.

Stangl, J. and Kane, M. 1991. "Structural Variables that Offer Explanatory Power for the Underrepresentation of Women Coaches Since Title IX: The Case of Homologous Reproduction." *Sociology of Sport Journal* 8: 47–60.

Sweet, S. and Norman, I. 1995. "The Nurse-Doctor Relationship: A Selective Literature Review." *Journal of Advanced Nursing* 22: 165–170.

Tantiwiramanond, D. 1998. "The Growth of Women's Collective Efforts in Southeast Asia." Presented paper for *Southeast Asia in the 20th Century, Southeast Asian Studies Regional Exchange Program*—SEASREP, University of Philippines.

Tantiwiramanond, D. and Pandey, S. 1997. "New Opportunities or New Inequalities: Development Issues and Women's Lives in Thailand." In *Women, Gender Relations and Development in Thai Society*, edited by V. Somswasdi and S. Theobald, 83–135. Chiang Mai: Ming Muang Navarnt.

van der Meulen Rodgers, Y. and Zveglich J. 2012. *Inclusive Growth and Gender Inequality in Asia's Labor Markets.* Asian Development Bank Working Paper 321. www.adb.org/sites/default/files/publication/30137/economics-wp321-inclusive-growth-gender-inequality.pdf www.adb.org/publications/inclusive-growth-and-gender-inequality.

Vasey, C. and Mitchell, R. 2015. "Gender Perceptions in Surgery: Is It Really a Level Playing Field?" *ANZ Journal of Surgery* 85(12): 898–901.

Vichit-Vadakan, J. 1997. "Women and Men in Thai Politics." In *Women, Gender Relations and Development in Thai Society*, edited by V. Somsawadi and S. Theobald. Chiang Mai: Chiang Mai University Press.

Vichit-Vadakan, J. 2008. "Women in Politics and Women and Politics: A Socio-Cultural Analysis of the Thai Context." In *Women and Politics in Thailand*, edited by K. Iwanaga. Copenhagen: NIAS Press.

Whittock, M. and Leonard, L. 2003. "Stepping Outside the Stereotype: A Pilot Study of the Motivations and Experiences of Males in the Nursing Profession." *Journal of Nursing Management* 11: 242–249.

World Bank. 2010. *Towards a Competitive Higher Education System in a Global Economy.* Bangkok: Ngandee Creation.

World Bank. 2016. "Thailand: Country at a Glance." www.worldbank.org/en/country/thailand.

Yin, R. 1994. *Case Study Research: Design and Method*, 2nd ed. London: Sage.

Yingchoncharoen, P. 2007. *Gender and Leadership in Thailand.* Bangkok: Ramkhamhaeng University.

Yukongdi, V. and Rowley, C. 2009. *The Changing Face of Women Managers in Asia: Opportunities and Challenges.* London: Routledge.

Index

For Product Safety Concerns and Information please contact our EU
representative GPSR@taylorandfrancis.com
Taylor & Francis Verlag GmbH, Kaufingerstraße 24, 80331 München, Germany

www.ingramcontent.com/pod-product-compliance
Ingram Content Group UK Ltd.
Pitfield, Milton Keynes, MK11 3LW, UK
UKHW020941180425
457613UK00019B/500